CAMBRIDGE STUDIES IN CRIMINOLOGY XLI
General Editor: Sir Leon Radzinowicz

Prisons Past and Future

THE HEINEMANN LIBRARY OF CRIMINOLOGY
AND PENAL REFORM

CAMBRIDGE STUDIES IN CRIMINOLOGY

PRISONS PAST AND FUTURE

Edited
for the Howard League
for Penal Reform
by

John C. Freeman

Faculty of Laws, University
of London King's College

HEINEMANN

LONDON

Heinemann Educational Books Ltd
LONDON EDINBURGH MELBOURNE AUCKLAND TORONTO
HONG KONG SINGAPORE KUALA LUMPUR NEW DELHI
NAIROBI JOHANNESBURG LUSAKA IBADAN
KINGSTON

ISBN 0 435 82308 6
© Howard League for Penal Reform

First published 1978

Publisher's note: This series is continuous with the Cambridge
Studies in Criminology, Volumes I to XIX, published by
Macmillan & Co., London

Published by
Heinemann Educational Books Ltd
48 Charles Street, London W1X 8AH
Printed and bound in Great Britain by
Morrison and Gibb Ltd, London and Edinburgh

CONTENTS

Part III

THE CONTRIBUTORS

INKERI ANTTILA, LL.D., Pol.D.h.c., has been Professor of Criminal Law in the University of Helsinki since 1961, but has been on leave of absence since 1974 to serve as Director of the Finnish Research Institute of Legal Policy. She is a member of the Scandinavian Research Council for Criminology, a Board Member of the International Society of Criminology and of the International Association of Penal Law and she is Vice-President of the International Penal and Penitentiary Foundation.

LOUIS BLOM-COOPER, Q.C., is Chairman of the Howard League for Penal Reform and has been a member of the Home Secretary's Advisory Council on the Penal System since 1966.

NILS CHRISTIE is Professor of Criminology at the Institute of Criminology and Criminal Law, University of Oslo.

RALPH ENGLAND (Ph.D., University of Pennsylvania, 1954) is Professor of Sociology at the University of Rhode Island. Author of various publications in his speciality, criminology, he is presently completing a monograph on John Howard based mainly on archival research carried out during two periods of sabbatical leave in England.

EDITH ELISABETH FLYNN is Professor of Criminal Justice, Northeastern University and Academic Director of the Northeastern University Criminal Justice Training Center, Boston. She is a member of the Corrections Council, National Council on Crime and Delinquency and also of the Joint Commission on Criminology and Criminal Justice Education, Standards and Goals. Formerly she served on the Task Force on Corrections of the National Advisory Commission on Criminal Justice Standards and Goals and was founder and Associate Director of the National Clearinghouse for Criminal Justice, Planning and Architecture.

DAVID FOGEL is Professor of Criminal Justice at the University of Illinois, Chicago Circle. He was formerly Commissioner of the Minnesota State Department of Corrections (1971–3) and was Executive Director of the Illinois Law Enforcement Commission (1973–7). He is the author of *We Are the Living Proof: The Justice Model for Corrections* (1975).

JOHN C. FREEMAN, J.P., barrister, psychologist and juvenile court magistrate, now lectures in criminal law, criminology and penology at University of London King's College. He is a member of the Scientific Committees of the International Society of Criminology and of the International Sociological, Penal and Penitentiary Research and Studies Centre, Messina; he is Treasurer of the British Society of Criminology and of the Division of Criminological and Legal Psychology and was formerly Chairman of the Association of Law Teachers.

T. C. N. GIBBENS, C.B.E., M.D., has been Professor of Forensic Psychiatry at the Institute of Psychiatry, University of London, since 1967 and has been Honorary Consultant to Bethlem Royal and Maudsley Hospitals since 1951. He was formerly President of the International Society of Criminology and is currently Chairman of the Institute for the Study and Treatment of Delinquency and Vice-Chairman of the Howard League for Penal Reform. He has served as a member of a number of governmental boards and committees, including the Parole Board during the years 1972–5, and has contributed extensively to the literature in his field.

ALBERT KREBS, Dr. phil., was formerly welfare officer and from 1928 Governor of Unter-Massfeld State Penal Institution, Thüringen. In 1933 he was dismissed for political reasons. From 1945–65 he was Director of Prisons, Hessen, and Head of the Prison Department in the Ministry of Justice, Wiesbaden. Concurrently from 1950 he was lecturer at Philipps University, Marburg/Lahn, where in 1955 he became Honorary Professor of Prison Studies and Criminology.

F. H. McCLINTOCK is Professor of Criminology in the University of Edinburgh.

TERENCE MORRIS is Professor of Sociology with Special Reference to Criminology, in the University of London. He is the author of a number of criminological works, including *Pentonville: The Sociology of an English Prison* and *Deviance and Control: The Secular Heresy*. His interest in prisons spans more than twenty-five years and ranges from that of a prison visitor to being a magistrate in a busy London court.

Professor Sir LEON RADZINOWICZ, LL.D., F.B.A., is Fellow of Trinity College, Cambridge.

The Reverend Canon L. LLOYD REES was ordained in 1942 to a curacy in Cardiff and served as Assistant Chaplain, H.M. Prison, Cardiff. In 1945 he joined the Prison Service as a full-time Chaplain and served as Chaplain of H.M. Prisons, Durham (1945–8), Dartmoor (1948–55) and Winchester (1955–62). He has been Chaplain General from 1962, Honorary Canon of Canterbury Cathedral from 1966 and Chaplain to The Queen from 1971.

The Rt. Hon. MERLYN REES, M.P., a graduate of London University, has been a Member of Parliament since 1963. Service with the R.A.F. during World War II ended with his attaining the rank of Squadron Leader. Later he became Lecturer in Economics at Luton College of Technology. Since entering Parliament he has held a number of offices, having most recently been Secretary of State for Northern Ireland (1974–6) and, currently, Secretary of State for the Home Department. In 1971 he was appointed a member of the Committee to examine the operation of Section 2 of the Official Secrets Act.

Judge ERIC STOCKDALE, B.Sc.(Econ.), LL.M., Ph.D., was a practising barrister from 1950–72 and since then has been a Circuit Judge. He is the President of the British Society of Criminology and a member of the Council of the National Association for the Care and Resettlement of Offenders (NACRO).

LAURIE TAYLOR is Professor of Sociology at the University of York. He has written widely on problems of deviance and penal policy. His principal publications include *Psychological Survival* (with Stanley Cohen, 1972), *Crime, Deviance and Socio-Legal Control* (with Roland Robertson, 1974), *Politics and Deviance* (edited with Ian Taylor, 1973) and *Escape Attempts: The Theory and Practice of Resistance to Everyday Life* (with Stanley Cohen, 1976).

J. E. THOMAS, Ph.D., worked for three years in Africa before returning to spend seven years in the governor grades of the English prison service. He has visited and studied prison systems in many parts of the world and has been a consultant on staff training. Dr. Thomas has written extensively about prisons, his best-known work being *The English Prison Officer since 1850*.

PREBEN WOLF took his degree in law in 1945. He served as Police Attorney until the following year and then held governing positions in penal institutions and administrative posts in the Prison Department from 1946–63. He became Research Fellow at the Institute of Criminal Science in 1963 and a year later Reader in Sociology at the University of Copenhagen. Since 1967 he has been Associate Professor of Sociology there.

MARVIN E. WOLFGANG is Professor of Sociology and Law, and Director of the Center for Studies in Criminology and Criminal Law, University of Pennsylvania. He is also President of the American Academy of Political and Social Science, a member of the American Philosophical Society and the author of many books and articles on criminology, including *Delinquency in a Birth Cohort* and *Crime and Justice*, in three volumes, edited with Sir Leon Radzinowicz.

GRAHAM ZELLICK is Lecturer in Laws at Queen Mary College, University of London. Formerly Ford Foundation Fellow in Criminal Law and Policy at the Stanford Law School, and Visiting Professor of Law at the University of Toronto, he served on the Jellicoe Committee on Boards of Visitors and is a member of the Council and Executive Committee of the Howard League for Penal Reform.

All the contributors to this volume, and the editor, have generously given their services without fee; royalties will go to the Howard League for Penal Reform. The Howard League is a charitable organization which exists to put forward constructive proposals for the reform of penal and social policies, to consider the principles on which such policies should be based and to spread information about the way offenders are treated. It receives no government grant, but is entirely supported by donations and the subscriptions of its members, many of whom also contribute to its policies from their experience in the administration of justice and the penal system.

Membership is open to individuals and organizations in any country who are concerned to bring about reforms. Details of membership will be sent on request by the Howard League for Penal Reform, 125 Kennington Park Road, London SE11 4JP.

CONFERENCE PATRONS

Inkeri Anttila

Ayush Morad Amar

Marc Ancel

James Y. Boamah

Pierre Bouzat

H. H. Brydensholt

W. Clifford

Paul Cornil

Sir Rupert Cross

Wolfgang Doleisch

Israel Drapkin

Rt. Hon. Lord Gardiner

Guiseppe di Gennaro

Erik Harremoes

G. J. Hawkins

The High Sheriff of Bedfordshire

Brunon Holyst

Hans-Heinrich Jescheck

Stanley W. Johnston

Hugh Klare

Gunnar Marnell

Wolf Middendorff

Luis Castillon Mora

G. Mueller

Amer Ahmed Al-Mukhtar

Sir Arthur Peterson

Jean Pinatel

P. G. Pötz

Sir Leon Radzinowicz

Manuel López-Rey

John L. Robson

Hira Singh

Denis Szabo

Jose Luis Vega

S.-C. Versele

INTRODUCTION

The year 1977, the bicentenary of John Howard's book, was recognized by the Howard League for Penal Reform as an opportunity for commemorating Howard and his work. However the League also wished to do more; to make a critical appraisal of prisons and the problems of prisons two hundred years later. Since its first foundation as the Howard Association in 1866, the Howard League has always worked as a potent stimulus for the evaluation and reform of the penal system. It is registered as a charitable organization and is accorded consultative status with the United Nations.

The planning of the Conference began with the support and encouragement of an eminent group of Conference Patrons drawn from more than a score of nations and including Gerhard Mueller, representing the United Nations and Erik Harremoes, the Council of Europe.*

An Organizing Committee was established comprising Professor T. C. N. Gibbens, C.B.E., Professor of Forensic Psychiatry in the University of London and Vice-Chairman of the Howard League; Professor A. W. B. Simpson, J.P., Dean of the Faculty of Social Sciences in the University of Kent at Canterbury; His Honour Judge Eric Stockdale; Professor Nigel Walker, Director of the Institute of Criminology of the University of Cambridge and Vice-President of the League; Martin Wright, Director of the Howard League for Penal Reform; and with myself as Honorary Conference Organizer.

The constraints of limited time and limited money in preparing for an event on such a scale were alleviated by the time given by Miss Clare Miller, then a law student at King's College, London, who was appointed part-time Administrative Assistant; by my wife, Margaret Freeman, who gave much energy to the social side of the programme; and by Carolyn Clark and Sheila Cooney, of the Staff of the Howard League. On the financial side, generous advance support was given by the Noel Buxton Trust, the Hilden Charitable Trust, Whitbread and Company Ltd. and the Swedish Prison and Probation Administration.

In choosing the University of Kent in the ancient cathedral city of Canterbury as its forum, the Committee was expressing a desire that a stimulating, yet economical venue should be found for a relatively small conference with adequate scope for discussion and intellectual interaction as well as for the presentation of more formal, invited contributions.

The papers which now form the chapters of this book were originally delivered to one of three principal sections of the Conference. In the first place, Section I looked again at John Howard's contribution, at the many changes since his day and at what lessons could be learned from two more centuries in the history of penal affairs. The papers of the Second Section centred around problems of the present day, developments in prison administration, prisoners' rights and so on.

* See p. x.

For similar reasons I have also published a review of current criminal justice policy.* This describes the development of policies since 1966 and considers to what extent assumptions so far made remain valid.

What would John Howard say now if he were to write a sequel to his book? He would find much of which he could approve. He might also conclude that much more needs to be done. He would find a fundamental change in the concept of imprisonment as a punishment. In the eighteenth century, except for debtors, it was a stage on the way to the gallows or transportation.

As for conditions, he would certainly find prisons both cleaner and less offensive with more acceptable food and bedding. He would see that they are healthier places, free from disease—in 1777 more prisoners died from gaol fever than were publicly executed—and their number was not insignificant. But he would be above all concerned, as we are, about the appalling overcrowding—the numbers of men crammed two or three in cells intended by Victorians, who designed and built them, for one.

There are no simple or easy solutions to this problem, which places such a great burden on our over-stretched prison system and its staff. Through major building programmes, now unhappily constrained by financial problems, and in terms of the liberalizing and enrichment of régimes we have done much. But the most important way to attack this problem is by keeping out of prison people who have no need to be there. That is why we have put so much emphasis in recent years on the development of non-custodial disposals.

ACPS Report

An important initiative has been taken by the Advisory Council on the Penal System which has recently submitted to me an interim report as part of its current review of maximum penalties. In the report, entitled *The Length of Prison Sentences,* the Council argues that prison sentences passed on the average offender for the ordinary, run-of-the-mill offence are in general too long, and could safely be reduced without any likely loss of effectiveness either from the point of view of the prisoner or from that of the protection of the public. The Council notes in its report that this view that prison sentences are on average too long is accepted by many informed observers today, and no doubt it is one which readers of a book such as this will endorse.

If sentences could be reduced, even by relatively small amounts, the effect upon the prison population could be significant. The reduction of the daily

* Home Office (1977): *A Review of Criminal Justice Policy 1976*

average population by a few thousand would bring a much needed relief to the system and to those who work in it, and release staff to some degree from the overwhelming day-to-day pressure of chronic overcrowding. It is a view to be commended in particular to those who have the heavy responsibility of sentencing offenders in the courts. If it is generally accepted that many prison sentences are too long, it is indeed wrong, as the Council points out, that this situation should continue. It would mean above all that the smaller number of prisoners would be able to serve their sentences in more tolerable conditions than they do today.

It is perhaps worth mentioning briefly factors which are now beginning to bear on reducing the size of the prison population. Following the Home Office circular to courts drawing attention to the recommendations of the Working Party on Bail, which have now been embodied in the new Bail Act, remands in custody have significantly decreased. The number being released on parole, as the most recent report of the Parole Board records, is steadily increasing. In the longer term alternatives to imprisonment are being developed and in recent years one of the most encouraging is the community service order.

Community Report

Considerable progress has been made in the two years since community service arrangements began to be widely introduced. There are now schemes in fifty-three of the fifty-six areas in England and Wales, and thirty-one cover the whole probation area. Over 9,000 orders were made in 1976 and the upward trend continues. The probation service has put great effort into setting up arrangements, and this at a time of mounting pressure on resources.

The Home Office is giving such encouragement and practical help as it can to the further expansion of arrangements, but it has to be faced that some areas will be prevented on resource grounds from moving ahead as fast as they would like. This makes it all the more desirable that community service should be carefully used. Its primary purpose must be to provide, where appropriate, a constructive alternative for offenders who would otherwise have received a short custodial sentence.

Drunkenness Sentences

It is often said that one group of people who could safely be removed from the prison system are the socially inadequate. Among this group are those who are imprisoned because of drunkenness offences, whether because they receive imprisonment as a sentence on being convicted of being drunk and disorderly, or, more commonly, because they are imprisoned in default of payment of fines for drunkenness offences.

Drunkenness offenders can be divided into two groups. There are the younger offenders, who are not dependent on alcohol, who drink excessively from time to time, for example on the way to football matches. They present a problem and it is clear the courts must be able to impose realistic fines if this sort of behaviour is to be deterred.

On the other hand, any increase in fines could result in a greater use of imprisonment for those older habitual offenders who find it difficult to pay fines, and for whom prison is no longer a deterrent. This is a knotty problem and I am pleased to be able to say that we hope to be able to resolve it to some extent with the Criminal Law Act. Broadly, we intend to increase the fines for the offences of being drunk or being drunk and disorderly but the maximum period in default of payment of the new maximum fines will be less than it is at present. We also intend to remove imprisonment as a penalty for the offence of being drunk and disorderly. The number of offenders concerned is not large, but we hope that our proposals will achieve a small but nevertheless welcome reduction in the prison population.

Young Offenders

Our young offender system is under acute pressure and is a matter of special concern to the Home Office. The continuing increase in the crime rate amongst younger age groups and increasing recidivism amongst the borstal population are causing severe overcrowding. The general philosophy under-lying the ACPS report, *Young Adult Offenders,* was an important statement and is generally consistent with our thinking. It is very disheartening, therefore, that the major resources that would be necessary to move significantly forward on this front are not available.

It will be necessary to make imaginative use of existing resources while continuing to seek fresh ways of gearing them more effectively to the needs of young offenders. There is a need for greater co-operation with the Probation Service, development of community work and extension of neighbourhood borstal concepts. Our overall aim must be to bring to bear a whole range of facilities for dealing with offenders of all ages, including imprisonment, and involve the public as well as voluntary bodies like the Howard League in the treatment of offenders.

All this necessarily makes considerable demands on staff who are hard pressed and working under considerable difficulty and constraint. It is timely and appropriate, therefore, that in recalling the work and philosophy of John Howard we should remind ourselves of the debt that is owed to the skills and dedicated work of the staffs of the services who are engaged in coping with the onerous and intractable problems of the penal system. No Home Secretary can fail to remember that, and I am sure that John Howard, too, would have understood the vital rôles that they play in bringing to fruition the ambitions of policy and purpose.

JOHN HOWARD

Professor Sir Leon Radzinowicz

These papers have been assembled here to mark the bicentenary of the *State of Prisons* and to pay a tribute to the work of John Howard. There are many ways in which this task might be discharged. But the way which most appeals to me, seems most appropriate to the occasion, and would also seem most congenial to the spirit of John Howard himself, is to ask, and attempt to answer, a series of concrete questions about what that work was and what impact if had upon the conditions of prisons and prisoners.

I could well have *raised* these questions, but I should have found it extremely difficult to *answer* them without the painstaking research carried out by Dr. Victor Bailey, and without the close collaboration of my friend, Miss Joan King. So to my questions.

* * *

First, how did it all begin? The story is typically English. No vast, beckoning vision, no grandiose project of enquiry, no all-embracing scheme of reform. Just a single specific injustice, which he noticed at Bedford gaol, when newly appointed High Sheriff for the County in 1773. He discovered that prisoners who were acquitted—often after spending many months in custody awaiting trial—were dragged back to gaol and locked up again until they could pay the fees claimed by the gaoler. Howard applied to the county justices for a salary to be paid to the gaoler, so that he need no longer rely upon what he could extort from the prisoners. But the bench demanded a precedent for so novel a payment. Confident that he would find the examples he wanted amongst his neighbours, Howard set out to look at the system in adjoining counties, only to find that the abuse he had thought local and exceptional was in fact the general rule. From then on his concerns, his enquiries, his travels spread out in ever-widening circles. Visiting gaols to investigate the injustice arising from fees, he met the horrors of gaol fever; discovering that some prisoners from county gaols had been transferred to houses of correction, he resolved that these also must be included in his investigation; not content with exploring the counties nearest his own, he went further and further afield. Looking back on it all, he explained: 'The work grew upon me insensibly. I could not enjoy my ease and leisure in the neglect of an opportunity offered me by providence of attempting the relief of the miserable.'

*   *   *

My second and third questions are also simple ones: *Where did he go?* and *How did he travel?* He certainly visited a formidable number of penal institutions: many enumerations have been attempted, but none is complete. Having gone from end to end of England and Wales, he moved on to Ireland and Scotland, then abroad, to virtually every country in Europe, and eventually into Russia. Nor was he the kind of enquirer who visits a prison for a day or two, a foreign country for a week or two, and thereafter claims first-hand knowledge of their conditions. He went again and again to see whether statutory reforms he had helped to bring about were in fact being implemented; to see whether his earlier criticisms had been met, his suggestions followed; to investigate the prevalence of yet more kinds of abuse he had discovered on his travels; to monitor changes for better or worse. There was something reminiscent of *Baedeker* in the way he handed out to each institution, with impressive impartiality, condemnation on some points, approval on others—and in the way in which he did not hesitate to upgrade or downgrade his report on it if, on a second or third visit, he found matters better or worse.

In achieving all this, it has been estimated that he travelled a total at least of fifty thousand miles; though some maintain it was closer to a hundred and fifty thousand miles. And that was not only before the days of cars and of planes, but before the days even of railways and decent roads. Moreover, he covered most of this on horseback, travelling by night as well as by day. He had tried using the stage coach only to discover it was hopeless. Such was the stench that clung to his garments after spending time in close contact with prisoners that he could not bear to travel with the windows closed.

*   *   *

My fourth question is again simple, but none the less revealing of the character of the man, his devotion to his task, his sturdy integrity and his fierce independence. *How were his travels financed?* He had no aid from charitable organizations. He refused a proffered government grant. He spent some thirty thousand pounds of his own money. Such have been the ravages of inflation that the Professor of Economic History in the University of Oxford tells me that would be equivalent to about half a million pounds today. John Howard was, in fact, his own Ford Foundation.

*   *   *

The fifth question needs longer consideration. *Did he meet with any obstruction in his visits, any resistance to his access to prisons or prisoners?* The short and surprising answer is 'Very rarely.' In only three cases was he unable even to get his foot in the door. These were all famous, or rather infamous, institutions: the sinister prison adjoining the Doge's Palace in Venice, the prison of the Inquisition in Rome, and the Bastille in Paris. He *was* allowed into a prison of the Spanish Inquisition, and allowed to see their collection of prohibited books and the pointed cap put on their victims. He was even permitted to go up the private staircase by which prisoners were brought to the tribunal, leading to a passage with several closed doors. But he was told that 'none but prisoners ever enter these rooms,' and when he asked to be confined for a month so that he could satisfy his curiosity, the reply was 'None come out under three years, and *they* take the oath of secrecy.' Faced with what seems to have been the true forerunner of the *Official Secrets Act,* Howard regretfully withdrew.

It is with some sorrow that I must also tell you that I can find only one instance in which the repulsive conditions in an institution themselves drove him back. His first sight of the Spin-house of Warsaw, in my native Poland, gave him so unfavourable an opinion of the way the country was run that he could face neither visiting the prisons of the provinces nor revisiting those of the capital, as was his constant practice elsewhere.

But rebuffs were the rare exceptions: in general Howard not only got into prisons, but was allowed to visit cells, even dungeons and torture chambers, and to talk freely to gaolers, turnkeys and prisoners themselves. How was it he had such freedom? There are not many places where we should find it today. I would suggest at least six things to account for it. Few countries had, in those days, a strong central bureaucracy, to lay down and enforce prohibitions of access. Penal institutions in general were far less cut off from the rest of the community than they are now: people went in and out to trade, to visit, to attend church services, and (in England) to have a look at the prisoners condemned to hang next day. Prison officials were a great deal less sophisticated, not to say less wary, than they would be today. They probably looked upon Howard as a well-heeled gentleman with eccentric tastes, who might as well be humoured, and they certainly would not have anticipated (at least on his first visit) the thoroughness with which he would observe, the severity with which he would record. Being the first in the field gives a certain advantage to any researcher, and there is no doubt that Howard exploited it to the full. On a *second* visit to one German prison he recorded: 'I perceived by the countenance of the gaoler and his unwillingness to shew me *again* the torture-room, that he had seen my publication.' At least in some countries, the squalor of conditions for the poor outside must have meant that gaolers had little consciousness that anything was wrong. Cleanliness, medical attention, adequate food and clothes, were beyond the means of many outside the prisons as well as inside them. Howard is said to have had great personal charm. He undoubtedly had both persistence and ingenuity. He records that, when he was denied entry to the prison of the *Grand Châtelet* in Paris, he unearthed a regulation which permitted the admission of people wanting to give alms. By this means he was able to see almost all of the prisoners.

*   *   *

My sixth question is this. *Was Howard simply a great humanitarian campaigner, albeit with a genius for research, or was he also concerned with devising a comprehensive scheme of prison reconstruction?* Certainly he saw it as his task to ferret out the abuses most needing to be eliminated, the initiatives most worthy of initiation. Certainly he devoted the third section of his *The State of the Prisons* to 'Proposed improvements in the structure and management of prisons', starting with where and how they should be built and equipped and going on to consider their staffing, regulation and régimes; thus transforming into detailed recommendations the quintessence of all he had learned in his travels, both evil and good. He gave some thought, too, to wider implications. He denied, for example, that his proposals would make prisons so soft that they would no longer be deterrent: on the contrary, the prohibition of all 'riotous amusement' would ensure that they were 'sufficiently irksome and disagreeable, especially to the idle and profligate'. Yet he advocated solitary confinement only as a temporary punishment for those who failed to respond to milder discipline. And his statement on the handling of prisoners is worth quoting in full:

> The notion that convicts are *ungovernable* is certainly *erroneous*. There is a mode of managing some of the most desperate, with ease to yourself, and advantage to them. Many of them are shrewd and sensible: manage them with calmness, yet with steadiness; show them that you have humanity, that you aim to make them useful members of society; let them see and hear the rules and orders of the prison, and be convinced that they are not defrauded in their provisions and clothes by contractors or gaolers; when they are sick, let them be treated with tenderness. Such conduct would prevent mutiny in prisons and attempts to escape; which I am fully persuaded are often owing to prisoners being made desperate, by the inhumanity and ill usage of their keepers.

If this advice had been followed, in all probability there would have been no Attica.

But to return to my theme. For all his investigations, and for all his recommendations, Howard did not see himself as the person to devise a fully developed new system of prison administration. That he saw as calling for a full-scale parliamentary enquiry followed by government action. Nor did he set up a coherent organization to press his proposals for reform. He sought to make his influence felt by arousing the consciences of influential individuals and stirring them to action. Looking back today, we may envy the speed with which some of his proposals were translated into legislative enactments. But he soon discovered that to have something on the Statute books was very different from having it enforced. Ten years after he first embarked on his journeys he recorded that he went again to several prisons he had previously known. 'I was sorry,' he reported, 'to find them confirm my suspicions, that our gaols are verging to their old state. Without much additional and unremitting care, the benefits produced of late years by attention to this object, will prove merely temporary.' The task was too vast, too long term, and too obdurate, for any one man, even though that man was John Howard.

In all this, his approach was practical and pragmatic, learning by what he saw, recommending what he thought would work. He has often been contrasted with that other outstanding name in penal reform, the Italian, Beccaria. Beccaria is known for his one brief and brilliant incursion into the field of penal philosophy, when caught up as a young man in the spirit of the enlightenment. *Crimes and Punishments* was all he produced, and in a sense it was more than enough. Howard was no philosopher. He did not embark upon his life's work until his early forties, but having once set his hand to the plough he never turned back. I prefer, in a way, to compare him with that other great Englishman to achieve international stature in his day—Jeremy Bentham. Bentham devoted something like sixty years to hammering out principles of punishment, elaborate schemes of prisons and penalties, which were yet curiously remote from real life and real men. Howard was very different. He did not question the right to punish, simply taking it for granted as part of the God-given order of things. What concerned him was that punishment should not degenerate into cruelty, abuse, injustice. His whole concern in this was with real men, whether statesmen or magistrates, gaolers or prisoners. It was at that level he thought and acted. The philosophy and the grand designs he left to others.

*   *   *

My next and last question is almost a cliché: shallow no doubt but hard to resist. As you may guess, it is this: *If John Howard were with us today, what would he think of the present 'state of prisons' throughout the world?*

Being not only a noble but also a shrewd man, he would soon have discovered the cruel truth that he could no longer hope to travel round freely, able to see for himself what goes on in prisons and prison camps (even in certain psychiatric hospitals). There is a passage in his memoirs where he tells of his visit to St. Petersburg (now Leningrad): he had no difficulty in seeing the prison and even the Empress wanted to meet him. A hundred years later, a moving tribute was paid to him by a Russian professor at the

that the prison was a backwater which scarcely came to the notice of the gentry or townsfolk. These assumptions, it is submitted, must be modified in the light of the evidence of various documents, quoted in the writer's book *A Study of Bedford Prison 1660–1877.*

The presence of John Bunyan as a prisoner in Bedford from 1660 to 1672 and again in 1677 (1977 also marks the tercentenary of Bunyan's final release) has not escaped the notice of Howard's biographers. The International Congress on the Prevention and Repression of Crime, meeting in London in 1872, heard the Rev. H. W. Bellows deliver a talk on Howard. He made the point, somewhat fulsomely but accurately, 'John Bunyan, a hundred years before—1660 to 1672—had made Bedford jail immortal by his *Pilgrim's Progress,* issued from his saint's rest in the providential confinement. John Howard was to make it immortal again, by commencing a Pilgrim's Progress from its walls.'

Bunyan had been imprisoned for refusing to worship in the restored Church of England after the Restoration of the Monarchy—like John Howard he was a Nonconformist. His imprisonment was certainly a matter which caused great concern to local people. For example, Paul Cobb, the Clerk of the Peace, visited him in prison and tried to persuade him to agree to conform. Although Bunyan did not trust him, Cobb was probably genuinely concerned to try and save him from the risk of execution or of exile, which risks undoubtedly existed. 'You may do much good if you continue still in the land, but alas, what benefit will it be to your friends, or what good can you do to them, if you should be sent away beyond the seas into Spain or Constantinople, or some other remote part of the world? Pray be ruled.' Fortunately, Bunyan did continue in the land, and did manage to do much good—much of it stemming from the important written work he succeeded in producing in the prison itself. Apart from some of *Pilgrim's Progress,* Bunyan wrote *Grace Abounding* in custody.

Once Bunyan was released from Bedford prison and was able to preach openly at the Old Meeting and elsewhere, and once he became known as the author of the most widely read book after the Bible, local people did not forget about his imprisonment. Howard was for many years a member of Bunyan's church, as has been mentioned, so that there was no chance of his overlooking his link with the prison. Bunyan had not been the only religious prisoner there. Apart from other Dissenters, there were many Quakers in the prison at the same time as he was. Many members of the community sympathized with them and were concerned about their imprisonment. Much the same may be said about the debtors who were under the same roof in the years before 1773. Many of them were respectable local tradesmen, and other members of the community did not forget about them. In 1730, for example, the Rector of Carlton helped to secure the release of a local butcher imprisoned for debt. He achieved the release by raising money from different well-wishers, including himself, and paying off the creditors. The last entry in the Rector's diary relating to the release reads: 'I paid then to the jailer, Mr. Richardson £5.7.0. His bill was £5.13.5.' The Richardson referred to was John Richardson junior.

Obviously there are not many documentary traces of minor signs of concern such as this, but the county quarter sessions rolls for 1752 contain another: a letter to the gaoler reading, 'The Duke of Bedford desires that Harbarts, and the old man you mentioned when his Grace was at Bedford, may be allowed the county bread, and he will be answerable for it.'

It would similarly be a mistake to think that Howard was the first Sheriff to interest himself in the prison building itself. Bedford has had a prison since 1165 and for several centuries it was on the same site in the centre of the town at one of the principal crossroads. The writer—with Howard's help—has in his book described the prison as it was when Howard first entered it. Various minor modifications and improvements had been made in earlier years, and Howard recorded that he saw a sail ventilator there. This had been installed in 1754 after the justices had ordered:

> It appearing to the said court that the common jail for the said county has been several times infected with a malignant fever, by means whereof several prisoners, as well debtors as felons, have lately died; and it having been presented into the said court by David James Esq., High Sheriff of the said county, that a ventilator would be extremely beneficial to the said jail by extracting thereout the foul and infectious air, whereby the lives of several of the prisoners confined therein would be in less danger; it is therefore ordered by the said court that Harry Johnson Esq. be desired to procure the said ventilator to be immediately erected as may be most beneficial to answer the purpose aforesaid.

David James, the Sheriff, may well have got the idea of installing a device for improving the air from Newgate in London, where a windmill sail ventilator had been installed in the preceding year. It is true that the Sheriff may have been concerned about gaol fever being brought into court and killing off the Sheriff and the judges (a very proper concern!) or about the fever spreading along the High Street rather than about the prisoners, but his interest nevertheless makes the point once more that the prison was not a forgotten backwater.

Although there is no doubt about the fact that conditions in the prison before, during and after Howard's time were bad, there is ample evidence in both state and county records that many sick prisoners received a degree of sympathetic consideration from the magistrates. There are many references to extra food being provided for such prisoners. Looked at from the point of view of the present day this is nothing much—especially since we are rightly shocked by any failure to provide for basic food and medical needs—but it is important when thinking about Howard, to put oneself back in his century and to apply the standards of his time.

The concern of the magistrates was sometimes communicated via the Secretary of State to the King. For example, in 1764 William Kirby was sentenced to death at Bedford assizes for sheep stealing, but was reprieved on the recommendation of the trial judge. Transportation for fourteen years was substituted as the penalty, but Kirby never made it to Maryland or Virginia, for he was shortly afterwards 'seized with a fever which totally deprived him of the use of his limbs and his understanding'. He was granted a free pardon by the young King, who had recently embarked on his sixty-year reign. The pardon itself is perhaps not surprising, but the covering letter from the Secretary of State reveals a remarkable degree of compassion on the part of different people.

> It having been represented to the King that were such sentence of transportation to be passed upon him it would be inevitably to his destruction, and the apothecary reporting that it is impossible he should either recover his limbs or his understanding, though it is possible he may live many years, and it having been further represented to His Majesty that the justices of the peace have hitherto ordered their Treasurer to add something towards his support, but that the jail is at the best but a very inconvenient place for the poor convict to live in, and that the poor woman his mother who lives at Biggleswade, is very desirous to receive her unfortunate son and to take care of him, and that the parish will very willingly contribute to his support, the King has been pleased to extend his further mercy to the said poor and unhappy convict by granting him a free pardon.

When Howard assumed the office of High Sheriff he also assumed responsibility for the prison and for the carrying out of the sentences of the courts in the county. When he first visited the prison, he was met by the gaoler Thomas Howard, and he recorded that he found a printed list of fees signed by T. Richardson, a previous gaoler: 'All persons that come to this place by warrant, commitment or verbally, must pay before discharge, fifteen shillings and four pence to the jailer and two shillings to the turnkey'.

The gaoler Howard was no relation of John Howard, but he was the nephew of the gaoler Thomas Richardson, whose brother and father had also held the post. Indeed, six members of the Richardson-Howard family held the job of gaoler for a total of some seventy years in the period 1711–1814. This is quite remarkable when one remembers that the High Sheriff changed annually, and that each one had to appoint the gaoler for the one year only. Some were content to re-appoint the existing gaoler; others preferred to appoint a fresh man or to give the post back to someone who had held it before. The word 'man' is used advisedly; whilst women gaolers occasionally held office elsewhere, there is no record of any woman gaoler in Bedford. It should be emphasized, however, that the gaolers' wives regularly helped to run their husbands' gaols, and even took complete charge on occasion, as when the gaoler was absent escorting prisoners from Bedford to a port for transportation to the Americas.

The documents relating to the appointment of gaoler are relatively few, but they demonstrate once again that the gaol was important in the community; and that the identity of the man appointed and his qualifications for office were matters of concern to magistrates and other citizens, as well as to the incoming High Sheriff himself. This is a part of John Howard's background which should not be overlooked.

The earliest remaining letter relating to the appointment of gaoler is one from a gentleman who had offered to act as Under-Sheriff, and was therefore presumably a lawyer in the county. He wrote in 1710: 'You were last night appointed High Sheriff. If you have not promised the jail, Mr. Bamford the present jailer is a good man and a friend of mine, whom I hope will you keep in.' The Sheriff rejected the advice and appointed John Richardson senior—doubtless after receiving advice from others.

The appointment of the gaoler was one of the most important tasks of the incoming Sheriff, and a letter from 1740 shows that he might well have had the benefit of the views of a number of people when making his choice. The Under-Sheriff, who had held office for some time, wrote to his new principal: 'The affair of the jailer has been a matter of no small perplexity since 'twas impossible to fix upon Stevens without giving offence to the Gentlemen on account of his maltreatment of the prisoners when jailer before.' The gentlemen referred to were the county magistrates before whom William Stevens, the then gaoler, had appeared some three years earlier, charged with assaulting one of his prisoners. Although prisoners were mentioned in the letter, there in no trace of any other prisoner having been maltreated by Stevens. The prisoner in question had not been a very attractive complainant. He was a recruiting agent for the King of Prussia and had lured a tall local lad to Potsdam to join the Giants' Regiment by means of various lies. The magistrates accepted the truth of the prisoner's complaint and bound the gaoler over to keep the peace generally and especially towards his prisoners. In his letter to the Sheriff in 1740 the Under-Sheriff specifically recommended a joint appointment of two men, one of whom he described as 'Mr. Richardson, the present jailer, a vigilant careful man, whose security is Mr. Battison, the coal merchant'.

Ten years later, in 1750, Thomas Richardson was sole gaoler once again but early in the following year he was replaced by Henry Tanner. In the papers of the Duke of Bedford's agent, Robert Butcher, is a letter stating: 'If it be determined to take the jail from Mr. Richardson and to place another in his room, I take the liberty to recommend the bearer, Mr. Henry Tanner, as a person who I believe would duly execute that office.'

On the same day Henry Hurst, who had married the widow of the disgraced gaoler William Stevens, also wrote to the Duke's agent, who had clearly asked him to make recommendations for the gaoler's post:

> I have turned my thoughts upon what you was speaking to me about at your house. There is five of our friends that are tolerably well situated for the jail, but I can't say that they are so well acquainted with life as I could wish. Whoever, if any of them, are thought well of, and they will think it a favour to be appointed as I told you, I will be ready at all times to assist, and my wife, whose first husband had the jail many years and almost the whole of the affair lay upon her to manage, and I, can be of great service to any person quite unacquainted with such an affair. The five persons are
>
> Liles Wooton at the 'White Horse', a tenant of Mr. Woodward;
> William Hill, lives on his own—the 'Star';
> Henry Tanner, a tenant to Mr. Bell at the 'Dolphin';
> John Cumberland at the 'Ram', tenant to Madm. Bell; and
> Richard Lane at the 'Bull', tenant to Mrs. Ann Day, executor to late Alderman Day.

Hurst then saw the letter recommending Tanner and added a note: 'I must own I think Mr. Tanner as proper a person as any I mentioned and his house as convenient as any.' It is interesting to note that each one of the five names suggested was that of an innkeeper, and that Tanner's house was the 'Dolphin', near the prison.

As the gaoler received no salary before John Howard's protests about that lamentable situation, he had to earn a living somehow, and he did so partly by providing food and drink to those prisoners who could afford it or who had it paid for them by the county, and partly by charging obnoxious fees, such as those which Howard saw listed when he first stepped into Bedford prison as Sheriff. It must be remembered that the magistrates had some control of the inns, then as now, so that they had some knowledge of the innkeepers, and some degree of hold over them for good behaviour. To that extent, having an innkeeper as gaoler, whilst having disadvantages as far as the supply of alcohol was concerned, had the advantage of providing some small degree of community control.

The fees which helped the gaoler to make a living were fixed by the justices at different times. As the predecessors of local government bodies they kept a fairly close watch on any expenditure. For example, in April 1741 the gaoler took seven prisoners on the overland stage of their long journey to the

Americas under a sentence of transportation. On his return he charged the justices a large sum for expenses, based on a similar charge for each prisoner escorted by him. In the following April, quarter sessions ordered: 'That the jailer for the time being be allowed £6 for conveying one felon to London in order for transportation, £10 for two felons, and £4 for each felon when more than two.'

In 1753 the justices authorized the following fees:

	s.d.
Of every prisoner charged in a civil action as an entrance fee	2·0.
Of every prisoner for chamber rent and the sole use of bedding and sheets per week	2·6.
If two in a bed then each to pay	1·3.
Of every prisoner for his discharge and fee	15·4.

Whilst the justices were obliged to allow the gaoler to charge fees in order to enable him to support his family, oddly enough there was no similar necessity in the case of the keeper of the house of correction. Although he had a very similar job to that of the gaoler—and their posts were to be combined in due course—the keeper was more fortunate in that he was paid a salary. An Act of 1575 had required the justices of all counties to set up a house of correction or bridewell. The one in Bedford opened ten years later, and the keeper could, from the start, rely on a salary, rather than on fees.

Thomas Howard, the gaoler who received John Howard in 1773, was succeeded ten years later by his brother, John Moore Howard. The latter soon earned substantial respect in the town, and twenty-one dignitaries recommended him to the incoming Sheriff in the following terms: 'We do hereby certify that Mr. Jno. Howard hath been jailer of the said county two years and during that time hath behaved with the greatest tenderness towards the prisoners and hath caused the jail to be constantly kept clean and wholesome, and from his care and sobriety we presume to recommend him as a person properly qualified in all respects for your nomination and continuance in the office of jailer.' It is true that some people would sign any petition placed before them, but this document is not without its significance. It shows once again the interest of the community in the post of gaoler, and this interest continued during John Howard's lifetime and also after his death in 1790 at Kherson in the Ukraine.

John Moore Howard was dismissed for misconduct in 1814. This was doubly unfortunate in that he personally had held the post for thirty years and, as his son wrote, 'during this long period has never entirely lost a prisoner'; and also as his family had been linked with the prison since 1711 or earlier. As soon as the news of the gaoler's downfall became public, Captain Mitchell, adjutant of one of the local militia regiments, set about getting the job, writing to various dignitaries for support. He clearly appreciated the fact that the appointment was a matter of concern to the gentry: one of the people he approached was the Rev. Philip Hunt, a magistrate who was to be most influential in prison affairs in the next twenty years. Another magistrate he contacted was the younger Samuel Whitbread, M.P., John Howard's cousin. In his letter to Whitbread the adjutant pointed out that he himself—unlike one of his rivals, who was a Dissenter—was a member of the Church of England. Whitbread rebuked him in terms which would have brought joy to John Bunyan's heart: 'I am surprised you should have thought it necessary to state so prominently that you are a member of the Established Church. I know of no office or station in life which more urgently requires that he who fills it should be in word and deed a good Christian, but it would never have occurred to me to have inquired whether you were of the Established Church or not.' The Rev. Philip Hunt wrote: 'I could not bear to see the unfortunate inmates of a prison under the control of a person of such illiberal and un-Christian sentiments as Captain Mitchell's letter contains.'

Whilst it is true that both Samuel Whitbread and Philip Hunt were outstanding magistrates who made their mark not only in the county but also nationally, concern about the character of the man filling the post of gaoler was not confined to them. Their views were typical of those of many magistrates of their time and of the whole of the eighteenth century. Such magistrates and such views helped to propel John Howard on the momentous journeys, the results of which we are remembering this year. Howard himself only gave us a small clue about the attitude of the magistrates. At the beginning of *The State of the Prisons* he described his concern about prisoners who remained in Bedford prison merely because they could not pay the fees of Thomas Howard, the gaoler. He continued with the immortal words (emphasis provided): 'In order to redress the hardship, I applied to the justices of the county for a salary to the jailer in lieu of his fees. *The bench were properly affected with the grievance, and willing to grant the relief desired:* but they wanted a precedent for charging the county with the expense. I therefore rode into several neighbouring counties in search of one.' The fact that the justices were both properly affected with the grievance, and willing to grant the relief desired, not only made it worth Howard's while to set off on his travels, but also confirms that there was in Bedfordshire a concern about the prison and its inmates which must have influenced Howard.

4

JOHN HOWARD AND HIS INFLUENCE IN AMERICA

R. W. England

John Howard (1726–1790) is one of the heroes of penology. He became a particular hero to Dissenter and Independent religious groups concerned with social reform, for he seemed to them a prime exemplar of non-establishment Christian piety, best shown by concern for social betterment, for the poor and downtrodden, for the brotherhood of man.

An extensive panegyric literature about Howard which began to accumulate at once after his death helped create a Howard image of such sanctimonious purity and goodness as would cause a saint to blush. This apotheosizing necessarily included Howard's efforts in prison reform with the result that he was popularly seen by later generations as the great mover and shaker of prisons in England and beyond. But someone seeking to uncover the foundations of his towering stature by learning precisely what his influence was finds, upon peeling off the layers of gilt plastered on him by successive admirers, that not only were his immediate achievements parochial and temporary, but that evidence of any larger impact on penology is tenuous.

Howard's reform efforts undeniably changed the ways in which some British local authorities handled their prisoners. These changes were accomplished mainly through personal initiatives carried by this persistent and determined country gentleman to Parliament, Lords Lieutenant, county justices and gaolers. Through prodigious tours of inspection Howard massively documented the miseries of English prisoners and the wide-spread flouting of statutes by county officials, and distributed his printed reports of his findings to persons of local and national influence.[1] He particularly endeavoured by personal visits to gaolers to persuade them to comply with such meagre statutory regulations as then existed including ones in the enactment of which he had played a part. The well-known result was that here and there about the kingdom occurred spotty improvements in prison conditions. Rules came to be posted in some places of confinement; extortion by keepers diminished; underground rooms were used less routinely; water supplies bettered; the sexes were separated in some new gaols. But these steps forward did not survive Howard's lifetime, for they were not part of any strong tide of prison improvement but eddies and chop stirred up by Howard's agitations. Upon his passing, English prison-keeping, its gadfly gone, relaxed into its old corrupt ways, to be undisturbed until a new generation of reformers began emerging after the turn of the century.

Though Howard's reforms were short lived, his detailed descriptions of English and continental places of incarceration during the latter part of the eighteenth century contain unique and invaluable historical data, and his example of selfless concern for the welfare of a despised under-class has inspired countless persons who followed him.

The facts that John Howard came to play any rôle in prison reform, and that this rôle took the odd style of endless inspections and chidings are themselves surprising. Howard's admirers, in accord with an earlier way of accounting for behaviour, attributed his reform activities to a great abundance in him of benevolence, philanthropy and Christian piety. But an analysis of Howard by the use of contemporary socio-psychological principles draws one's attention to much more than 'character' traits. John Howard, it happens, had a personality considered peculiar by people who knew him, and his early personal history likewise contained anomalies. In my opinion, these hold the key to his reformist efforts including both his accomplishments and his failure to seize a particular opportunity to accomplish far more than he did. I cannot, in this brief space, present more than an outline of my hypothesis on the sources of Howard's motivations.[2]

Raised by his business-oriented Calvinist family, Howard lived the first half of his life in and around London, where his associates were mainly successful City tradesmen, artisans and manufacturers. Howard had been directed towards a City career in the grocery business but for reasons unknown never finished his expensive apprenticeship. He came into his inheritance in his early twenties, living thereafter without gainful employment on an income quite modest for a man of leisure in those times.[3] Howard's London years are curiously empty of any recorded activities which could have foretold his later eminence. He did succeed in gaining membership of the Royal Society (1756) through the intercession of John Canton, a one-time weaver's apprentice turned experimenter in physics, and joined the Society for the Encouragement of Arts, Manufactures, and Commerce in 1758, his chief sponsor being a City jeweller. Howard seems to have travelled frequently to Europe and within the British Isles during this period. When at home he resided, as an unmarried man, in the Middlesex village of Stoke Newington and in London. There is sketchy evidence that Howard dabbled in science in those years, though he could point to no particular achievement therein when he submitted his application to the Royal Society. Several of his friends were scientists (as the term was then used), and he would, as the country gentleman he later became, conduct some impressive agricultural experiments at his country estate.

Mindful that most books and other writing about Howard after his death in 1790 were heavily panegyric, that many undocumented assertions about him got into print and came to be perpetuated as authentic Howardian lore, I undertook a search for first-hand accounts of the reformer recorded by contemporaries who had met him. These accounts are few, but they are either in fair agreement or they complement one another.

The reformer was a small, dark-complexioned, rather plain man of rapid speech and quick, vigorous movements. He could be waspish when crossed. Fastidious in his person, abstemious in his appetites and fussily punctilious in his habits, to some he appeared spinsterish and prim. In no way did John Howard match the stereotype of the extroverted, fun-loving eighteenth-century gentleman: he was a dour Calvinist.

The obscurity of his London and Middlesex period is due, I think, to his having become a gentleman too soon. When he was a boy, his family and its connections had been at the social rank of successful City of London entrepreneurs; it was that cultural level for which Howard was best prepared, but from which he—on his own—rose when he abandoned his apprenticeship at twenty or so, attained his patrimony, and set forth as a gentleman of leisure. In the long run, humanity would benefit from his decision, but at the time, it left him in a nether world of marginality. As the first leisured gentleman of his line, he forswore a business career but was, in personality, religion, upbringing, tastes and interests, not really suited for the idle life. Some vague early ailments of a 'nervous' kind, which included one of such severity as to cause a prolonged invalid episode culminating in his egregious first marriage, I am inclined to interpret as rooted in a distressing social plight with which he could not cope.

It was during this early period too that Howard commenced his frequent domestic and Continental touring, an avocational interest which he would combine with prison inspections after 1773. John Aikin, Howard's associate and first biographer, said that the reformer initially travelled in search of improved health, but presented no evidence for this. The rigours of Howard's later documented tours convince me that his constitution matched those of the horses on whose backs he customarily rode around England. At any rate, travel would have helped fill young Howard's time, as would the reading of medical and scientific writings which presumably occupied him at home.

The contrast between the anonymity of his urban years and the fame he gained after he moved to the rural parish of Cardington, Bedfordshire, in

about 1760 is striking. I suspect that Howard's marginal status was too
keenly felt in the City, that he was too apprehensive and discomfited there
for his potential to be realized. But as a principal resident landowner and
landlord in a quiet country parish, peopled by a handful of families of the
smaller gentry and a few hundred obsequious labourers, his life as a country
gentleman would release and nurture expression of his strong Calvinist sense
of social responsibility.

Howard's reformist fame has overshadowed two other important achievements accomplished or begun during his pre-sheriff country years. Too
briefly, these were: his development of model housing for the labourers in
Cardington parish, and his highly successful experiments with a variety of
potato which he caused to be widely adopted here and in Ireland, and for
which he won a gold medal from the Society of Arts.[4]

Intellectually, Howard was little given to the speculative, the philosophical,
the literary. His interests and temperament were compatible with science,
technology, engineering and the practical arts. Before his prison tours began
in 1773 he had had a decade of experience in Cardington parish personally
overseeing the building of numerous modern brick cottages, keeping a
particular eye on problems of drainage, ventilation and hygiene. He had also
served for two years as his parish's road supervisor during which time he
constructed a unique causeway road into Cardington village.

So it was as a man with practical experience in construction and housing
that Howard began inspecting prisons. His two books reflect this experience.
He was appalled by overcrowding, lack of sanitation, damp and ill-lighted
quarters, disorder, corruption. *The State of the Prisons* and *Lazarettos* contain
quantities of detailed technical data pertaining to room dimensions, window
counts, staircase heights, space usage, water supply, waste disposal, bathing
facilities, bedding and other aspects to which the attention of a paternalistic
landlord would be drawn. In the final editions of his books there are thirty-
two finely-detailed plates of prison and hospital plans and elevations, with
many of the measurements apparently made by Howard himself. Numbers of
these plans represented particularly institutions whose physical features (and
sometimes their management as well) Howard approved of as models for
wider adoption. Most of these, ironically, he had found on the Continent,
there being too few in his own country to serve as examples of good
planning.

Howard's published works, taken together, contain two broad categories
of information, somewhat confusingly intermingled: one category constitutes a heavily-documented indictment of the cruelties then being visited
upon prisoners both in the British Isles and in Europe (but especially in the
former); the second category amounts to a kind of 'plans and specifications'

handbook on institutional housing few of which, if any, then existed.

Howard himself drew up a model plan for a county gaol.[5] Among its details were unusual features adopted so closely by Philadelphia authorities as to support the argument that the Philadelphians copied parts of Howard's plan (a matter of historical importance). These features were: an arcaded construction to ward off damp and discourage escape attempts; felons to be locked at night in solitary cells to prevent moral contamination and encourage repentance; cells to be furnished with an inner door of iron lattice and an outer door of solid wood for guards' safety; and high, vaulted cell ceilings to prevent suffocation in case of fire.

In Britain's American colonies the conditions of prisoners in the seaboard settlements were no better than those in the mother country. There had been much chafing by the colonists under the colonialized versions of Britain's harsh penal laws, so it is not surprising that soon after the Declaration of Independence the former colonists began to replace hanging, mutilation and branding with deprivation of liberty for all but a handful of felonies.

It is important to be mindful that the original United States of America comprised, as they still do, a federation of political entities which severally retained all powers not specifically reserved to the Federal government. Each state was (and still is) allowed the full machinery of government organized in the three branches of executive, legislative and judicial. Consequently, each state was free to adopt its own criminal statutes and its own prison system for felons (lesser offenders being generally tried and punished under county or township authority). Each state was free to establish felony prisons along any lines it wished. But what should these lines be? The technical knowledge of collectively housing numbers of persons which had accumulated in Western cultures by the end of the eighteenth century was already considerable, though insufficient to answer fully the unique needs of felony prisons. Europeans and to a lesser extent the American colonialists were experienced with asylums, houses of correction, gaols, warships, hospitals and monasteries where scores—sometimes hundreds—of persons were housed. These establishments had been obliged to reckon with problems perpetually attending all human habitations: those of light, heat, sleeping arrangements, feeding, hygiene, and the rest. But the relatively abrupt emergence of the felony prison idea presented the Americans with urgent new problems, answers to which were scarcely available in the technology of institutional operations as then known. The basic problem was: how to sequester numbers of presumably depraved and dangerous felons under conditions at once humane, totally secure, and free from corruption and moral contamination? The American states, therefore, were confronted by pressing custodial needs but with means of fulfilment not ready at hand. It is not difficult to prevent prisoner escapes: shackling is highly effective; so is immuring in a sunken dungeon; a ball and chain works well—but these and other custodial measures which had long been known were now to be abandoned as cruel, but without compromising the fundamental requirement that escapes must not occur. American authorities then, were confronted by pressing custodial problems with no easy solutions.

The several states necessarily embarked on makeshift and trial-and-error solutions for a period of about forty years after the Revolution. Some of these solutions were dreadful. The worst was probably that of Connecticut, where the site of a worked-out copper mine near East Grandby was used as a felony prison from 1776 until 1827. An estimated 800 felons of both sexes served time there during those years, the men being confined at night in little sheds erected in the mine tunnels, and making nails and shoes above ground during the day. The mine was entered by descending a nineteen-foot ladder into Stygian black and chilling damp. Fractious prisoners were flogged at a surface whipping-post or shackled to the wall of an unlighted chamber at the end of one of the tunnels, where the shackling-hasps are still in place.

Another awful prison experiment was that of the State of Maine. Security and isolation were assured at night by locking prisoners singly in fifty-two stone-lined underground pits entered by retractable ladders through openings in their ceilings. Maine winters are severe; a feeble system of piping heat into the cells did not prevent numbers of inmates from dying of exposure or contracting pulmonary diseases. By day the prisoners mined granite from a quarry enclosed within the prison's walls.

Most of the states in this early era however relied heavily on the use of numerous guards for security, with prisoners being locked at night in rooms built for multiple occupancy, in an architectural variant of asylum and poor-house design. A few efforts were made to group inmates by degrees of criminality and thereby minimize contamination, but communication could not effectively be prevented by this measure.

It was during this forty-year interim of floundering that John Howard might have played a key role in American prison history. The colony of Pennsylvania had been founded as a Quaker refuge late in the seventeenth century by William Penn. Its chief city, Philadelphia, soon became the heart of American Quakerism and of social reform activities led by this Dissenter sect. The Quakers had eagerly kept abreast of European and British reformist writings during the hundred years preceding the American Revolution to guide their governance of the colony. Possibly inspired by the first two editions of Howard's *The State of Prisons,* the Quakers organized in 1783 The Philadelphia Society for Alleviating the Miseries of Public Prisons. Leaders of this body particularly studied Howard's books. The Society, in fact, sent him a flattering letter in 1788 requesting suggestions for a prison they were seeking to improve.

There is circumstantial evidence that Howard answered the Society, for a pamphlet it published in 1790 contained many details of a new county bridewell in Wymondham, Norfolk, put up by Sir Thomas Beevor. Although Howard briefly described this institution in *Lazarettos* (1789), the Quaker pamphlet contained information not published by Howard. An American historian has maintained that Beevor's plan was the basis for the construction of a 'Penitentiary House' erected in the yard of Philadelphia's Walnut Street Jail in 1790 as a prison within a prison for holding troublesome felons.[6] But this building contained three of the unusual features recommended by Howard in his county gaol plan: it was arcaded; its sixteen cells were vaulted; each cell held a latticed door and a wooden door. Additionally, a particular type of ventilator screen favoured by Howard was used in the building. The probability seems to me high that the presence of these four in the Quakers' structure, each an original concept of Howard's, must be attributed to him.

For some years after 1790 the Walnut Street Jail and its Penitentiary House enjoyed the reputation of a model prison, copied in its layout and programme by several state and local governments. But it eventually met the usual fate of American prisons: rapid population growth resulted in severe over-crowding, with consequent idleness, hygienic problems and moral contamination. It was replaced by a unique and extraordinarily massive structure designed by a young English-born architect, John Haviland. Haviland was commissioned by the State of Pennsylvania to devise an escape-proof, easily-guarded institution for male felons who were to be imprisoned under perpetual but humane solitary confinement of a type disallowing any communication between inmates. The result was the historic Eastern State Penitentiary at Philadelphia, opened in 1829. In effect, this prison was the 'Penitentiary House' enlarged many-fold with some new features invented by Haviland. At enormous expense, it met the specified conditions. Within a stoutly walled enclosure were erected seven long cell blocks, extending out from a central observation rotunda. Flanking the narrow corridor in each block were large, double-doored, vaulted cells, these opening not into the corridor but into walled exercise yards appending each cell. Granite walls eighteen to twenty-four inches thick separated the cells, which were floored by twenty-eight inches of concrete and granite slabs. Food slots opened onto the corridors, for no prisoner was to be allowed out of his cell and yard area for the duration of his stay. Escape from either enclosure and communication between enclosures was virtually impossible.

Haviland, as concerned as the Quakers that solitary confinements be humane, provided for each prisoner roomy, well-ventilated, heated cells, each containing a simple flush toilet. A remarkably secure and unique structure, it had an original capacity of some four hundred inmates.

This prison was duplicated in smaller versions chiefly in New Jersey and in some counties in the United States. But a rival felony prison system had been developing in New York State under far less humane leadership than the Quakers provided. This system, known as the silent-congregate, was physically characterized by multi-tiered honeycombs of tiny cells back to back in great stone and concrete blocks which were enclosed by surrounding shells. Individual prisoners occupied the cells at night; days, they worked in gangs under rules of silence enforced by on-the-spot whippings.

This rival system eventually predominated in the American states, for its severity and the ability of its prisons to pay their own way—albeit by what amounted to forced labour—appealed strongly to the rough-and-ready pieties and economic sentiments of a rural America.

In 1831 Britain's Home Office commissioned William Crawford of the London Prison Discipline Society to examine the prisons of the United States as possible models for a national prison system in this country. His voluminous report, published in 1835,[7] strongly advised the adoption of Pennsylvania's system of solitary confinement. His advice was followed. The first result was Pentonville Prison, erected in the Caledonian Road, Middlesex, and opened in 1842, a half-century after Howard's death. Pentonville lived up to its old nickname, 'the Model', for its radial plan and its roomy cells and skylighted corridors were imitated widely in England and in dozens of other countries. One could say indeed, that it became the standard prison throughout much of the civilized world.

So some of Howard's prison ideas very likely detoured to America, underwent maturation through Quaker foster-parentage, and recrossed the Atlantic as healthy offspring. That this detour happened at all can perhaps be explained by a particular error in judgement by the reformer. D. L. Howard suggested some years ago that Howard's personal shortcomings might have reduced his potential influence.[8] I quite agree. Howard seemed incapable of harnessing his reformist zeal to sustained co-operative endeavour. After passage of the landmark Penitentiary Houses Act of 1779, stimulated principally by publication of the first edition of *State of the Prisons* (1777), Howard was appointed by the Privy Council to be one of three 'supervisors of the buildings' whose immediate task was to find a site suitable for the first of two national prisons authorized by the Act. But disagreement and quarreling among the three blocked selection of a site; after two fruitless years Howard's patience ran out and he resigned his post in a dudgeon.

What did Howard do after resigning? Press on the Government the need for forthright action? Carry his case to his influential acquaintances in and out of Parliament? Despite the fact that his efforts had played a major rôle in creating public and official sentiment leading to the Penitentiary Houses Act, Howard simply resumed his inspection of gaols, travelling additional thousands of miles and nearly bankrupting himself in the doing. But Britain needed no further proof of its cruelty to prisoners; now convinced, it had been moved to the threshold of profound prison innovation. Strong leadership by Howard probably could have seen it crossed and his life's achievements much augmented by having put his country in the forefront of penological development. Howard's umbrageous withdrawal at so crucial a juncture of prison history thrust the Penitentiary Houses Act into limbo; no national prison for felons would be built in England for sixty years. The momentum of the country's prison reform movement slowed to a crawl until Evangelical and Utilitarian reformers began emerging three decades later.

On the other hand, as a quasi-public official concerned with actual prison construction and management on which he was the expert, Howard's tours might necessarily have been curtailed or even ended. But his dogged return to travelling allowed him to collect vast additional data, published as much enlarged versions of *The State of the Prisons* and the first edition of *Lazarettos*, to the enrichment of our knowledge of incarceration conditions in Howard's era.

The reformer apparently had been criticized by some as overdoing his inspection tours, particularly regarding a projected visit to Russia and beyond, for he was then past sixty. But he avowed a Calvinist sense of calling; '. . . let not my conduct be *uncandidly* imputed to *rashness* or *enthusiasm*, but to a *serious, deliberate* conviction that I am pursuing the path of *duty* . . .'[9] The following year on 20 January 1790, he perished from typhus in distant Tartary.

References

1. *The State of the Prisons in England and Wales,* Warrington, 1777, 1780, 1784; *An Account of the Principal Lazarettos in Europe,* Warrington, 1789.

2. A book in progress will contain my full argument and its supporting data.

3. His income never exceeded £500 *per annum.*

4. *See* England, R. W. (1976), 'The Cluster Potato: John Howard's achievement in Scientific Farming', *The Agricultural History Review,* Vol. 24, pt. II: pp. 144–8.

5. *The State of the Prisons,* 1784: pp. 19–43.

6. Barnes, Harry Elmer (1927), *The Evolution of Penology in Pennsylvania,* New York, Bobbs-Merrill Company: p. 77.

7. Crawford, William (1835), *Report of the Penitentiaries in the United States,* London.

8. Howard, D. L. (1963), *John Howard: Prison Reformer,* New York, Archer House Inc.: p. 166.

9. *Lazarettos:* p. 235. Italics are his.

JOHN HOWARD'S INFLUENCE ON THE PRISON SYSTEM OF EUROPE WITH SPECIAL REFERENCE TO GERMANY

Albert Krebs

To reform prisoners, or to make them better as to their morals, should always be the leading view in every house of correction and their earnings should only be a secondary object.

John Howard, *The State of Prisons*, 4th ed., 1792.[1]

I

On 5 April 1777 John Howard dedicated his book *The State of the Prisons in England and Wales, with Preliminary Observations and an Account of some Foreign Prisons* to the English House of Commons.[2] Its publication at that time had a far-reaching effect, like the ripples from a heavy stone cast into water. The bicentenary of the publication of this book is also a fitting time to consider its significance for the present day. It is my task to attempt to show how the questions raised by Howard influenced Europe, and especially Germany, like the rings emanating from the stone that was thrown. But I would like to state that Howard's influence can only be realized on an international level. To see Howard in context, we must remember that during his lifetime he witnessed the effects of the Enlightenment, saw the rise of England's supremacy and heard the first rumblings of the French Revolution. I presuppose knowledge of his biography. The quotation with which I began is the key to understanding his influence in the field: 'To reform prisoners, or make them better as to their morals [and their conduct] should be the leading view in every house of correction and their earnings should only be a secondary object.' He himself characterized his life's work with the words: 'I labour to bring the torch of human love into these distant parts, for in God's hands no instrument is too weak.'[3]

His work, as is evident from this 'profession', was inspired by his religious attitude. As an adult, in 1770, he made his covenant with God and renewed it shortly before the end of his life.[4] This religious attitude can only be mentioned briefly here. It alone impelled and enabled him, despite every risk and danger, to undertake faithfully the tasks which he felt had been assigned to him by God, from the time of his appointment as Sheriff in 1773 until his death at Kherson, in the Crimea (1790). He felt it was his mission to make a thorough investigation into the conditions in prisons and hospitals, where diseases and epidemics were rampant. Then, with accurate data, he made a survey of his findings, fearlessly demanded that the defects be remedied and finally proposed a new system. In religious instruction he saw the opportunity to exercise a lasting influence and bring about a change of heart. Religion alone could enable completion of the desired improvement.[5] He unassumingly acknowledged that the reform itself should be entrusted to other 'men of genius'.[6] He saw himself as a forerunner of change, rather than as a man who achieves it.

On seven large-scale journeys to many European countries from 1775 to 1790, he sought out the major prisons and hospitals in the countries he regarded as important. In his book published in 1777, he wrote down the experiences of the first two journeys.[7] After three further journeys he supplemented it with further observations in 1784.[8] On the sixth journey which took him to the Near East in 1785, he investigated plague hospitals with particular care and wrote about them in his second great book *Account of the Principal Hospitals and Lazarettos* in Europe (1789). He also wrote about the forty-two days he spent in the plague quarantine station in Venice.[9] On his seventh, and last journey, which took him as far as the Crimea, John Howard died of the plague at Kherson, on 20 January 1790.[10] He had used this journey also for the study of hospital conditions and to draw up suggestions for fighting the devastating epidemics.

II

With regard to my task of evaluating the influence of John Howard on the prison system of Europe, with special reference to Germany, it is essential to trace his ideas. I make no claim to a full coverage of his effectiveness and achievement. I do intend to sketch the arrangements he felt would bring about 'moral improvement'. His 'General Heads of Regulations' of 1784, drawn up by him in the light of the real situation in prisons of the time, show great specialist knowledge, a logical way of thinking and an unusual strength of will. He knew prison reform must be tackled in a dynamic fashion.

In the course of his journeys in Britain and many continental countries he conducted his investigations free from any illusions. As he financed these ventures out of his own pocket[11] he could maintain complete independence.

His exciting experiences were described not only in his two books, but in diary records and letters.[12] All the documents show the exertions and dangers he had to undergo to fulfil, with body, mind and soul, the self-imposed tasks, which he felt had been laid on him by God.

In his work some basic questions can be identified, eight of which will be examined in more detail here. They concern:

1. Living standards in prison
2. Régime: sucurity, health, diet, clothing, lodging, heating, religious instruction and morals
3. Means of coercion
4. Reception and discharge
5. Work
6. Prison employees
7. Boards of Control
8. Human rights

His notes on safeguarding human rights in the areas he investigated are an impressive reflection of his personality.[13]

1. *Living standards*

John Howard considered the overall standard of living in an institution as well as the sanitary arrangements to be most important. He noted details like the construction of prisons near rivers,[14] the regular whitewashing of the internal areas[15] and the installation of baths and ventilation equipment.[16] He substantiated these needs with the sober remark: 'I am convinced that in England more prisoners die at present as a result of sickness than through execution.'[17] Only through prudent health precautions on journeys and visits to institutions did John Howard survive, even during the stay in quarantine at Venice.[18] What response did such statements and demands elicit?[19] In England the House of Commons introduced countermeasures in the light of Howard's criticism. With the general improvement in the standards of living of the free, living standards also rose in prisons and hospitals. His achievement is that by exhortation and accusation, he was the first to point out the deplorable state of affairs, and to give it suitable publicity.[20]

2. *Régime*

John Howard tackled very seriously the problem of the régime of confinement. He knew the meaning of the words written later by Radbruch: 'Group confinement makes men worse, solitary confinement makes men weaker.' He also knew that of necessity, one can 'only be trained for society in society'.[21] Was he then really concerned with the relationship between the particular and the general? The answer must be yes. In the description of the prison in

Ghent he rated very highly the measures taken 'to make the prisoners useful members of society in the future.'[22]

The three main systems of confinement which developed after Howard's death were the Philadelphia or Pennsylvania system, the Auburn or New York system, and finally the Irish system which was a combination of the first two. They will not be considered further here. A large majority at the first International Meeting for Prison Reform in 1846, at Frankfurt am Main, called for solitary confinement by day and night.[23] The debate on this subject was continued at the International Criminal Law and Prison Congresses, and the issue remains alive today. John Howard's view was that the prisoner should be allowed a single room, at least for his night-time quarters.

3. *Means of coercion*

Coercive measures, such as trial by inquisition and torture, are alien to English law as a legal practice. Its legal processes therefore could have served as an example to the world as the dangers of inquisition and torture became increasingly recognized from the time of the Renaissance.[24] For this reason, the practice of these coercive methods made a particular impression on John Howard during his observations on the Continent. His account of his visit to the inquisition prison at Valladolid reveals the inner tension of the visitor. Certain areas there were barred to him. 'None but prisoners ever enter these rooms,' it was said. Frustrated, he answered provocatively: 'I would be confined for a month to satisfy my curiosity.' He was told: 'None come out under three years, and they take the oath of secrecy.'[25]

Before his appointment as Sheriff, and during a visit to Italy, he had already formed his opinion on torture, the cruellest of all inventions, and thanked God that he had been born in a country where there was now religious toleration.[26] In this rejection of torture he referred to Beccaria.[27] The decision of King Frederic the Second of Prussia to forbid torture, thereby giving Germany an example of the censure of this cruel practice, won John Howard's unreserved approval.[28] He was horrified by a particularly harrowing form of torture in the town of Osnabruck (in the ancestral country of the English King),[29] and also by similar methods employed in the free imperial cities of Hamburg[30] and Nuremberg.[31]

4. *Reception and discharge*

Even the simplest routine in the institutions of those days could bring problems: reception, for example, entailed the cruel custom by which prisoners forced the newcomer to 'pay or strip'. The gaoler supplied brandy, in return, and this was drunk by all in lieu of an entrance fee. John Howard was disgusted and called this a fatal custom, particularly because the removal of his clothes could bring sickness or even death to the victim.[32] Another deplorable custom in the house of correction at Mannheim revolted him just as much. There the newcomer was received with a 'welcome', i.e. beaten with a device specially made for the purpose.[33] The welcome was officially graded as 'small', 'medium' and 'large'. The same practice was occasionally employed as a 'farewell'.[34]

The idea of deterrence discernible in these methods became an increasing influence as the houses of correction changed to penal establishments.[35] However, these abuses also led to attempted remedies. The prison chaplain of Halle, H. B. Wagnitz, who always paid grateful tribute to the influence of John Howard, condemned this form of deterrence as 'barbaric' and pressed for the introduction of an enquiry into the prisoner's character on his admission.[36] John Howard also made the first steps towards a new approach to discharge, examining both the preparation for it and the event itself, and he made suggested improvements. He knew 'our prisons, these stages and schools of idleness and vice' and he formulated the new aim of influencing the prisoners' moral development and motivating them to behave well. The willing and industrious should be encouraged by an improvement in their accommodation and diet. On release they should be given a 'good character'.[37] Such a reference might build up self-esteem, particularly in those discharged without means who might go vainly from door to door seeking work. Moreover, even the penitent ex-prisoner could be driven by almost insuperable pressure to fall back into his old way of life.[38]

I will return later to possible connections between Howard's influence and attempts at prison aftercare by the 'Philadelphia Society for Alleviating the Miseries in Public Prisons'. One of their tasks was to prevent any severance of the ties that unite the human race. The prisoner was still human! Later generations were, at least in theory, prepared to accept these conclusions. H. B. Wagnitz, in his day, raised the matter of how one should treat discharged prisoners.[39] Systematic aid to discharged prisoners first began with the establishment of 'Prison Societies'. In 1805 such a society was founded in London, and this set up places of refuge for discharged prisoners.[40] Even so, Elizabeth Fry, at the beginning of her work at Newgate in London in 1813, found prison conditions in the same state as John Howard had found them.[41] In 1815, she founded the British Society for Promoting the Reform of Female Prisoners.[42] In 1823 Theodor Fliedner founded the Rhine-Westphalia Prison Society on this English model.[43] In 1828, stimulated by this example, the physician, N. H. Julius, took part in the establishment of the Berlin Association for the Reform of Prisoners.[44] Numerous other welfare associations were then established in all civilized countries.

5. *Work*

The period in which James Watt discovered the steam engine, in 1766, and Adam Smith published his *Enquiry into the Nature and Causes of the Wealth of Nations* in 1776[45] saw the beginning of a new sense of the importance of work, both in free society and in prisons. Since the establishment of the Amsterdam House of Correction in 1595, the importance of work in prison had been acknowledged, but this example had lost effectiveness. In England, as John Howard had discovered, the county gaol might be both a bridewell and a workhouse and therefore nobody, unless sick, should have been without work.[46] The reality was otherwise; only rarely was there work done in workhouses.[47] On his journeys through many European countries, John Howard noted that prisoners there were usually forced to work. He rejected the view that enforced work contradicts the English idea of freedom, and that work is the privilege of the free.[48] From this viewpoint, he made a detailed description of the House of Correction in Ghent, as being a model of its kind. With exemplary zeal, they strove there towards the goal of making prisoners useful to society. In this Ghent prison he saw people blossom out,[49] but he also saw some deteriorate when the authorities forbade them to work.[50]

However much John Howard campaigned for work, he knew its limitations, as the quotation at the head of the paper shows. If the question of earnings in prisons has often in the two hundred years since then been of principal importance, this is in no way the result of his efforts. Almost a hundred years ago, Karl Krohne, an expert on the prison service in Prussia of that time, made this statement, developing Howard's ideas: 'Work in prison must be considered from a three-fold point of view—the moral, the penal and the economic. The moral right to work makes it our duty to organize work so that it does not become an affliction or reduce the prisoners to slaves. From the economic point of view, it is essential that the work of prisoners be of real value, and attract the highest possible pay, thus doing no harm to free labour.'[51] John Howard earlier supported a similar material reward for the work performance.[52] The International Prison Congresses considered these problems again and again. It was fitting that, in the 1920s, the Howard League for Penal Reform proposed Minimum Rules for the Treatment of Prisoners, which also included recommendations on work. At the First United Nations Congress on the Prevention of Crime and the Treatment of Offenders in Geneva in 1955, recommendations regarding the employment of prisoners were compiled, after thorough consideration and debate by the competent authorities.[53]

6. *Prison employees*

In *The State of the Prisons*, Howard insisted that the first task of the prison administration must be to find a good man for gaoler, one who is honest, energetic and humane.[54] John Howard always held to this view,[55] and his observations while visiting more than three hundred prisons only strengthened it. How did reality match this? We have an engraving of 1729 by William Hogarth, the English artist and social critic: 'The prison warder Bambridge being tried by a Committee of the House of Commons'. He was charged with aiding the escape of several debtors and unlawfully putting others in chains and locking them in dungeons with the result that they died. Bambridge was dismissed and sentenced to a term of imprisonment.[56] John Howard knew that after a gaoler had been appointed in the light of the qualities already stipulated, his work conditions must also be properly laid down and scrupulously maintained. He was fully aware of the danger of the misuse of power, inherent in the gaoler's position. Bambridge was a warning example! Howard's call for 'cleanliness' certainly also included 'inner purity'.[57]

Safe custody, with the least possible severity, was for him the essential basis of well-ordered detention and imprisonment. He noted an excessive attention to security in Russia where the army exclusively manned the prisons. In all other European countries which he visited, paid civilians were used.[58] But reasons of expediency as well as security did cause entire prison institutions, as for example in Prussia, gradually to assume a military character which sometimes still remains today. After the end of the war, around 1813, the demobilized forces appointed to the prison service set up 'an institution on the model of a battalion, the governor corresponding to the commander, inspectors resembling officers, subordinate officials in place of non-commissioned officers, and prisoners in place of troops.' But Karl Krohne, who reported this, knew of the inherent dangers: 'This military framework meant that the staff and above all the governor, were invested with great power which only too often developed dangerously into capricious despotism.'[59] The position of prison staff as a group is still developing today. New occupational groups have joined the 'turnkey' of 1777 and they perform the old tasks and also an increasing number of new ones which now form part of the prison régime.[60] Here, especially, improvements must go forward.

7. Boards of Control

It was also one of John Howard's basic opinions that an inspector should be appointed for each prison, either from the ranks of his colleagues in the municipal administration or by Parliament. Sheriffs and town councillors already had powers of inspection, but 'individual sheriffs neglected this part of their duties . . . evidently in part because of the health dangers associated with it.'[61]

The instructions of the supervisory authorities on the Continent for prison staff were first concerned with regulations on general behaviour and then duties to prisoners. The general instructions began with the residence obligation,[62] the maintenance of security by careful supervision of cells,[63] the strict observance of the prescribed daily routine and ended with the threat of punishment for infringement of these orders.[64] The instructions concerning duties towards prisoners began with the need for faithful service and also forbade the acceptance of gifts to avoid the development of special relationships.[65] Regulations about conduct at reception, treatment at work and control of supervised free time, e.g. a prohibition on card-playing, followed.[66] In his account of Paris, John Howard noted a form of instruction to inspectors.[67] He showed a particular appreciation of the Amsterdam 'College of Regents' which had been adopted in the Hanseatic towns.[68] These accounts and suggestions all betray a certain bitterness at being left alone to carry out the duties of sheriff. Even the dedication of his book of 1777 to the House of Commons sounded a note of distress. The gravity of this problem, even at the present time, is not to be disputed. Further developments certainly followed these lines of thought, but each generation also returns to the main questions afresh. In the draft of a law concerning the reform of prisons and prison discipline for the State of Louisiana, which became the Livingstone Code of 1827, the rights and duties of all responsible, both prison staff and inspectors were defined, and in the introduction Juvenal's celebrated question: *'Quis custodiet ipsos custodes?'*[69] was posed yet again with a new meaning.

8. *Human rights*

For what reasons did John Howard press for well-thought-out rules of conduct, with which prisoners, of course, were to be fully acquainted? Is it possible to speak of a legal status of prisoners as early as 1770? His factual mind throws light on such questions.[70] In the three hundred or more institutions he visited, he found a price list for food in more than one-third; however, other regulations were only announced by notices in about twenty prisons.[71] In the summary of his book of 1784, he called for such notices[72] and also for penalties for their unlawful removal.[73] He demanded order and discipline to protect the peace of the institution. He did not differentiate between the rules of behaviour for prisoners and the work regulations for the officials.[74] The solution of this problem remains difficult since the idea of the equal protection of the law for both groups must be upheld.

There has been a steady development in the concept of human rights, which since the Bill of Rights of Virginia in 1776 has included prisoners' rights.[75] The relationship between rights and duties has always been central. We know from experience that the institutional microcosm cannot survive if this balance is missing. It was a crucial point in the German development when the Frankfurt Professor of Criminal Law, Berthold Freudenthal, emphasized the legal status of prisoners in 1909.[76] The previously mentioned 'Minimum Rules' which are binding on all civilized nations, have regulated the subject since 1955 in accordance with John Howard's precepts.[77]

III

The fundamental questions which John Howard perceived as essential in the course of his journeys of inspection in Britain and his study trips on the Continent indicated even then the additional problems which would appear in the eighteenth century. A detailed discussion of these would go beyond the scope of this paper. Nevertheless, brief mention will be made here of John Howard's attitude to the forms of imprisonment in Philadelphia and Auburn. The systems developed there strongly influenced prisons in all civilized countries in the nineteenth century.

The widely travelled philanthropist had not visited the prisons and hospitals of North America, as did many specialists at a later date. However, he studied the current political and penal problems of the 'New World'. He approved of the independence movement in the developing states which he witnessed before the publication of his standard work in 1777. He counted himself among those who were delighted that 'America refused to accede' to the demands of the mother country and he 'gloried in the outcome'.[78] The repercussions of this also affected prisons in England, as the suspension of transportation[79] added overcrowding to existing ills.

How did the people of 'New England', especially in the States of Pennsylvania and New York, with their prisons of Philadelphia and Auburn respectively, react to the fundamental questions posed in the large surveys of 1777 and 1784?—John Howard's work was well known there. A letter to him, dated 1788, from William White, President of the Philadelphia Society for Alleviating the Miseries in Public Prisons, is preserved.[80] In it White says: 'The Society joins with all friends of humanity in Europe in gratitude to you for having made the unhappy persons detained in prison the subject of increased general attention and sympathy.' In addition, the President thanked him for having 'pointed out ways not simply of alleviating suffering, but also of preventing crimes and other distressing circumstances which lead to crime.' The letter ends 'with sincere wishes that your worthwhile work may long continue and that, in the service of humanity, you may also have the joy of seeing the success of your work in every part of the globe.' A reply to this letter is not preserved. If it ever reached its intended recipient in the spring of 1788, it would have found him working under pressure on the interpretation of the findings of his sixth journey and the editing of the *Account of the Lazarettos*. However, an indirect reply could be seen in this work.

John Howard knew of the work of the Philadelphia Society[81] and he offered to subscribe £500 if a similar project were started in England.[82] We have further details of his connections with the New England prison system. A French contemporary, the Duc de la Rochefoucauld-Liancourt, affirmed at the beginning of his travel notebook, *The Prisons in Philadelphia* (1795): 'Howard's teachings and system were carefully adopted in Philadelphia many years ago.'[83] De la Rochefoucauld-Liancourt then considers further the introduction of the new Pennsylvania legislation based on reason and justice which replaced the death penalty with solitary confinement.[84] The title of the travel notebook in the German edition is: *Howards praktisches System auf die Gefängnisse in Philadelphia angewandt*.[85] The scholar who in our own time was most closely connected with establishment of a prison system in Pennsylvania, Negley K. Teeters, also referred in various publications to the way in which John Howard's views were of influence in Philadelphia. Teeters starts out from the thesis that Howard was a genuine advocate of solitary confinement as a means of reformation. He also refers to the English prisons at Wymondham and Gloucester which were organized on the basis of Howard's ideas on solitary imprisonment.[86] 'There prisoners slept, ate, and worked in single cells.' He summarizes his studies in a single sentence: 'The influence of John Howard is discernible throughout.'[87]

However deep the influence of this great man on the prison system in North America may be judged to have been, the reformers there had detailed knowledge of developments in England. They were aware of his indisputable influence. They knew of his substantial surveys, of the imperfections they revealed and of his proposals for improvement.[88] As F. H. Wines has said, 'The modern humane movements in our field began with Beccaria, the philosopher; Howard, the man of action, increasingly turned the attention of the authorities to the plight of those deprived of liberty.[89]

This development took place in three phases, from 1777 to 1871, from 1871 to 1918 and from 1918 to date.[90] During the first period, which began with the publication of Howard's standard work, we may see, in Germany for example, the fundamental influence of this pioneer on the growing literature of penal reform. His exemplary surveys revealed the existing shortcomings to the experts and the interested public, and stimulated reforms. Although the continuing influence of Howard's work cannot be so exactly demonstrated in the second and third periods, it is a fact that each generation of specialists since then has tried to build on the experiences of the practitioners and theorists working before them and to follow the example of John Howard.[91]

I will now consider the possible impact of Howard's ideas on the prison system of the then leading European power, France. The sharp contrast between England and France even affected the private lives of the citizens. The ambivalence of John Howard's reaction to France is evident. Apart from his harsh experiences as a French prisoner of war in 1756, he formed lasting impressions on repeated study trips. The anonymous translator of the French edition of *The State of the Prisons*, published in 1788, in contrast to the translator and editor of the German edition, refrained from making any personal comment.[92] Since French at that time was the language of the upper classes throughout the Continent, it was through this translation that all interested people learnt of his investigations and proposals.

In the publication of de la Rochefoucauld-Liancourt, referred to above, John Howard's basic idea was maintained: the ultimate purpose of criminal sentencing must be not only to punish but to reform the criminal.[93] A description of 'separate confinement' followed, and then we are told that the new system developed far more successfully than Howard would have dared to hope.[94] The interest in this subject in contemporary France must have been great, for even the Finance Minister of the time, Jacques Necker, drew up plans for prisons,[95] and prizes were offered for research into the best ways of improving convict prisons. This also happened in Germany.[96]

L. R. Villermé, a doctor, also reported on developments in France, and referred to the English philanthropist, in his book: *Prisons As They Are and As They Should Be* (1820), which he dedicated to de la Rochefoucauld-Liancourt. Villermé discussed prison buildings, hygiene, morality and political economy, and described, in a style very close to that of his English mentor, different French prisons. His favourite saying was the slogan of San Michèle: 'It is of little advantage to restrain the bad by punishment unless you render them good by discipline.' Villermé agreed with the conclusions of de la Rochefoucauld-Liancourt, who recommended solitary confinement in particular for all serious offenders, in line with the accepted laws in Philadelphia. Villermé then remarked that this was only rarely implemented in Europe. The period of solitary confinement should be determined on the individual merits of each case. Finally, he advocated the appointment of honorary inspectors who should use their influence to alleviate the severity with which rules were enforced in prisons.[97]

The development of solitary confinement on the Philadelphia model continued in France as in the rest of Europe. The German judge Noellner maintained in 1841 that of the European Commissioners sent out to North

America to look at the prison system, not a single one on his return did not prefer the Philadelphia system.[98] The First International Prison Reform Conference in Frankfurt am Main in 1846 also commended solitary confinement with only a few dissenting votes.[99] Specialists in the civilized countries had already reached a large measure of agreement on the subject.

Shortly after John Howard's death, the previously mentioned Halle prison chaplain, H. B. Wagnitz, published his *Historical Accounts and Observations on the Major Houses of Correction in Germany* and dedicated it to 'Howard's spirit and those on whom it rests' (1791). In the preface, he said, 'How good it would be if a German with the same researcher's eye and warm feeling for the sufferings of his fellow men were to visit and examine the prisons, houses of correction, lunatic asylums and hospitals of his own country as the Englishman did in his.' He continued a little later: 'People everywhere are more concerned with human rights, and prisoners are certainly now in the forefront of attention. Rulers who have not done so in the past are now fulfilling their duty of fatherly care towards them.'[100] The plan of his book corresponds with its model to a large extent, but while John Howard reported exclusively on institutions he himself had seen, Wagnitz also borrowed accounts from other published works.[101] Questions of funds, the administrative structure, and the treatment of prisoners were considered on Howard's model. Wagnitz developed personality investigation further following Howard's suggestions. He then pressed, like the German Herder, for recognition of diversity, i.e. for individualized treatment. He objected strongly, for example, to an intended imposition by Joseph II of one uniform educational system in all the states under his rule.[102] Wagnitz also recommended a systematic training for prison officials in training colleges. Through Wagnitz[103] Howard influenced the Prussian and also, at least in writing, the German prison system. This influence was especially telling, as the Prussian Minister of Justice, von Arnim, had a high opinion of Wagnitz as a man of practical abilities.[104] Von Arnim himself influenced the Prussian 'General Plan' of 1804, by which a better penal system was to be introduced and prisons were to be improved. This, of course, was not put into effect immediately since the Napoleonic Wars commandeered all the forces.[105]

Justus Gruner, who was promoted to Governor-General of the Rhine region of Prussia in 1813, is another important figure. He published three books on the subject.[106] In his survey of the Westphalia prisons conducted on the model of John Howard (1802), he refers time and again to the 'noble Briton who became the comforter and guardian of unfortunate prisoners'. Gruner takes up Howard's account of his visits to German prisons, particularly Osnabruck, and remarks respectfully if very critically: 'The noble Briton has been unjust to this institution, unless it has been improved since his visit, which I doubt, for certainly it does not now deserve such criticism, despite its shortcomings.'[107] In his attempt to find the most just and suitable form of public security institution, Gruner comments: 'I have often found that Wagnitz's valuable reports are unsatisfactory because they were second-hand. To make a valid judgement of public institutions, it is essential to view and inspect them oneself.'[108] Gruner followed this specialist report with a personal record of his journey of 1803[109] and he had the courage to dedicate the specialist work to the then King of Prussia, Frederick William III and the report of the journey to the Queen, Luise. The dedications were accepted.

In the years that followed, there was a continuing debate on the Continent as to whether and how imprisonment could best serve as a means of combatting crime, and what should be learnt from the North American experiences at Philadelphia and Auburn, which were frequently visited by European specialists. The physician, N. H. Julius, to whom the later expert on the Prussian prison system, J. H. Wichern, gave the honorary title of the 'German Howard',[110] became a resolute spokesman in the debate about solitary confinement. In the Netherlands the honorary title of a 'Dutch Howard' was conferred on a businessman named Suringar, who was then becoming known in international prison reform.[111] Such titles should honour both John Howard and their recipients.

The Prussian prison reformer, Karl Krohne, who played a leading part in promoting reform partly by his attendance at the major international criminal law and prison congresses[112] summed up his evaluation of John Howard in his *Textbook of Penology* of 1889 in the following sentences: 'By the nature of his work, but even more by his personal character, Howard has become the model for all who are engaged in prison reform. No ordinary philanthropist, he was free from all sentimentality and romanticism, which make the criminal an object of maudlin pity. He upheld the moral seriousness and just severity of punishment, and simply desired as a just religious man to remove from punishment and its execution everything that is contrary to the rights and dignity of those who punish and those who are punished.'[113]

Since John Howard, as I have tried to show, has the undisputed merit of having exhorted civilized nations to humanize their prison systems, it appears to me that his life and death still have significance today. Born in England in 1726 in a time of revolutionary change, he became a spokesman for suffering men, and died in Russia in 1790, in the firm conviction that a charitable mission had been given to him by God. He endeavoured to bring about an understanding between the strong and the weak of his time. He overcame frontiers and staked his life on the endeavour to promote concord between East and West, between which a barrier existed even then. We may

6

'A GOOD MAN FOR GAOLER'?—
Crisis, Discontent and the Prison Staff

J. E. Thomas

John Howard was not the first to focus attention on prison staff, any more than he was the first to try to excite concern about the plight of prisoners. His distinction seems to lie in the way in which he sustained his interest, and the prodigious amount of work he did to interest others. But in the earliest documentation about prisons, there can be found appeals for improvement, including many recommendations to correct that staff misbehaviour which sprang from the manifest defects of what we would call today 'organizational structures'. Many were to be echoed by Howard, such as this, which dates from the mid-sixteenth century:

> It were more convenient, that the keepers of prisons had a stipend appointed unto them than to live by bullying the poor prisoners and to augment their sorrow.[1]

Howard's special contribution was to emphasize the need for a 'good man', and to prove, beyond doubt, that in the ramshackle system he described, such men were in rather short supply. Further, he was sufficiently expert and sufficiently sophisticated to appreciate and, in the rather intangible way in which such things happen, to disseminate his appreciation that there could be no real change unless the overall organization of prisons was improved. Unless staff were properly paid, for example, there would be no end to the exploitation of prisoners, which characterized the English, and some European systems, for so many hundreds of years. And so he added his voice to the demand that good quality prison staff should be recruited, and that, once appointed, they should, by being properly paid, retain some hope of remaining of good quality.

In terms of trying to understand modern systems, much had happened since Howard. The purpose of this chapter is to try to trace the development of his shrewd aphorism, with the aim of helping us to understand present-day staff. In this development lies the key to much staff discontent, a feature of modern prison services which ought to be of the greatest concern. I wish therefore to discuss three things: The evolution of prison staff structures which, throughout the world show a remarkable homogeneity; the effects on uniformed staff of the introduction of reformative policies, for which reform organizations have often canvassed; and the relationship between reform bodies, notably the several Howard groups, and the uniformed staff. I shall draw illustrations mainly from England, but, as will become clear, the English system is usually an example of a world-wide pattern, since the evolution and practice of prison policy in advanced societies shows a notable concordance.

If my business in this paper were narrowly confined to an account of how the modern English prison system came to take its basic shape, I would begin, and almost end, with three officers of the Royal Engineers. These three architects of the system were Sir Joshua Jebb, who was Chairman of Convict Prisons from the inception of the service in 1850 until 1863; Sir Edmund Henderson, Chairman from 1863 until 1868, and his successor, Sir Edmund Du Cane, who ultimately took on the responsibility, as Chairman of the Prison Commissioners, for administering every prison in England and Wales. This was in 1877, when all prisons were brought under central government control. The third quarter of the nineteenth century was distinguished by the attempt to 'professionalize' many areas of public life. These military officers were the product of a relatively advanced segment of the army, the Royal Engineers, whose Royal Military Academy at Woolwich had been established, as the Royal Academy in the mid-eighteenth century.[2] Standards were quite high, and from 1825 to 1849 there was a failure rate of a quarter.[3] The calibre of Du Cane may be gauged from the fact that he came out at the top of his term.[4]

What is clear from a review of penal development at the time is that the several major reforms which were introduced, such as the abolition of patronage, the eradication of prisoner 'staff', and most important, the establishment of a para-military staff structure, were the consequence, not so much of the reformative zeal of earlier people, as of this new conglomerate of 'efficiency' and 'professionalism', which characterized much of the debate about public administration, and is exemplified by the Royal Engineers. So much was this evident, that Henry Labouchère remarked:

> Whenever the government was in difficulty in finding an officer of high capacity for civil administration, the right man was sure to be obtained among the officers of the Royal Engineers.[5]

Apart from the embarrassing presence of antiquated buildings, from Wormwood Scrubs in London, to Fremantle in Western Australia,[6] the most persistent and controversial legacy of these years is the para-military structure. The founders of the Service were not the first to recruit soldiers, or to advocate their employment. Nor is the para-military structure only found in prisons. Many institutions have adopted it as an appropriate means of organization, notably psychiatric hospitals. As far as prison services are concerned, most are organized along these lines, and attempts to modify the structure because of its incompatibility with therapeutic desiderata, have generally failed. It is, therefore, appropriate to dwell on its purpose and function.

The main function of the para-military structure is to deal with crises which arise in a community, such as a prison, where there is absence of commonly agreed assumptions about the laws which are established there. Prisoners, like other groups living in what they perceive to be an oppressive régime, are likely to conform only under duress. Such conformity can be ensured in two ways. The first of these is by the use of naked force. Because of the relative numbers of staff and prisoners this cannot easily be sustained, especially since most modern prison systems allow prisoners to 'associate' and thus propel staff into a vulnerable position. The alternative is to operate a reward system where staff offer inmates a wide variety of incentives which encourage conformity. These range from being allowed to eat in association to being released on parole.[7] The combination of the separate system, which in Victorian England precluded association, and the para-military structure which like its Army forebear can handle disorder if it *does* arise, leads to a subdued, if sterile, prison régime.

But, to the Victorian administrator, the para-military structure seemed to have other, very definite advantages. The ruling of oppressed people tends to lead to abuse, since a characteristic of being subject to oppression is powerlessness in respect of law-making and lack of redress in case of injustice. This, of course, is precisely what the current attempts to assert prisoners' rights are all about. This danger of abuse was reduced by an important component of a para-military régime. This is the way in which staff discretion is circumscribed, by precise delineation of authority at each level in the hierarchy. This close supervision by the senior rank of the junior rank next below, was intended by the Victorian administrators, as many of their instructions made clear. In 1877, for example, officers were warned that any ill-treatment would be severely dealt with,[8] and Du Cane was as rigid as ever in the instructions about the use of weapons and 'any abuse of power on the part of an officer'.[9]

Thus, through such a hierarchy, staff discretion was clearly prescribed, and indulgence in any excess was likely to lead to punishment. Such precision helped staff to understand what was expected of them. Officers, like most workers, wish to eliminate as much vagueness as possible, especially in prison where passions run high, and allegations and counter-allegations are endemic.

But such authoritarianism had a positive, if rather paternalistic aspect. As well as closely supervising staff conduct, Du Cane ensured that they were looked after. While abuse of prisoners was punished, abuse of staff was similarly attended by sanctions. And there are many examples of material assistance to staff, including the building of staff quarters where it was difficult to obtain lodgings.[10]

Even allowing for the hyperbole in official pronouncements and the familiar gap between the alleged and the actual, there is sufficient evidence to conclude that, within the tasks defined by the Government, Du Cane's contribution to the development of a competent administration of English prisons was colossal. More generally, since the mid-nineteenth century as far as the everyday life of prisoners in England is concerned, the work of these three officers of the Royal Engineers, for good or ill, eclipses anything effected by penal reform bodies, or by individuals. The only person of comparable status was Alexander Paterson, who was a Commissioner from 1922 to 1947, and who is best remembered for his shaping of the borstal system.[11]

What did the Howard Association make of this? *Fundamentally*, Tallack, who was Secretary for almost the same period as Du Cane was Chairman of the Prison Commission, approved of the general direction of the policies. Naturally, Tallack from time to time manifested that ambivalence about which of the two groups in the prison to support, which has always characterized reform bodies. He was often critical of individual cases of ill-treatment, as in the case of a convict called Fury who committed a murder in 1882, allegedly so that he could be put out of his misery.[12] He also described some officers as 'great brutes' to the Gladstone Committee, a remark which he was unable to justify.[13] But, Tallack, also supported staff especially in their morally-neutral battles with the Treasury for more pay and better conditions.[14] What Tallack did approve of was the separate system.[15] It is often not sufficiently stressed in historical evaluation of the penal system that a dominant theme in the views expressed by reformers from Howard onwards was a wish to restrict the freedom of prisoners and so to curb 'contamination'. This agitation culminated in the separation of the sexes, the prevention of drinking, and the institutionalization and victory over the silent system of the separate system which, whatever other features it may have, at least prevents contamination.[16] When separation was rigidly enforced, Tallack approved. Indeed, although he did not like the policy of recruiting ex-servicemen, who fitted easily into the para-militarism of the service, he seems to have conceded that separation was effectively enforced by the para-military structure. There were in fact periods in the history of the rather interesting relationship between Tallack and Du Cane when there was little stress.[17]

This para-military structure, with its overall task of control, was consonant with what was the official goal of prison policy—deterrence. Living in a separate system is substantially a punitive experience which, in the view of the classical policy-maker, is calculated to deter. Confusion arises when, as typically has happened in advanced societies in recent years, reformers press for more 'training' or 'treatment' in prison régimes. This usually results in a great deal of uncertainty about the para-military structure, which, nevertheless, remains the linchpin of prison administration. The latter years of the nineteenth century witnessed a culmination of these pressures for change. There were the International Congresses of those years in Europe, the influence of the Elmira reformatory in New York State, and various Inquiries. Such Inquiries reveal that the cadre of people who were interested in prison was spread throughout the world. In Western Australia for example, in 1898-9, there was a Royal Commission, provoked by a radical Parliamentarian, in the course of which the opinions of Du Cane and Tallack were quoted and discussed.[18]

In England, the turning point was the well-known Gladstone Committee.[19] Their principal, and most famous, recommendation was that:

> prison treatment should have as its primary and concurrent objects deterrence, and reformation.

This statement created an atmosphere in which major steps were taken, over the next seventy years, to make the experience of imprisonment less cruel. There is little need to describe these steps in detail, since they form the corpus of several standard accounts of the English prison system which allege and recount the abolition of Victorian barbarism, and its replacement by a kind of penal Enlightenment.[20] Sympathetic governments, such as the Liberal Government of 1905, individual Home Secretaries, such as R. A. Butler, and charismatic figures such as Paterson and W. W. Llewellin, all combined to make the English prison system, in the first half of this century, an examplar of prison reform. Vestiges of this are plentiful. For example, each year, despite the dismantling of the British Empire, groups of senior staff from the Commonwealth attend long courses at The Prison Service College, Wakefield, a practice begun in the 1930s. Some of the innovations were the establishment of the borstal system for young offenders, and the abolition of separate confinement, the broad arrow, and the convict crop. Others ranged from 'open' establishments and home leave, to education programmes and the hostel scheme.

Above all, as professions made their claims to expertise, they were introduced into the prison service. They included teachers, psychologists, pharmacists, direct entrants into the governor grades, and, latterly, social workers. Each introduction has been applauded, or in some cases—that of social workers for example—encouraged by the reform pressure groups. This has been the pattern, as has already been pointed out, not only in England, but in most countries which aspire to the accolade of being described as civilized. What has also been universal is a blank refusal to examine and deal with the reaction of uniformed prison staff, throughout the world, to these changes. What I wish to do in this last section is to give some account of this reaction. This is necessary for several somewhat unrelated reasons amongst which there will be, I hope, at least one which will appeal to each reader.

The first is the need for historical completeness. No assessment of a prison system in historical terms can be complete without some account of staff. Yet, very little indeed has been written about prison staff, except in terms which apologize for their apparent intransigence. Next, there are, crudely, operational reasons for pondering the attitudes of staff. No prison system will move in any direction without their co-operation, and to suppose otherwise is to indulge in the familiar fantasy of the governor or superintendent who believes that *his* contact with the prisoners is paramount. Finally, since a good deal of this volume is concerned with the rôle of reform organizations in penal policy, such organizations should try, in some cases harder, to understand staff attitudes. This is a most urgent question, if the hostility which is prevalent in the relationship between the two is to be modified.

As conditions of imprisonment have improved for inmates (although this must not be exaggerated), so the milieu in which staff operate has changed. Parallel with the easing of restrictions on prisoners has been increasing uncertainty and uneasiness on the part of staff. It is my belief that this has now reached such proportions (in some countries more than others) that some prison systems are on the point of organizational, if not total, collapse. Some people welcome this, or advocate it. What I am concerned with is the more limited question of how this has come about.

The whole of the events since the definition of rehabilitative aims should be viewed against the sheer intrinsic stress of prison work. It has this in common with other forms of what Goffman in *Asylums* calls 'people work', during which, we may assume, people are put in a situation where they have to depend upon others, usually reluctantly. The tension and hostility in a prison system, even allowing for the collusion of staff and inmates, are considerable. In addition, rehabilitative policies introduce degrees of uncertainty with the following consequences.

A preliminary, and concomitant, feature of such policies is that prisoners have more freedom of movement, notably the freedom to associate. As a result, staff, being outnumbered, feel vulnerable to attack, although this too varies from country to country, and should not be exaggerated. There is a generalized feeling that they are no longer in control, and yet that if they lose control, the critical attention of the community will be drawn to the prison, and staff will he held to ridicule. This is, almost invariably, an immediate consequence of manifest loss of control. An example from the English experience occurred when one of the mail train robbers escaped in 1964. *The Times* which had always treated reform in prison with great sympathy, now adopted the pose which staff suspected such bodies would. In a leader, the newspaper opined that this escape was 'a monumental scandal', and that it made 'the prison service a laughing stock among the criminal classes'.[21] And we have all heard of Attica.

The next point is that officers observe that in a situation where they are in competition with prisoners for scarce resources, those resources go to prisoners. Nor can such observations be regarded as unduly fantastic. Cool observers have noted instances where they are correct.[22] And can one too hastily ignore the following complaint, which is replicated in prison officers' magazines throughout the world?

> —our psychologist friends will shortly be taking up residence in two new suites of interview offices. These have been recently built at untold expense with all the refinements; that is except air conditioners but these are probably on order. One of these would be nice perched on top of the wall in replacement of the disgusting structures called Gun Posts, but then it would be a waste of time. The guns are only manned 24 hours a day.[23]

The particular example illustrates another source of discontent which has grown up as prisons have become progressively liberalized. This is the rôle of those 'specialists', or 'professionals', who have been recruited into prison services with increasing gusto. Officers' apprehensions about these have several dimensions, although it is by no means agreed that all, or any, of their apprehensions are justified. Where they are, there may be found specialists who try to deal with them. The first of these is that they are physical evidence of staff suspicion that a great deal of money can be spent on prisoners, when less is available to them. Next, the staff note that prisoners, because of the attention of the specialists, are receiving a great deal of assistance in areas where they themselves feel defective. The most easily verbalized and almost universal example of this is in respect of education. In England, as in some other countries, prison education is in the hands of professional teachers, often working in the bureaucratic structures which professionals elaborate as soon as their claim to special status is agreed. Prison officers maintain that they would like further education, and regard it as unjust that they do not get it. This provides certain confirmation of the depressing of their status and the elevating of that of the prisoner. In England, for example, officers supervise prisoners who are given time off from the working day to study for degrees of the Open University. Whether this is just or unjust is not at issue in this discussion. What has to be recognized is the colossal potential for resentment in this situation.

The third aspect of the attitude of the staff to specialists is somewhat confused, indeed contradictory. It is that, in respect of certain specialists, the uniformed officers could do the job equally well. This is especially so with regard to social workers in England, many of whom now work in prisons. Some officers feel that, with training, they could undertake such work, arguing that they come from the same background as the prisoners, and that they know them well. Yet, the officers suspect that much of the specialist activity is valueless, that the prisoners do not benefit from it, and that prisoners regard specialists as ripe for manipulation.[24]

But the most serious reservation which uniformed staff have about specialists is a belief that the latter have more sympathy with the prisoners than they have with the staff. They sometimes feel that the unity of purpose between uniformed officers and the non-uniformed senior staff in their task of controlling events in the prison has been undermined by rehabilitative policies, and considerably exacerbated by the presence of élite specialist groups. In some countries, notably England, this phenomenon may be reinforced by a drawing together of those who enter senior grades directly, and specialists, who then, together, display more interest in prisoners than in uniformed staff. This realignment of interests and loyalties amongst the groups of people who work in the prison is an important contributor to what is perceived as 'low morale'. It may be emphasized again that these attitudes may not be justified, and also that they are felt in varying degrees, from time to time, and place to place. But their existence is indubitable.

With regard to the reform organizations which are a feature of most advanced societies, a divorce between them and uniformed officers generally occurs early. As early as 1915 in England, the *Prison Officers' Magazine* observed that one unnamed society (clearly the Howard League) 'has committed the almost unpardonable error of liberating the prisoner and chaining up the officer'.[25] In some cases the result is entrenched mutual bitterness which is sterile, and in the pursuit of which the parties soon lose sight of prisoners' welfare or rehabilitation. Once again this is, in part, a result of the seemingly inescapable clash which is typical of prison life, and in the course of which reformers, it seems to staff, side with the prisoners. But it is more significant than this.

Prison officers often, and with justice, feel that they are insufficiently consulted about penal affairs. They express the view in their magazines, that, as with car workers or university staff, their experience ought to be taken into account when policy is made. However, what in fact happens is that certain people, able to exercise power at key points in the decision-making process, influence the direction of penal policy. Since much decision-making is both inexplicable and important in penal administration, staff in the field are forced to conclude that nobody is concerned with their opinions, while 'the reformers' have a large say in how things happen.[26] The cynicism which is often the outcome of reflection on such events, may perhaps be understood by reference to one English example. The Mountbatten Report[27] recommended the development of a new prison to cater for long-term prisoners. The Radzinowicz Report[28] recommended, instead, 'dispersal' of such prisoners to several prisons. This latter recommendation was accepted, despite the fact that, *inter alia,* the Prison Officers' Association opposed it, and continues to do so. The Radzinowicz Report pointed to the closure of Alcatraz as support for its recommendation, whilst neglecting to point out that it was replaced by the maximum security US Penitentiary at Marion, Illinois.[29] But a member of the Radzinowicz Committee, Mr. Leo Abse, in a very honest fashion, has since explained that he was determined to ensure that dispersal was accepted, and so introduced discussion about unlikely issues, such as that of carrying firearms, not presently employed in England, to deflect discussion from the main issue.[30]

There is another most important source of friction between reformers and prison staff, which is a reflection of relationships in the wider society. It centres around social class differences. One of the statements about prison officers in England which was made persistently in the Victorian period, was that they were not 'gentlemen'. It is a constant theme in views expressed at the time. Peek, Chairman of the Howard Association, and Tallack, for instance, wrote to *The Times* that the chief warder in charge could not deal with chaplains and surgeons who are 'really his superiors . . . by reason of their higher social position'.[31] At a time of growing inter-class animosity, such patronizing comments angered officers, and continued to do so for very many years. Whether or not this is relevant today, the heritage is present, as is the identification of middle-class people with reform. The parallels with America where segments of middle-class society have identified with the black revolt against prison authority are obvious enough.

Several other important factors need to be listed, briefly, to illustrate how conflicts have been sharpened at the present time. One of these is the abolition of capital punishment in many countries, which has led to the prospect of some prisoners spending most, and sometimes all, of their lives in prison. This part of the prison population, together with those who are serving extremely long sentences, see little purpose in colluding with staff by seeking reward in the traditional fashion. This reality, which was an important strand in the events leading to the Mountbatten Inquiry, makes prisons more difficult to manage. This difficulty, in turn, is compounded by a political radicalization of prisoners because of an increased awareness of race as a factor in imprisonment. Emanating largely from the United States, this has affected countries with racial minorities who are disproportionately represented in prison—New Zealand for example, or Western Australia, where a Royal Commission was set up recently to investigate alleged ill-treatment of Aboriginal prisoners.[32] Finally, there has been, in several countries, a widening of the division between staff, and newer, more radical groups who have no interest in improving prison conditions, and are intent on abolishing prisons altogether.

The present position is, as a consequence of all that has been described, that prison staff in many countries feel themselves to be alienated from the organizations which employ them, from the society which causes the organizations to come into existence, from the reform bodies who in various ways monitor and seek to influence the direction of prison affairs, and from increasingly large numbers of prisoners. The response of staff is usually to determine on resistance, if only by expressing their views forcefully, as in this example from Australia:

> How would you like to be assaulted, without offering any provocation in the course of your duty and then see the culprit (a native) be given every piece of legal aid required. To have the Community Welfare call you a liar and to see some sort of concocted lies appear in the Court. To have the Legal Aid representative call you a liar and then to have eventually a Magistrate who at least, was able to see that the offender was lying, convict him and give him one month concurrent for unlawful assault on a prison officer.[33]

In England, officers in some areas are displaying resistance amounting to militancy in dealing with the authorities. Some join extreme right-wing political parties, which promise a return to a support for authority.

In New York City, to take one American example, a team for election to a correctional officer organization gave as its platform:[34]

Adequate staffing
Basic civil rights for officers too
Elimination of our second class citizen status
Improved public image
Elimination of our 'no win policy'

They concluded by stating that:

> The time has come to tell the inmates when they are wrong. Nothing can be gained by long drawn out talk sessions that make them feel important and cost the city of New York a fortune. As your elected leadership we will push to regain the control we need to make our prisons safer for every officer and also the inmates who are most often the victims of lawlessness.

These examples are a fair summary of the current concern of prison officers in many countries.

Developments in prisons in recent years make Howard's dictum, in the title of this paper, seem simplistic indeed. The fact is that societies, more than ever, are confused about their prisons, and so it is hardly surprising that staff are equally confused. Until the community is a little clearer about the aims of its prisons, and until staff are encouraged to help formulate those aims, the milieu can hardly be created which will encourage the recruitment and development of 'a good man'.

In closing, may I stress that the burden on the reform bodies, especially the more influential ones, is considerable. Some have tried to engage the goodwill of prison staff, others frankly refuse to try. It is fair to say that none have consistently succeeded in maintaining a dialogue with staff which would serve to prove to the latter that reformers are concerned to understand them. But, if prison reform, as an activity, is to survive, then it is to staff that some attention should be paid. Because of the complexity and sophistication of some of the problems discussed, reformers might be forgiven for not doing so, arguing that it is too late. I hope that I have demonstrated that, apart from any other considerations, this would be a tactical error.

References

1. Meadows, J. (1874), *Henry Brinklow's Complaynt of Roderyk Mors,* Cowper, Early English Text Society, Kegan Paul, Bench, Trubner and Co. Ltd.: p. 28.

2. Harries-Jenkins, G. (1977), *The Army in Victorian Society*, Routledge and Kegan Paul: p. 113.

3. ibid.: p. 114.

4. For a biography of Du Cane *see:* Hasluck, A. (1975), *Royal Engineer*, Australia, Angus and Robertson.

5. Porter, W. (1889), *History of the Corps of Royal Engineers,* London, quoted in Roberts, D. (1960), *Victorian Origins of the Welfare State,* Yale University Press: p. 157.

6. For a history of prisons in Western Australia *see:* Thomas, J. E. & Stewart, A. (1978), *Imprisonment in Western Australia,* University of Western Australia Press.

7. For a discussion of 'power sharing' in prison *see:* Sykes, G. (1958), *The Society of Captives,* Princeton.

8. (1877), *Annual Report of the Directors of Convict Prisons*: p. VIII.

9. Du Cane, E. F. (1885), *The Punishment and Prevention of Crime,* Macmillan: pp. 165–7.

10. ibid.: p. 97. For a detailed discussion of the establishment of the English prison service *see:* Thomas, J. E. (1972), *The English Prison Officer since 1850,* Routledge and Kegan Paul: ch. 3.

11. For an account of Paterson's work *see:* Thomas, op. cit.: ch. 8.

12. (1882), *The Times,* 31 May: p. 4.

13. (1895), Minutes of Evidence taken by the Departmental Committee on Prisons with Appendices and Index, Q. 6898 and Q. 6912–20.

14. *See* for example: (1882), *The Times,* 7 June: p. 4.

15. Rose, G. (1961), *The Struggle for Penal Reform*, Stevens and Sons Ltd.: p. 20.

16. *See:* Fox, L. W. (1952), *The English Prison and Borstal System*, Routledge and Kegan Paul: pp. 32ff.

17. Rose, op. cit.: p. 46.

18. *Royal Commission appointed to inquire into the penal system of the colony, 1899, Western Australia. See:* Thomas, J. E. & Stewart, A., op. cit.

19. *Report from the Departmental Committee on Prisons, 1895.*

20. *See* for example: Fox, L. W., op. cit.

21. (1964), *The Times*, 13 August: p. 11.

22. *See* for example: (1958), *Report of the Committee on Remunerations and Conditions of Service of Certain Grades in the Prison Services*, Cmd. 544 (Wynn Parry Report).

23. (1975), *Western Australian Prison Officers' Union Newsletter*, September: p. 18.

24. *See:* Thomas, J. E., op. cit.: ch. 9.

25. (1915), *Prison Officer's Magazine*, February: p. 44.

26. For a discussion of prison staff and penal policy *see:* Thomas, J. E. (1977), 'The Influence of the Prison Service' in Walker, N., *Penal Policy Making in England*, Cambridge.

27. (1966), *Report of the Inquiry into Prison Escapes and Security*, Cmnd. 3175.

28. (1968), *The Regime for long-term Prisoners in Conditions of Maximum Security*, A.C.P.S.

29. (1976), *Federal Prison System Facilities*, Washington D.C., Bureau of Prisons: p. 13.

30. Abse, L. (1973), *Private Member*, Macdonald: pp. 121ff. For a discussion of the issue of concentration/dispersal *see:* Thomas, J. E. (1974), 'Policy and Administration in Penal Establishments' in Blom-Cooper, L., *Progress in Penal Reform*, O.U.P.

31. (1891), *The Times*, 10 February: p. 10.

32. (1973), *Royal Commission appointed to investigate: Various allegations of assaults on or brutality to prisoners in Fremantle Prison: and of discrimination against aboriginal or part aboriginal prisoners therein: and upon certain other matters touching that Prison, its inmates and staff*, Western Australia.

33. (1976), *Western Australian Prison Officers' Union Newsletter*, February: p. 9.

34. (1977), *The Toffel Team News*, Correction Officers of New York.

7

THE CENTRALIZATION OF GOVERN-MENTAL CONTROL OF NATIONAL PRISON SERVICES, WITH SPECIAL REFERENCE TO THE PRISON ACT, 1877

L. J. Blom-Cooper

Introduction

A decade after both the death penalty had ceased to be the penalty for virtually all crimes (except murder) and the last convict had been transported to the Australian colonies the prison system of England and Wales was nationalized. Yet the transfer of more than a hundred local prisons of varying size, from the small lock-up to the large prisons that disfigure our major cities, from local administration to central government, hitherto the responsibility of the local justices of the peace, was unaccompanied by any penological considerations. The modern penal system that was being ushered in by the use, for the first time, of imprisonment as a punishment for crime (and not just as a staging post to the gallows or the hulks on the Thames) evoked no response of a penological kind from the legislators, or indeed from penal reformers, in 1877; indeed the legislation was passed with little fuss or bother. Least of all was any thought given to local involvement in the treatment of offenders who would return to their communities after serving the sentences, although the local justices, rather as a matter of *amour-propre,* retained their links with the prisons through the Visiting Committee of Justices. The prison was then a place apart, shut off from the community it sought to serve.

When the new prison service was established under the Prison Act 1877, and administered by the five Prison Commissioners (who took over on 1 April 1878), it had conferred on it an administrative distinction that has remained untouched by a century of developments in local government. Unlike the hospital service, the education authorities, the social services or the dwindling number of police forces, the local community has had, and still has no statutory administrative function in respect of penal establishments sited in its limits. Many of the prisons, by the accident of history, are embedded in the heart of densely urban areas of our industrialized society. The sole local connection, even to this day, is the Board of Visitors (remote as that is), and it is not concerned with finance, staffing or penal policy. Before trying to make good these assertions, I must describe the penal scene as parliamentarians found it a hundred years ago.

The background to the centralization of the prison system has been described with deftness by Dr. J. E. Thomas in his work *The English Prison Officer since 1850,* but I must traverse some of the same ground. Parliamentary concern for prisons was a late starter. It is hardly to be found before the mid-eighteenth century, and when it came (the earliest Act is 1758) it was perfunctory and limited. Broadly speaking, the early legislation required local justices simply to make rules for the management of prisons. John Howard's monumental work however quickened public concern and prompted the parliamentarians to action. The first code of rules for prisons was to be found in the Gaols Act 1823. As the Webbs wrote in their famous work *English Prisons under Local Government,* this 'was the first measure of general prison reform to be framed and enacted on the responsibility of the national executive'. The Act provided for quarterly reports by the justices to the Home Secretary, systematic inspection by the justices, payment of salaries to gaolers, abolition of private trading by gaolers, improved accommodation, and above all reports from the gaoler, the chaplain and the surgeon were to be presented to quarter sessions. There was also insistence on productive labour, education and religious observance. As a code of prison accountability to both local and central government, it was an impressive piece of legislation. It was, however, limited to a minority of prisons—those of the county justices of the cities of London and Westminster, and seventeen provincial towns. The London debtors' prison and 150 gaols in the boroughs were excluded. But more significant was the fact that there was no machinery for enforcement, and no inspectorate. It was only too apparent that further direction from central government was vital. The inspectorate came in 1835. After Parliament passed the Act of 1835 'for effecting greater uniformity of practice in the government of prisons and for appointing inspectors of prisons in Great Britain' the inspectors' annual reports record the gradual application of a uniform policy even though for some time there was no agreement about what that policy should be.

The greater involvement of central government in the control of prisons was accompanied by the growing disenchantment with transportation (a *punishment* not just an ugly Americanized word for 'transport'!) In August 1838 the Select Committee on Transportation (the Molesworth Committee) issued a report critical of all transportation. If that Committee's recommendations bore little relation to the evidence presented to it (but more to the conceptions of Molesworth and his disciples), the issue of what to replace transport by was thrust firmly on central government. The end of transportation did not come until 1867, before which time central government became increasingly aware of the disparities between the local prisons administered by the justices and the handful of convict prisons for which it was directly responsible. The increasing concern in England about the efficacy of transportation was matched by the growing unwillingness of the Australian colonists to take any more convicts. The Molesworth Committee's recommendation of detention in penitentiaries became the only viable alternative. And in 1853 an Act was passed to allow the substitution of a sentence of penal servitude which could be served in England, for all crimes punishable by transportation for less than fourteen years.

During the middle of the nineteenth century, while methods of dealing with offenders were being adapted to meet the inevitable ending of transportation, the local prisons remained in a very unsatisfactory state. A series of reports culminated in the important Select Committee of the House of Lords on Prison Discipline in 1863. It catalogued the chronic deficiencies of local administration. The 1865 Act was based upon these recommendations. It established a detailed code of rules. The gaoler, for example, was under a statutory obligation to visit the whole of the prison daily and see every prisoner. He was 'at least once during the week' to go through the prison 'at an uncertain hour of the night' and record his nocturnal visitation in his journal. Particular duties were laid upon the prison surgeon and upon the chaplain. The financial grant from central government to the local authority could be withdrawn if the latter failed to comply with the Act, and the Secretary of State was empowered to close an inadequate prison. But this could not be done unless another authority was willing to receive the 'redundant' prisons; hence closure, which occurred on a large scale after 1877, could be achieved only when the administration was in the hands of one national authority. Moreover, despite the unifying purpose of the 1865 Act, uniformity of management and treatment was not achieved—at least not before it was too late to resist nationalization.

The 1877 Take-over

The situation was ripe for a national take-over. The central government was immersed in penal policy resulting from the ending of transportation; it had not succeeded in effecting any marked change in the conditions of local prisons and there was no concerted opposition to centralization among the political parties. It was paradoxically the Disraeli administration, with its record of hostility to central administration, that took the plunge of the first extreme case of nationalization.

The Conservative Government returned to power in 1874 was committed to a reduction in rates. The centralization of the prison system was one of the ways in which that could be effected. And in June 1876 Mr. Asheton Cross, the Home Secretary, introduced his Prisons Bill. A year later, on 12 July 1877, it received the Royal Assent; it came into force on 1 April 1878.

The Bill proposed the transfer of management on the grounds that (a) the condition of the prisons, and (b) the expense of their management, dictated such a measure. The relief for the local rates and the imposition of a uniform system of discipline were in fact the exclusively insistent themes of the debates, which were not very extensive. The Webbs considered that the Act encountered 'even less opposition than had been expected'. The opposition lacked nothing in volume, however, mainly through the advocacy of the Member for Burnley and a Committee member of the Howard Association, Mr. John Rylands. On the second reading of the Bill on 22 June 1876 he moved an amendment to the effect that, while recognizing the necessity of Members to secure economy and efficiency in the management of prisons, 'it would be inexpedient to transfer the control and management of prisons from local authorities to the Secretary of State'. He specifically did not rest his argument on the question of local taxation, although he thought it a great 'mistake to transfer large sums from local rates to the exchequer'. His theme was that there might be some economy, but it would be achieved at the risk of undesirable local inconvenience. He foresaw the conveyance of prisoners over long distances, and he thought that the provision of accommodation to cope with the 'cycles of crime' could be more efficiently organized locally than nationally. And he did not think that the cost of maintaining prison buildings would be saved. He instanced how 'at Borstal, a prison entirely and positively under government control, with 315 prisoners the cost per head is £55 per year, compared with Pentonville, with 970 prisoners at a cost of £30 per head per year.'

But underlying Mr. Ryland's long and well-documented report was the loss of authority of the local justices. He denied the lack of uniformity, save in respect of prison diet and labour. And any reform in the development of prison industry could be carried through better under local than under central authority. He bemoaned the fact that the justices' authority was limited to keeping up the visiting justices who 'might inspect the prisons, and if they saw anything wrong, they might inform the assistant inspector'. And as a final fling he taunted the Home Secretary with the observation that every argument for centralizing the prison system applied with equal force to taking over control of the police. Taking all the borough police and the county police under a single authority 'would effect a great economy of management, would employ a less number of police at less cost'.

Apart from a passing reference to the 'cycles of crime', the argument was directed solely to the conditions and management of the prisons. Nothing was said about the purpose of imprisonment, the community's responsibility for crime and the treatment of offenders, other than in the context of the functioning of the prison. The argument was thus solely focused on the responsibility for administration. Rylands moreover was not entirely in step with the Howard Association that had perseveringly advocated improvement in the administration of prisons. In its annual report in September 1876 the Association welcomed the Bill, in particular the provision that would empower the Secretary of State to discontinue a large number of unnecessary gaols. It noted the various anomalies of prison administration—the widely differing punishment inflicted in various gaols for the same class of disciplinary offences, the greatly varying cost, from £25 per prisoner in one gaol to £105 in another, and the extreme variety in the scale of prison earnings. It reflected Rylands' stance only to the extent that it hoped that the Home Secretary would not insist upon the *extreme* centralization which he seemed disposed to sanction. In a deputation to the Home Secretary, the Howard Association members were concerned only marginally with the continued functioning of the visiting justices and that certain powers might yet be conceded to local authorities.

A year later the Howard Association, after the Act had been passed, reiterated its long advocacy for the 'diminution of needless small gaols and a *consolidation* of the general prison system' and viewed with great satisfaction the long-denied reform in the Prison Act. It did however express unhappiness at too great an adherence to the principle of centralization. It hoped that the new central organization would not abandon the silent and separate system, so passionately propagated by the Association's secretary, William Tallack. And the Association went on to urge the ultimate diminution of the number of prisoners, with due attention to the deterrent and reformatory influence of this rigid separation of prisoners from evil communications with other offenders. There was however no reference to the state of crime, the community's responsibility for its offenders or its involvement in the use of imprisonment as an instrument of crime control. The reformers were preoccupied with the condition of imprisonment, as much as the politicians were concerned with their proper administration.

In essence, it was the unsuitability of the areas administering the hundred or so local prison authorities, coupled with the diversity of these authorities themselves (not to mention their shortcomings in administering the prisons) that compelled their demise as autonomous prison authorities. None of the local authorities acted for areas of sufficiently large populations to warrant separate administration of one penal institution—many local gaols had a daily average population of less than a dozen inmates. If the transfer was inevitable, it embodied the persistent political error of assuming that the pendulum must swing to the other extreme. As the Webbs pointed out 'the opposite of the wrong is seldom, if ever, to be found to be the right'. If prison administration by the county and borough authorities had become inadmissible there was no guarantee that a department of central government was necessarily the best, or more correctly the only alternative.

	Local Prisons	*Convict Prisoners Serving Penal Servitude*
1877	17,806	*circa* 10,000
1913	14,300	2,700
1918	7,000	1,200
1920	8,400	1,400

The concessions made by the 1877 Act to the claims of the local authorities were minimal, indeed swiftly the prisons began to disappear. The Act envisaged the closure of a large number of unnecessary gaols. (In 1876 the daily average prison population was 17,806. Forty of the larger prisons provided accommodation for 20,000 prisoners, the remaining seventy provided accommodation of between two and forty-eight cells.) Within a year of the Prison Commissioners taking over on 1 April 1878 the number of prisons was reduced from 113 to 68. But where discontinuance was effected the original prison authority had to be notified of closure and on payment of £120 in respect of each prisoner belonging to the prison authority for whom cell accommodation had been provided on 12 July 1876, the prison would be reconveyed to the local authority. If not, the Secretary of State could sell the property and after recouping the cost of sale would pay the surplus to the former prison authority. It was only in 1972 in section 59 of the Criminal Justice Act that the prison sites became the exclusive property of the Crown.

Such was the completeness of centralization in practice that few if any of the local authorities bought up the discontinued prisons. By the early 1880s the local authorities displayed an almost total abandonment of interest in prisons; they simply had given up the struggle. The public interest in the buildings, many of them of great architectural interest, was so lacking that most of the prisons were sold by tender to private citizens who allowed the buildings to become derelict and sold off the valuable land. In some instances the stout building materials were sold and used by local worthies to build private residences for themselves.*

The only remnant of local administration is the form of local supervision by the justices of the peace. Section 13 of the Act set up Visiting Committees appointed to each local prison by the local court of quarter sessions or local bench (or benches) of magistrates. A Member of the Committee was to have free access to every part of the prison, to every prisoner at all times. Additionally members were to visit at frequent intervals and hear any complaints which might be made to them by the prisoners and, if asked, privately. This vestigial remainder of local control involved three functions: inspection, adjudication in the most serious disciplinary offences and being the receptacle for prisoners' complaints.

This is not the place to rehearse the recommendations of the Jellicoe Committee on Boards of Visitors or the most limited report of the official Working Party on Adjudication Procedures in Prisons. It is sufficient for the purpose of this paper to note what the various committees have said about the rôle of the visiting justices. The Gladstone Committee in 1895 (p. 7) said that visiting committees' had for the most part acquiesced in the supremacy of central administration, had discharged their duties perfunctorily and had not exercised the [very unsuitable] functions laid upon them by the Prison Act.' The inquiry conducted by Hobhouse Brockway in 1921 led them substantially to endorse the view of the Gladstone Committee (*English Prisons Today* (1922), p. 389ff). The Franklin Committee, to review Punishments in Prisons, Borstal Institutions, Approved Schools and Remand Homes, said in its report in 1951: 'The Visiting Committees carried out their judicial functions, but on other matters they were rather overpowered by the forceful new Commissioners, and the evidence of the Gladstone Committee showed that only a few visiting committees were taking any interest in the running of the prisons.' The Jellicoe Committee noted that procedural improvements in the judicial function no doubt took place as a result of the Franklin Committee's proposals but that 'it seems unlikely that this other work would have been done any better.' And in my own limited knowledge it is not much more than perfunctory.

The convict prisons—that is the non-local prisons—were given boards of visitors under the Prison Act 1898. Unlike the visiting committees they were

---

* One or two local authorities did exercise their right to re-acquire any local prisons which the Prison Commissioners were intending to close, for example at Beau Maris, Anglesey, which was purchased by the local authority and, until recent times, was used for the local constabulary and in 1972 was converted into a museum. (The museum itself contains the only extant tread-mill.) Other authorities similarly repurchased closed prisons, for example Northleach in Gloucestershire.

required to have only two magistrate members. By the nature of the prisons they were concerned more with long-term prisoners and were not concerned with matters relating to the remand function of local prisons. The Courts Act 1971 abolished the courts of assize and quarter sessions. Consequently the selecting body for visiting committees disappeared, and now all penal institutions have a board of visitors. Magistrates no longer exclusively staff the boards on local prisons, but still have at least 50 per cent of the composition. This hardly reflects a direct interest by the local community, let alone influence upon prison administration and more importantly upon penal policy.

With the passing of the 1877 Act, penal policy and practice shifted irreversibly to central government, to the powerful Prison Commissioners: Du Cane, Ruggles-Brise, Paterson, Fox were names to conjure with. Their influence was immense and conceded nothing to local factors. Local government ceased to have any say in penal policy; and local participation in the running of prisons was restricted to the lay magistracy and a small number of citizens from the neighbourhood of a penal establishment. Until very recently there has been little, if any, official or even unofficial, local authority involvement in penal institutions within the authority's area. Sir Lionel Fox's description of the function of boards of visitors and the visiting committees as 'most valuable'—the committee acting as 'an impartial, judicial and non-official body' is valid only (if at all) in respect of the disciplinary and supervisory function. It pointedly takes no note of the potential link between the prison and the local community in terms of penal policy.

The characteristic features of a centralized administration that are peculiar to prisons, and are in my view inimicable to public understanding of the penal system that should lead to a sound penal policy, can be itemised.

1. *The Lack of Public Awareness*

Although many prisons are sited in the centres of dense urban population, prisoners are out of sight and out of mind of the public. High prison walls are not just physical barriers; they seal off the inmates from the populace. Although the traffic of people in and out of the prison gates today is large, nevertheless the prison is a silent world still shrouded in mystery. Few people other than the families of prisoners visit them and then only see little of the real life of the place. Much has been done to counteract this fact. The Home Office in recent years has accorded television teams a greater freedom of access to prisons, as a result of which the general public has now been afforded new opportunities to learn something of the realities of prison life. Had local administration continued in the prison system over the last hundred years the corrective to public unawareness of penal problems would have been earlier and more effective. It is noteworthy, as Sir Leon Radzinowicz has observed,* how the decentralized prison system of two hundred years ago presented no obstacle to John Howard. Although a journalist today might be able to visit as freely, this would not have been true ten or twenty years ago.

2. *The Lack of Voluntary Involvement*

A national administration tends to deal with voluntary associations that are closest to its own administration. The relationship of the Howard League or NACRO with the Prison Department of the Home Office, whatever its nature, tends to centre around issues of national penal policy and practice. The voluntary bodies necessarily confine their activities to general issues and direct their campaigns at the central authority. To some extent this limitation has been acknowledged. A few years ago the Prison Department reorganized itself by setting up regional departments. The Howard League in its turn has begun establishing branches in provincial towns and NACRO has directed much of its field work to selected centres of population. Had the growth in local government taken in some responsibility for prisons, the local voluntary agencies would have been activated. By contrast it is noticeable how in a country like Holland local voluntary bodies are more engaged in penal affairs, mainly because voluntary work, locally based, has always been a feature of Dutch life.

3. *The Lack of Local Inspection*

Whenever the power and responsibility for government is exclusively in the hands of one authority and the inspectorate is in the care of another authority, there tends to be a much greater degree of impartiality, more fearless criticism and a greater willingness to countenance change in practice. The most effective period of the prison inspectorate was in the years before the 1877 Act, when national government sought to control the local administration by a national inspectorate.

If there is no turning back on the prison system erected in 1877 there are ways in which the pervasiveness of centralization could usefully be mitigated. There are signs that this is actively desired by some local authorities. The London Borough of Islington, which uniquely has *two* major prisons within its area—Holloway and Pentonville—has already made a move. It has made three major proposals. First, it seeks the direct representation on the board of visitors of the two prisons. Linked to this is a proposal to provide direct access of prisoners to local councillors on matters concerning the Borough

* ante p. 9.

or where a prisoner's family lives in the Borough. Direct representation would not necessarily improve the links, but clearly the Home Secretary should exercise the power of appointment in such a way as to allow greater participation by local politicians. Direct access is available and should be encouraged.

The third proposal involves inspection. The Association of Metropolitan Authorities is being urged to have inspection under the Health and Safety at Work Act delegated to local authorities, and that Crown property should no longer be exempted from inspection by local authority officers under the provisions of the Food and Drugs Act. These proposals raise difficulties that need resolving, but the idea behind them is sound—greater responsibility for aspects of social life occurring locally, prisons as part of the locality, not just geographically but socially.

Such proposals lead one to a simple observation. If it is desirable to move towards greater local involvement in penal policy and practice—and I believe it is—it should not be wholly impracticable for the Home Office to set up local committees in areas where there are penal establishments to perform some of the functions of prison administration. With the growing need of prisons to rely upon local hospitals, local psychiatric services, after-care hostels and other social services for prisoners' families and ex-prisoners and their families, it is time for some accommodation to be made by the central administration to the applicability of the services of local authorities. The problem of social control and the treatment of offenders is becoming more and more community-based. The shift is away from custody to non-custodial treatment; and custody itself is no longer a one-off treatment but properly is part of an on-going programme of social intervention in which local authorities are under a statutory obligation to be involved. The need to involve local authorities in the penal system is pressing.

The centenary of the Prison Act 1877 is a moment to acknowledge that our Victorian legislators did well to put an end to abuses and to facilitate vast improvements in our prison system. But, with hindsight, they saddled us with a system that is open to the grave objection that it isolated the prison from the communities it sought to serve, to the point where the local communities wash their hands of a problem that is properly theirs.

That indefatigable penal reformer within the prison system, the Rev. W. D. Morrison, the Canadian-born chaplain at Wandsworth Prison, wrote in 1894:

> It is not to be denied that the local prison administration in operation before 1878 had its faults and undoubtedly required radical alterations. But it had its virtues too. Prisons can never be successfully administered without a practical knowledge of the prison population, and an intimate acquaintance with the prison staff. Both of these requisites the county magistrates possessed, and as a result prisoners

were never mechanized into mere pieces on a chess-board, and the prison staff was never rendered impotent as a reformative agency by a smouldering spirit of disaffection. In fact the old local prison administration was a system which kept the ruling classes in touch with social miseries in their acutest forms. Local power created local interest and a sense of local responsibility.*

* Morrison, Rev W. D. (1894), 'Are our prisons a Failure?' *Fortnightly Review*, Vol LV: p. 461.

8

SHARED RESPONSIBILITY

The Rev. Canon Lloyd Rees

John 19[18]
'There they crucified Him and two others with Him, on either side one, and Jesus in the midst.'

Above the altar in the Chapel of Winchester Prison there hangs a rather remarkable crucifix—the work of a young sculptor, David Noble. The crucifix which shows Christ as a young, virile person in the act of offering Himself to the Father hangs against a dead white background and by an accident of lighting throws two shadows. It was Harry, the Chapel red-band, who first noticed the shadows and asked me if the sculptor had intended them to be there. I replied that he had not, but how appropriate they were—for on the green hill outside the city wall there were three crosses not one, and there were three men not one.

So it is worth asking the question: 'Who were these two men who hung alongside Jesus in the hour of His death, sharing suffering with Him?' Tradition tells us that they were political revolutionaries, men who had banded with others to overthrow the tyrannical government and who had faced the consequences of their being taken prisoner. One publicly admitted his responsibility for what he had done and for the situation in which he now found himself. 'We indeed suffer justly, for we receive the due reward of our sins.' Some people, we hope, would not have been so harsh in their judgement and would have recognized that there were others who shared responsibility with them—those who set the task, those who participated but were not caught, those who imposed the tyranny—responsibility was shared.

But what was Our Lord doing there—He who was Himself without sin—what was He doing there on His Cross of suffering and of punishment? There are many answers which can be given to this important question, but I am attracted by the explanation given by Bishop Hughes of Croydon who says that if priesthood toward one another can be understood as the shouldering of necessary responsibility, then Jesus was there exercising His priesthood, coming where others were, accepting and expressing responsibility for us and for them. I have described this picture of the Winchester crucifix—and the two others—because it is only in this context that we can begin to think about the prisoner and our relationship to him.

First of all the picture asserts the truth that the prisoner himself has a responsibility for what he has done and for his situation. To suggest to him that he has no responsibility and that his actions can be totally explained in terms of factors outside himself is to do him a disservice and to rob him of his freedom as a moral agent. If he has no freedom, then he is not culpable and we have no right to punish him or deter or reform him. We need to help the offender face and answer the question 'How far am I responsible?', for my pastoral experience leads me to think that it is not until that question is honestly faced and answered that the process of healing can really begin. Moral growth takes place precisely as the offender is brought to face the true significance of what he has done. But the same pastoral experience makes me realize how cautious we need to be in trying to assess the degree of responsibility which any one offender has—for many are themselves the victims of the ignorance and insensitivity of others who share responsibility with them and for them. 'Every single prisoner is one single piece of evidence that responsible relationships have broken down all round.' Responsibility is shared—not only the offender but the society which judges him are characterized by failure and wrong-doing, the solidarity of human existence is a solidarity in sin and in expecting the offender to become more law-abiding we need to be remedying those aspects of society's life which contribute to his behaviour.

The responsibility of the State towards the offender is not discharged merely by arresting him, establishing his guilt and committing him to prison —it is not discharged until everything possible has been done to help him become a stronger and more hopeful person. The prisoner has rights because he is a person—he has the right to be treated as a person and not as something less, he has the right to be understood, he has the right to emerge from prison at least not more damaged than when he went in. And those who discharge this responsibility on our behalf—prison administrators, governors, officers, probation officers and the like—are entitled to our understanding and our care and our support. Theirs is far from an easy task, maintaining a system, coming to terms with some prisoners who are bitter and unresponsive and aggressive and with a public which has conflicting expectations of the system. Not only the prisoner but everyone involved in prison symbolizes and suffers the failures of the whole society. But if they are to have that understanding and support, they need to share with others in the dialogue, in discussion of their views and experience and conclusions. For there are others, too, who express their responsibility in study and research and in questioning and in challenging. But that challenging needs to be from a position of knowledge and identification and integrity and co-operation.

It needs to be rooted in a presumption that the people who are challenged are themselves people of integrity and knowledge and achievement. For there are fundamental questions to be discussed—questions about the whole notion of punishment, its necessity, its justification, and its effect; questions about alternatives to imprisonment; questions about decriminalization and diversion; questions about treatment and containment and after-care. In that discussion, all need to be involved—the criminologist, the anthropologist, the psychiatrist, the sociologist, the theologian, the judge, the police, the prison officer—all have their contribution to make, all have their insights and experience to express. Too often the holders of conflicting views remain polite to one another but present their views, if at all, at a respectable distance from one another, but dialogue alone can produce understanding and respect—and charity; and understanding and respect and charity are more likely to produce co-operation.

And in that co-operation let each look to John Howard and his courage and his zeal and his humility, and echo his words:

'To God alone be praise! I do not regret the loss of many conveniences of life, but bless God who inclined my mind to such a scheme.'

Dame as the Goddess of Reason. Not all the enthusiastic concern for rationality took so dramatic or so sacrilegious a form, but there was a new and fundamental questioning of the basis of political and social institutions. By the time *The State of the Prisons* appeared the American Declaration of Independence held certain things to be self-evident and inalienable and Howard's contemporary Adam Smith had produced that quintessential analysis of political economy, *The Wealth of Nations*.

The rational test of any social and political institution was two-fold. To be acceptable it needed to do no violence to the fundamental dignity of Man and at the same time it needed to be practically effective in achieving its imputed objectives. Clearly, the eighteenth-century penal system did neither in that it was both cruel *and* ineffectual. Howard, like Dr. Benjamin Rush and the members of the Pennsylvania Prison Society, was not slow to see that cruel and degrading treatment was also ineffectual as a means of controlling crime.

It was hardly surprising then, that the penal system came to be one of the concerns of the Utilitarian movement. Bentham, that lawyer whom lawyers seem so often reluctant to acknowledge as one of their own kind, saw crime as a perfect example of a situation in which the hedonistic calculus might be applied, the function of the criminal law and the penal system being just sufficient to tip the balance in the direction of law observance. Bentham's concern with the schemes for a national penitentiary that would take the place of transportation are well known, but the influence of Utilitarian philosophy upon other institutions of social control is no less important. When the 'model' convict prison at Pentonville opened in 1842 it was in its architecture and its ethos astonishingly similar to the many workhouses that were being erected all over England in response to that all too devastatingly rational Utilitarian analysis of the Poor Law made by Edwin Chadwick in 1834. Self-help was to be stimulated among paupers by the knowledge that public relief was only to be had in an institution that treated its inmates in such a way that every rational pauper would do all in his power to avoid entering its portals. Law observance among the criminal classes was to be achieved by prison conditions that would ensure that the happiest convict was still less happy than the most unhappy law-abiding citizen outside.

Not of course that the simple notion of rational deterrence was without its uses. It had been able to demonstrate how the increasing severities of the criminal law in the eighteenth century far from reducing crime, had actually contributed to its increase through the law of diminishing marginal returns. The disutility of a death penalty applied to hundreds of offences became all too clear. But the critics of the extreme utilitarian view tended to reject the idea that crime was no more than a rational response to the balance between the pleasures of law-breaking and the pains of the penal system; it suggested a view of Man that hinted at a state of semi-automatism in which free will was either attenuated or non-existent. At worst it denied the moral nature of Man in that it denied that when he acted virtuously he did so because he knew the difference between right and wrong and did not merely refrain from crime because the consequences would be painful.

Now if Man were seen as not merely a rational being but a moral being— and the two are by no means mutually exclusive—then there could be more to a penal system than the provision of rational deterrence. It was possible to develop a new dimension, that of rehabilitation. Rehabilitation is, of course, a word with several possible meanings. Certainly for the early pioneers of the Pennsylvania Penitentiary it meant that kind of moral and spiritual regeneration that would ensure that there would be no return to crime. That the Pennsylvania system should have broken down in its attempts to achieve this end is scarcely surprising when one considers the moral imperfections of those law-abiding citizens entrusted with government. Those penal administrators who have been committed to this view of rehabilitation over the years have, on the whole, been regarded with some suspicion by those with a more practical concern for the business of government. Mary Carpenter and Alexander Maconochie were regarded by their contemporaries as both eccentrics and embarrassments. At the same time there was another interpretation of the idea of rehabilitation which permitted its fusion with the more direct concerns of rational deterrence. This consisted of an adaptation of the Protestant ethic albeit in a grossly distorted form; work was to be equated with virtue, and idleness (which included economic survival through crime) with vice. Thus if prisoners could be put to work it would be positively good for them in permitting them to act virtuously while if the work were irksome it would provide that element of deterrence that would dissuade them from continuing in crime. They would be trained in the habits of industry which was as much their duty as it might be their pleasure. One must compare this view with that which enjoined working people everywhere to accept with good grace the duties of the station in life to which they had been called. Servants ought to be cheerfully subject to their masters and not to question their authority. A modification of this view was based upon the idea that by improving the economic life-chances of offenders their commitment to honest labour might be the greater and their chances of enjoying economic security correspondingly enlarged. Thus the unskilled man ought to be taught skills, the illiterate taught to read, and so on.

Penal practice in the nineteenth century was beset with difficulties and criticisms which have an astonishingly contemporary ring. Let us take, for instance, the application of utilitarian deterrence. It was not possible so to organize prison régimes that the lot of the happiest convict was still worse than that of the most unhappy man outside. To have done so would have meant a programme of deliberate starvation and disease, indeed, of going back to the conditions of the congregate gaol of the eighteenth century in which apart from the gallows the most effective check on the size of the prison population was the epidemic. Thus in the interests of hygiene alone, the housing and nutrition of prisoners had to be substantially better than those of the poor outside. Yet this denial of the principle of less eligibility, particularly when prisoners were also set to useful labour and were able to improve their chances in the labour market, was an affront to those who felt that in no circumstances ought crime to pay any dividends. The criticism is still with us. I have heard participants in public debates refer to prisoners as 'living like lords' enjoying television and much else besides. That prison food usually leaves much to be desired, and the availability of television could be a dubious privilege is one thing; few 'lords' sleep two or three to a small room and must endure the odours of each other's nightsoil. Yet at the same time it is probably true to say that even such an inmate enjoys marginally better conditions of life than a vagrant alcoholic turned out in the early morning from a common lodging-house to seek what shelter he can from the rain and cold.

The question is not so much one of determining ways of enshrining the principle of less eligibility in differential standards but of establishing minimum criteria of physical decency below which prison standards, whatever the condition of the most marginal groups outside, cannot be allowed to fall. Usually these resolve themselves as the standards necessary to maintain the inmate in reasonably good health and free from disease (although they may not pay much attention to the inmate's mental health save in extreme circumstances). In this context it is not unimportant to observe that virtually all prisons in the western industrial world approach these standards, or at least attempt to do so; only in the prisons of the Soviet Empire and other openly totalitarian states is there any deliberate divergence from such a policy which, whatever its humanitarian virtues, usually commends itself as the course most likely to avoid trouble.

The combination of the stimulation of virtue by the provision of disciplined work with that of deterrence through the provision of irksome experiences is still very much with us. Why should the borstal system provide morally undeserving youths with the chance to learn a trade when boys who have chosen not to commit offences have poorer opportunities? Unfortunately much of the work that is available to prison inmates is of a dull and irksome character, yet contemporary prison administrators would be loath to take satisfaction in the idea that they would have pleased certain nineteenth-century penal theorists. The fact is that much prison work, even when it has an economic value, is no more and no less irksome than the sort of work which characterizes the industrial system of the world outside. Where it differs is in the extent of economic reward, which results in prison labour having the characteristics of serfdom rather than free labour. Nor does it follow that the simple acquisition of skills, resulting in an improvement in the inmate's economic chances, provides any insulation against future crime; that must depend upon a range of factors not least important of which is that of personal commitment to law observance. It was abhorrent to the nineteenth-century public that wrongdoers should lie in idleness, even in gaol; therefore they ought to be employed at something, even if that something was from an economic point of view, utterly futile.

One may ask the question, and in seriousness, of how far prisons have advanced since the time of Howard. Now much must depend upon a clear understanding of the objectives; if these are unknown then the question is unanswerable. Since Howard's day the overt function of the prison has changed from being a place where for the most part criminals awaited the sentences of death or transportation, to being one to which they are consigned for a variety of purposes which different interests rate with varying priority.

The nineteenth century placed deterrence high on the list, together with expiation for wrong done. Our century has become sceptical of deterrence and because it is a strikingly amoral age the idea of expiation is largely meaningless to it. We talk, instead, of rehabilitation and 'treatment'.

Much of the responsibility for this we must lay at the doors of those who have followed in the Positivist tracks of Lombroso in their search for those objective identifying characteristics of the criminal which set him apart from the rest of mankind and which, at the same time, divest him of his moral responsibilities for crime. I include here all that farrago of nonsense which stems from the argument that because it is not possible accurately to determine criminal responsibility in the moral sense we should proceed on the basis that such responsibility does not exist at all. It has given us the 'treatment' model of penology, to which we may add the like terms of 'training' and rehabilitation.

In a physical sense, prisons are less nasty. That is undeniable since not even the most enthusiastic member of PROP can point to a death from gaol fever in the last five years. But it does not follow either that nastiness is limited to things like death from gaol fever, nor that progress has been achieved simply because the objectives have changed.

My argument is that the state of prisons is parlous, both in this country and in many abroad. Let me say initially that I believe that there are many worse prisons in Europe than those in this country. I should not like to be imprisoned in Italy, nor in France, nor, I think, in West Germany. I would regard a sentence served in many prisons in North America as one of living death subject to homosexual rape. But because things may be worse elsewhere, it does not follow that they must be good here. In what sense, then, is the state of prisons parlous?

Firstly, because in the confusion of their objectives they succeed in achieving virtually nothing. They are expensive to run. They do not prevent crime. They do not reduce crime. They do not, as far as we can tell, turn a significant number of criminals into non-criminals. They do not, in many cases, present to the public any credible equation between the heinousness of crime and just punishment.

Secondly, although they attempt to make provision for the physical decencies of life they do not always succeed. Here one must make a distinction between the long-term prison and the local establishment in which the problems of overcrowding and physical degradation are at their worst. Can we really be satisfied at the sanitary arrangements that prevail in local prisons? Or more important, that those whose more serious crimes apparently deserved longer sentences enjoy better conditions than those who, for less serious crimes receive shorter terms?

Thirdly, there is substantial evidence that the prison system contributes to divisions in society in that there is a differential liability between particular social classes to suffer imprisonment at all; and if they do suffer it, to the ways in which they do so.

Prisons have always acted as instruments of social control, never less than in the nineteenth century when the gaol was a tangible symbol of the power of the state to control and in certain cases repress the lower orders when their challenge to the established order exceeded the margin of tolerability. Six months for the thief, six months for the striking miner. Prisons and jails in the southern states of the US still, I suspect, play a similar rôle in relation to those 'uppitty niggers' who get above themselves and make trouble for white folks. If contemporary British prisons are not so starkly concerned to help control the lower orders, it remains a fact that unless one assumes that certain social classes have a monopoly of vice, then strangely the majority of prison inmates come from the bottom of the social scale. Not all, but the majority. The reasons for this are not hard to discern; they spend their time predominantly in public social space where their deviant activities most readily come to the notice of law enforcement agents. Their commitment to the value system of a property-oriented society is often marginal and they are frequently the victims of stereotype and prejudice to which they equally frequently respond as to self-fulfilling prophecies. Thus those at the bottom of the heap, our marginal brethren, enjoy a greater chance of being convicted, and the more frequently one is convicted the greater the possibility of being

sent to prison. And once imprisoned, the greater is the chance of re-incarcer-
ation. We may all sleep soundly in our beds tonight in the knowledge that
Her Majesty's prisons hold safe within their television-scanned and Alsatian-
patrolled walls, a large number of social nuisances and a much smaller number
of serious social menaces. Not so, however, for the white collar criminal who
because of the restrictions imposed on sentencing first offenders is less likely
to get a prison sentence in any event, and, if he does get a sentence, may quite
often have it suspended. But assuming the worst, and the prison gates close
upon him, how long is he likely to remain in durance most vile? The answer
is not long, since those who run the open prisons are anxious to receive every
potential candidate. Without corrupt councillors, dishonest architects and
greedy public servants (some of whom find that their pensions have been
restored to them on release) open prisons might be even emptier than they
are now. There are, of course, parallels in the US following the Watergate
trials.

   Now how one can justify this sort of thing in terms of the objectives of
treatment, training and rehabilitation I do not know. I do not know how one
begins to train some of those whose names one forbears to mention (now that
white collar criminals are so well protected by the Rehabilitation of Offenders
Act) or for what. Nor can one see how the nature of the prison experience,
as distinct from the imposed stigma of conviction, can be in the least appropriate to any degree of responsibility for the damage done to the image of the
integrity of those in public life, especially local public life. The effect of such
uses of imprisonment tends only to emphasize the socially divisive qualities
of the criminal justice system, and, one must suspect, alienate still further
the most marginal groups in society who suffer quite disproportionately for
crimes of lesser magnitude.

   Fourthly, I would argue that things can only go from the present bad to a
future worse since the current confusion of objectives is now made more
difficult to resolve by the commitment of penal administrators and their
advisers to actions which relate more to the need to find immediate solutions
to immediate problems than to the formulation of socially acceptable long-
term policies. Prisons being overcrowded, means are sought to empty them.
For young offenders the borstal term has been shortened and detention centre
remission substantially increased. Suggestions have been made to increase the
terms of remission for adult offenders too, but the greatest contribution has
undoubtedly been made by the development of the parole system. This is
probably not the place in which to launch a full-scale attack on the parole
system but one must note the way in which its protagonists, seeking to
justify their continuance of the system, are prepared to go to considerable
lengths to ignore its defects, not least of which is the manner in which the

parole system is an affront to natural justice. The intervention of the Executive to over-ride a judicial act, ought, in any but a totalitarian society, be both rare and limited to the most special circumstances. To the extent to which the executive acts of the state devised in secret on the basis of arbitrary criteria increase, the status and authority of judicial acts must decline. But more bluntly, for a man not to know the numbered days of his imprisonment, nor to know how best he may please his captors to secure his early release, nor to know why he has failed to please them, nor to have benefit of counsel, such as he was entitled to have at his trial, is an affront to natural justice. And it is of no avail for the Parole Board to suggest that because a gratifying proportion of those who have found favour in its sight have not returned to prison it is justification of the system. That is egregious nonsense.

That parole systems, especially when linked to indeterminate sentences, are now under intense criticism in the United States ought in all conscience to be having some effect here. But not so, and one suspects because the development of parole achieves two purposes. On the one hand it helps to relieve the pressure on prison space, while on the other it promotes the image of liberal penology. Now before we talk of ways of relieving pressure on prisons we first ought to address ourselves to whether those who are there taking up so much space need be there at all. Ironically, the kind of prisoners who take up the most space and who suffer the grossest overcrowding are those least likely to be even eligible for parole. Alternatively, as the Advisory Council on the Penal System has suggested, there may be a good case for reducing the length of many medium and short sentences.

But in its promotion of the image of a liberal penology the parole system is particularly dangerous. For although executive acts can rectify judicial error, whether of fact or of justice, it remains that executive justice is among the best-loved weapons of tyrants. It is the backbone of the penal system of the Soviet Empire in which the judiciary are the creatures of the bureaucratic state itself; it is in essence capable of expressing the fearfully capricious whims of the Amins and Pappa Docs of this world. Now if it is suggested that 'nothing like that can possibly happen here' I would urge reflection upon the way in which political extremists of both left and right have emerged in our society. The political climate is more volatile than many believe, and he seems to me a brave man who can absolutely guarantee that a penal system embodying a substantial element of executive interference in the judicial process could not be manipulated to political advantage by a government of either extreme right or left.

But leaving that frightening prospect aside one may still be troubled at the imagery of liberal penology. In this respect one must consider the effect it has upon prisons and the penal system generally. For longer now than anyone living can remember, the great cry of penal reformers has been to make prisons both more humane and more effectual in turning offenders away from crime. In this they have been encouraged by those who believe, through their commitment to the heresies of positivism, that 'treatment' is a real possibility and that 'treatment' must of necessity assume the moral condition of the offender to be irrelevant. In so doing questions which are essential moral questions—and they include those which relate to justice—have been brushed aside in the interests of practical questions. The fact that Fabian criminology as it has been termed has proved to be a ruinous failure is a sad but not altogether unwelcome event since its success would undoubtedly have encouraged the extension of bureaucratic intervention at the expense of judicial activity. The sorts of questions which a genuinely liberal penologist ought to ask are not, for instance, whether a sentence of six months on a shoplifter is more or less effective than one of three months—and leave it at that, but whether it is right that a shoplifter gets six months while a brutal sex offender goes free with a suspended sentence. Or whether we should happily sentence the woefully-provoked perpetrators of domestic murders to life imprisonment while a driver with a long record of serious motoring offences who then kills through his drunken driving receives a sentence of nine months. A liberal penology must be concerned with both the appearance and substance of justice.

Yet perhaps is this nowhere better demonstrated than in the area of prisoners' rights. It is no cause for congratulation that the UK has had to be taken to Strasbourg on more than one occasion, yet probably prisoners are as well treated here as anywhere in the Western world. It remains, nevertheless, that prisoners still have great difficulty in establishing the dimensions of their legal rights once they are incarcerated. The illiberal view assumes that imprisonment must extinguish all rights, reducing the inmate to the status of a slave, but that is scarcely acceptable. It is commonly argued that the system of Boards of Visitors is an effective check on prison management, but that is debatable. It has not prevented serious troubles in recent years, some of which must be in part the consequence of less-than-adequate management. The identification of Boards, or more commonly the Chairmen of Boards with the prison authorities in times of trouble, stimulates no confidence in their objectivity; after riots have been quelled the powers of Boards to impose what are in effect serious penalties are exercised in situations in which the position of the indicated inmate is far from satisfactory. If inmates regard these as kangaroo courts they can hardly be blamed. They are vulnerable to the collusion of witnesses against them, they have no right to counsel, their right to call witnesses in defence is limited both by the Board's discretion and by the fact that defence witnesses may think themselves vulnerable to various reprisals from which there is scant protection. What is perhaps more troubling is that in recent years when prison riots have assumed proportions more serious than at any time in this century, the policy of the Prison Department has been to eschew the traditional practice of establishing a public inquiry and, instead, to consume as best and furtively it can, its own unhealthy smoke. If the situation with regard to the Hull riot is modified, it will only have been in response to public pressure and the realization that the conduct of such inquiries in secret can only be damaging to the public image of the prison system. The government had the chance to think again about the way in which prison discipline might be enforced when the report of the unofficial Jellicoe Committee was published,* yet it preferred to retain the *status quo*, encouraged by the report of its own internal Departmental Committee which did little more than to decide that things were really very well as they were. That the Jellicoe report stimulated hostility, not least among some of the Boards of Visitors, can hardly come as a surprise, but it ought to be reflected upon that a report produced jointly by *Justice*, NACRO and the Howard League should have been held in so little regard. Similarly with the question of prisoners' rights. When the first conference on human rights met in 1972, although it was presided over by a most distinguished member of the higher judiciary, not one official representative of the Prison Department was present. It was left to a long-retired Prison Commissioner to talk about the prison administrators' side of the problem.

I shall of course be accused of exaggeration, but I shall not be deterred from saying that I do not believe that there is now, in fact, any discernible penal policy, save that of seeking to resolve the immediate problems of the prison system by means of expedients which have at the same time the complexion of a progressive liberalism, thus making them seemingly attractive to the insistent critic of the system. Nor do I believe that unless and until the Advisory Council on the Penal System ceases to concern itself with what are predominantly practical issues—ways of keeping the ship afloat so to speak—rather than with policy—or where the ship should be headed—will there be any effective check on the present drift.

Parliament has been far from ineffective in the past in debating penal questions, but usually only when Members have been well informed by groups that have made it their concern to ensure that they are. The need for such groups to galvanize and to bring pressure to bear upon Parliament has probably been never greater. I shall be accused of cynicism if I say that Advisory Councils, composed of the 'great and the good' are never likely to

* Report of a Committee set up by *Justice*, the Howard League for Penal Reform and the National Association for the Care and Resettlement of Offenders (1975), *Boards of Visitors of Penal Institutions*, Chichester and London, Barry Rose.

exert a very powerful influence since the chances are that the only part of their advice which is likely to be taken is that which is already acceptable to the minister and his permanent officials. One only has to see what was done with the report of Earl Mountbatten* to see how radical suggestions may be effectively neutralized. Nor am I persuaded that Royal Commissions are the most fruitful of endeavours in this field. That on the penal system which wound itself up in 1967 did not flinch from recognizing that the size of the task was too great.

What is needed, I would suggest, is that the penal debate, including both the prison system and its alternatives, should be regarded as being of no less importance than the great education debate. In the last analysis it is in Parliament that the public resolution of that debate can be translated into legislation. Such resolution need not be the crude expression of the *vox populi* and it would be undesirable if it were to be so. But still less ought we to be content with policies devised by 'experts' who are decidedly lacking in either the talents or the authority of philosopher kings.

* Home Office (1966), *Report of the Inquiry into Escape and Security,* Cmnd. 3175.

10

THE EFFECT OF PRISON ON CRIMINALITY

Preben Wolf

The Prison as a Total Institution

The prison is mentioned explicitly by Erving Goffman (1961)* as a clear example of what he has called 'total institutions', i.e. places of 'residence and work where a large number of like-situated individuals, cut off from the wider society for an appreciable period of time, together lead an enclosed, formally-administered round of life'. The total institutions are roughly categorized by Goffman into five groupings according to type of inmates and primary functions. His categorization includes institutions for the care of the harmless handicapped, the less harmless handicapped, the more or less dangerous but not handicapped, institutions in order better to pursue certain instrumental tasks, and institutions serving as retreats from the world.

Historically these five categories of total institutions may be said to have grown up together. In the very old days the tasks of the various types of total institutions mentioned by Goffman were mainly left to be carried out by private persons. Confinement rarely lasted for a very long time, and it was hardly ever intended to serve any particular purpose in itself, neither punitive, curative, reformative, nor educative. People in confinement were simply kept there only until their cases could be decided, execution take place, controversies be settled, demands fulfilled, or simply in order to prevent them from doing harm to others by spreading contagious diseases, betraying the king, the feudal lord, the tribe or clan to hostile powers. The clientele was hardly differentiated at all. Even if specific categories were recognized and confined in institutions, they were often mixed with other categories in the same institution or type of institution.

Whether a community sometimes uses confinement of some of its own members or not seems to depend largely on the resources, technology, and social organization of the community in question. It is not possible to indicate a definite point in time or stage in the development of a society at which it began to use confinement in one form or another. Like most other

* The References for this chapter are listed at the end (pp. 103–4) in alphabetical order.

social phenomena, several forms of confinement and restraint appear at the same time within different areas and are often overlapping through long periods of time within the same area. Placing in institutions, nursing in hospitals, compulsory school, quarantine, imprisonment, forced labour, concentration camps, sanatoria, orphanages, internment, etc., emerge, differentiate, and replace or supplement each other concurrently with economic development and the divisions of labour in society. This happens in relative independence of the normative culture and the prevailing ideologies in the different societies at different times (Philip, 1947). The various ideologies are important when it comes to the formulation of justifications of confinement, the definitions of the clienteles to be confined, and the treatment given to clients during their stay. Up to a point it may be said that the total institutions we are talking about here have a common history. The single types of institutions begin their own histories concurrently with the process of making special diagnoses and sorting out their particular clienteles from a hitherto undifferentiated mass of inmates.

When John Howard wrote his book on *The State of the Prisons* this process had already begun, and it has not stopped yet.

The Functions of Prisons

From an economic or technological point of view, it seems natural to emphasize that the increasing use of confinement from the Middle Ages and onwards may very well have been conditioned by the state's need for (cheap) labour. The Church, the King, the feudal lord, and the city council were the public agencies of the Middle Ages who might be in need of man-power. Furthermore they had at their disposal buildings which were suitable for keeping the workers indoors. In short they managed the technology and controlled the economy.

The Church was able to solve its labour problems through abbeys, monasteries and convents. The secular powers sent prisoners to work at fortifications, as shipbuilders for the navy, or to row in the galleys. Beggars were a nuisance everywhere, but the problem was accentuated in the northern and western parts of Europe after the Reformation. The establishment of Bridewell in England and of *Zuchthäuser* in Germany and Holland has induced some authors to put forward hypotheses indicating that such new institutions for forced labour were particular manifestations of the Protestant ethic and puritanical ideology. Maybe so, but one should not forget that the Reformation increased the current problems of keeping peace and order, as well as the problems of maintenance and support in the now

Protestant parts of Europe. True enough the *tuchthuis* in Holland was established by Calvinists, but in Catholic France Jesuits were responsible for the corresponding *hôpitaux generaux*, and in France as elsewhere in Europe scarcity of labour was urgent at the time (Mathiesen, 1972).

This was at the beginning of the mercantilistic epoch in economic history with its manufactures, its textile and colour industries, the advocation of complete state control of national trade, and the development of new nationalized industries with cheap labour in order to bring about a steady extension of the commercial and military powers of the nation. Prisons were part of the national economy. In the eighteenth century and later when industrialization and free competition broke through, the spinning-houses and similar manufacturies lost their importance for the national economy of the European nations (Wolf, 1972). Jeremy Bentham's attempt to have the previously state-managed correctional manufacturies changed into panopticon prisons under contract management was understandable in the first flush of Adam Smith's new economic revelation.

Like the public managers of prison industry during the mercantilistic period, the new liberal utilitarians believed that prisoners should pay their way. Prisons should be productive units and fill their place in the national economy. But according to Bentham prisoners should also share in the profits of their labour and be reformed by learning a profitable trade. He was prepared, by use of public contract with the governor of the prison, to make punishment a source of private profit. The governor's profits would depend on his success in rehabilitating the prisoner. Bentham's plans were never completely realized, but a number of ideas and practical suggestions were adopted, in part at least, and entered into the prison reforms and the law reforms of many nations. John Howard, the great humanitarian, had exposed the horrible state of the prisons. It was for Bentham to draw the practical and theoretical conclusions (Seagle, 1947).

Bentham deduced from his psychological pleasure-pain proposition that punishment could prevent unwanted behaviour. This could be done by restraining the offenders in prison for a period of time. This both caused them to suffer the pains of restraint and rendered them harmless, as long as they were kept inside the prison walls. At the same time Bentham wanted to maximize the amount of liberty, defined as absence of restraint, in society. From this principle it follows that not even criminals should be detained beyond the point in time when the punishment has had its effect. Bentham was the first penologist to suggest that imprisonment could be used effectively to control social behaviour and at the same time to help to maximize the amount of liberty in society. He was also the first penologist to formulate a scientific theory about the effects of prison on criminality. His theory is essentially behaviourist, based on the use of reward and punishment to modify behaviour. His plans for a model prison were never carried out, his hypotheses never tested, and his theory based on the pleasure-pain calculus is now considered obsolete. But to him the question put to us today about the effects of prison on criminality was crucial. He never succeeded in getting an answer to that question. It has been asked many times since then, but a conclusive answer has not yet been found.

Effects on Criminality

(i) *General prevention*

To be sent to prison for an offence against the law is by definition a punishment; it is intended to be a punishment, and it is generally assumed that the offender gets the feeling of being punished by his imprisonment. The stipulation in the criminal law that certain human actions will be followed by imprisonment of the perpetrators constitutes the threat of punishment. Psychologically speaking, a punishment is a noxious stimulus, which the subject will tend to reject, avoid, or escape from. When confined, men reflexively struggle and break free (Skinner, 1973; Solomon, 1964). One way of avoiding punishment is to behave in conformity with the law. This is what legal scholars may call the deterrent effect of prison and other means of punishment.

Professor Andenæs of Oslo University, who has cultivated the idea of the general preventive effects of punishment, tried to make the terminology clear in an article in 1975: 'In the literature of English-speaking countries deterrence is used as a technical term: *general deterrence* to signify the effects of threat of punishment, *special deterrence* to signify the effects of actual punishment on the individual offender' (Andenæs, 1975). As pointed out by Andenæs in the same article, there is the difficulty with the term deterrence that it tends to narrow down to influence by fear, and to neglect other influences of punishment, e.g. moral effects, educative, socializing, attitude-shaping, norm-strengthening influences, etc.

In German and Scandinavian literature this difficulty is avoided by using the term *general prevention*. In a similar way *individual* or *special prevention* is used instead of special deterrence. Another terminological difficulty is also mentioned by Andenæs in the same article: 'General deterrence (or general prevention) is sometimes defined as the restraining impact which the punishment of offenders has *on others*' (Andenæs, 1975). This according to Andenæs is an unfortunate definition, because it concentrates on actual punishment in isolation from the threat of the law. From a general preventive point of view the main function of actual punishment is to make the threat of law credible.

Another reason for Andenæs to reject this definition is that it tends to give you a feeling that 'somebody is being sacrificed for the purpose of instilling fear in others, that the use of the deterrence mechanism is, therefore, in some way unjust or improper' (op. cit., pp. 342–3). Maybe so, but I fail to see that it is much better to 'sacrifice' people in order to make a formulated threat credible, than to 'sacrifice' somebody in order to communicate a threat.

Some of the more notable studies of the general deterrent effect have been concerned with the death penalty, and the outcome of most of those studies has been seriously questioned recently. But here we are concerned with prison only. Andenæs has reviewed a number of studies concerned with the general deterrent effects of various aspects of imprisonment (op. cit., pp. 344–7). The aspects taken up by several researchers in the United States concern certainty and severity of prison sentences and make an attempt to assess the incapacitating effect of imprisonment. The outcome of studies of the latter suggests that the incapacitating factor is not an important factor in deterrence research, but it will of course have to be taken into account. As far as the other aspects are concerned, Andenæs contends that the research studies reviewed by him do not say anything conclusive with regard to the differential effects of certainty and severity of punishments. 'What the research does suggest is, first, that the use of *imprisonment* acts as a deterrent for traditional crimes, and secondly, differences in *length of imprisonment,* at the *levels of use in the United States,* do not seem to have much impact on crime' (op. cit., p. 347).

I think that Andenæs may be right in insisting that general deterrence research should concentrate on punishment or threat of punishment as such and, apart from possible incapacitating or rehabilitative effects, not concern itself specifically with the penalty of imprisonment. It is difficult, if not impossible, to single out the particular impact of prison on crime rates. The effect of certainty of punishment is logically independent of the kind of punishment used, and severity is an ambiguous concept.

The rôle of the prison as a communicator of threats is difficult to assess. The mere sight of a prison may, like the visible presence of the police etc., serve as a reminder of a threatening punishment or of a valid norm. The Bastille may have had a frightening effect on the Parisians of its time, but of course this possible effect must be less important today than it might have been earlier. In his book on *Dickens and Crime* (1968) Philip Collins tends to ascribe Dickens' preoccupation with prisons partly to the fact that prisons dominated the London scene much more in his time than in ours. Confinement of offenders is also realized through arrests and detention before trial. It is a precondition for the system of bail and is used in case of non-payment of fines, etc. In addition it is assumed that the activities of the police, the prosecutors and courts have their direct punitive effects. So if general prevention is effective at all, its effects are brought about by a long process through which individuals may conceivably end up in prison. The intended punishment is not the only threat, not the only punitive element in the process, and perhaps not even the most important one.

Andenæs recognizes some of these particular difficulties in an indirect way by his contention that 'the rates of clearance by arrest give a better approximation to certainty of sanction than do the rates of imprisonment. Moreover, arrest in itself, although not a penalty in any legal sense, in fact acts as a kind of sanction, carrying both unpleasantness and some social stigma' (op. cit., p. 347). This is another reason to agree with Andenæs' insistence not to base general deterrent effects on a single element in the punitive process, but rather to consider the process as a whole.

We must—I think—accept the truth in Homans' observation in his analysis of social control in Whyte's Norton Street Gang '. . . that the effectiveness of control lies in the large number of evils a man brings down upon himself when he departs from a group norm' (Homans, 1951). We all know that the loss of personal freedom is not the only, and not always the most serious, punitive consequence of a prison sentence.

(ii) *Special Prevention*

In an official discussion on crime policy, which was held in Denmark about ten years ago, the late Professor of Criminology at the University of Copenhagen, Karl Otto Christiansen, put forward the following remarks: 'We know nothing about the general preventive effect of punishment, so that effect we believe in. We know quite a lot about the special preventive effect, so that we do not believe in' (Wolf, 1971).

During the past ten years the situation described by Christiansen may have changed considerably. A great deal of research has been done on both types of prevention or deterrent effects of punishment. The many research projects concerned with special prevention have added virtually nothing to our knowledge in this field. We still tend not to believe in its positive effects on criminality. The more recent upswing in research on the general deterrent effects may have given us some knowledge which we did not have before, but believers in general prevention will still have to rely more or less on faith.

In what I have said so far about the general deterrent effects of punishment in general and of imprisonment in particular, I have already drawn heavily on Andenæs' work (1975). Maybe a quotation from the concluding part of his most recent article will be an appropriate bridge from the topic of general deterrence to the topic of special deterrence (prevention): '. . . deterrence is, no doubt, *one* of the perspectives which can and ought to be used in explaining human behaviour, with all of us on the receiving end' (Andenæs, 1975).

The crucial question to those 'on the receiving end' as well as to those who are responsible for the distribution of punishments, concerns the type of reaction towards criminals which will yield the most effective contribution to the prevention of recidivism (Christie, 1972).

As mentioned before, a great deal of research on special or individual prevention has been done in the past thirty to forty years, particularly in England and in the United States. Some of these studies are very simple in their methodologies, others are more sophisticated.

I shall not go into methodological problems here. I take officially-registered relapse into crime as the given criterion of failure, whether it be defined as a reconviction or maybe takes the form of a revocation of parole only, and I am not concerned with the various types of evaluation studies done (Wilkins 1969; Weiss, 1972). Nor shall I survey the results of research to date in any detail. Most textbooks in criminology have done that, and in addition a number of surveys and reviews are available in separate publications. W. C. Bailey (1966) reviewed 100 correctional outcome studies completed between 1940 and 1959. Less than 25 per cent of these pieces of research were experimental, more than half of them were unsystematic, uncontrollable, empirical studies. As far as results are concerned, almost half of the research studies found favourable outcomes of correctional treatment, but some of the most carefully planned and most systematic studies, according to Bailey, showed more detrimental than favourable effects of institutional treatment, or they were not able to show any effects at all.

Lipton, Martinson and Wilks have published a similar survey report (1975) about the effectiveness of correctional treatment, covering studies published during the period from 1945 to 1967. In Scandinavia, Britta Kyvsgaard, University of Copenhagen, is doing a similar survey covering outcome studies from 1960 to 1976. The main preliminary results of her survey do not differ much from the results of previous surveys mentioned here. Studies purporting to measure the effectiveness of group psychotherapy, group counselling, individual psychotherapy, or other type of therapy carried through with inmates of correctional institutions, show that results are no better or worse than 'ordinary' institutional treatment, i.e. standard training and/or work programmes. Studies concerned with different programmes for offenders on probation or parole are equally inconclusive, and so are studies comparing recidivism after institutional treatment with recidivism after non-institutional treatment. By no means all of the studies reviewed by Kyvsgaard (1977) have produced negative results, but research showing positive results has mainly studied the effects of very special arrangements and not used recidivism as a criterion of failure.

Even for the studies mentioned which show positive results, it must be said that it is difficult to tell what elements in the successful treatment have been mainly responsible for the favourable result (Berntsen and Christiansen, 1965). Furthermore we do not know, as a rule, if the results are permanent or not, nor to what extent they are accompanied by unfavourable side effects. Most of all this is well known to everybody concerned with criminology, penology, and crime policy, so I need not go further into these questions. Those who might be interested in Scandinavian research in this field can be referred to Berntsen's and Christiansen's report in *Scandinavian Studies in Criminology*, vol. 1 (1965), concerning short-term offenders, to Nils Christie's summary in the same series, vol. 3 (1971), and to Norman Bishop's article 'Beware of treatment' in the publication of the Scandinavian Research Council for Criminology, *Some Developments in Nordic Criminal Policy and Criminology* (1975).

The most interesting among recent studies of the impact of imprisonment on criminality in Scandinavia is a study by Ulla Bondeson from Sweden (1974). She studied thirteen institutions—youth reform schools, youth prisons, and other prisons. Through her research, which includes a 1967 study of a training school for delinquent girls (Bondeson, 1968), Ulla Bondeson has shown various negative effects of inmates' adaptation or socialization to the prison community. In her first study in 1967 she showed plainly how the process of socialization into the criminal subculture of a training school for girls correlated with later recidivism. Her more recent study of the prisoner in prison society (1974) also indicates that prisonization has a negative effect on rehabilitation as measured by later adaptation to life outside the prison. Her latest work is a study of intentions and reality of non-institutional treatment of criminals in Sweden (Bondeson, 1977).

In this study Bondeson has made a direct attempt to assess the impact of differential treatment during probation and of the special Swedish form of it called 'skyddstillsyn' which could be translated as 'protective supervision'. Among other things it is a characteristic of protective supervision that it may, as part of the treatment, be combined with a stay in an institution. So in comparing the effects of different forms of probation and protective supervision, Ulla Bondeson has also taken the opportunity to make comparisons between the effects of protective supervision with and without institutional treatment.

She uses registered recidivism (indictable offences) within a two-year period as the criterion of failure, and she finds thus that only 12 per cent of the ordinary probationers (no special treatment) become failures according to these criteria. So do 30 per cent of those sentenced to protective supervision without institutional treatment, and as many as 61 per cent of those given protective supervision with institutional treatment. A prognostic instrument based on about forty background variables and with a good predictive efficiency was used to classify probationers etc. into risk categories. Keeping these risk categories constant Mrs. Bondeson still found large and statistically significant differences in recidivism between probationers who had been sentenced to different treatments within the field of probation and protective supervision. Since we are not here interested in differential effects of non-institutional treatment it suffices to say that protective supervision with institutional treatment had by far the highest level of recidivism within each of the risk categories, and it was also seen to reach these levels in the shortest time.

A multiple regression analysis of the material further demonstrated that the kind of reaction applied within this field was capable of explaining more of the actual results in recidivism than any of the other variables studied by Mrs. Bondeson, e.g. stability of work, residential conditions, unemployment after sentence, abuse of alcohol, previous sentences or age of probationer (Bondeson, 1977). Ulla Bondeson's fundamental hypotheses are that inmates are being socialized more or less permanently in their correctional communities, that negative influences, e.g. criminalization, drug addiction, institutionalization, stigmatization, alienation, and a deterioration in social conditions outside the institutions outweigh the positive influences, e.g. rehabilitation. She has suggested that these effects are determined primarily by the loss of liberty and detention within a total institution. Both social learning theories and functional theories can be brought in to explain these aspects of inmate subculture. Her hypotheses seem to have been borne out by her empirical work dating from 1967, 1974, and 1977.

I think the original and perhaps most important contribution to this kind of research by Mrs. Bondeson has been her use of an 'argot test' for the existence of a criminal subculture (1968). Her book in 1974 and some of her results in 1977, are not only important for crime theory and criminological methodology, they have also important practical implications in pointing out existing subcultures of crime, and the rôle of institutions as virtual schools for crime (Wolf, 1977).

Ulla Bondeson actually concludes her interpretations (1977) with the simple hypothesis of Leslie Wilkins: '. . . that the least that it is possible to do with offenders, the better the outcome!' (Wilkins, 1969, p. 83). But she does not stop there. She adds an interpretation in terms of the sociology of law in addition to the criminological interpretation just mentioned, and here she touches upon a question also put by Andenæs in his discussions of the general preventive effects of punishment (1975). The question concerns the effects of stigmatization, which is recognized as one effect of punishment which may be both detrimental and beneficial in its impact on criminality. Ulla Bondeson contends (1977, pp. 327–8) that individual or special prevention may be unsuccessful because of stigmatization through the interaction of a number of legal and extra-legal factors. Several authors will agree to that, while others will disagree and hold that stigma may result in deterrence or prevention, as well as in reinforcement of the deviant behaviour in question. This may be true, but Bondeson's contention has much more support in current research. At the same time it must be said that Andenæs and others are probably right when they hold that stigma is perhaps the most important deterrent element in punishment (Andenæs, 1973). This controversy is one of the dilemmas of penal policy which has not yet been resolved by research.

The Interchangeability of Penal Measures

The trouble with punishment is not that it does not work, because it does. Punishment can effectively suppress undesirable behaviour, but unfortunately it may also suppress highly desirable behaviour in the process. If it sometimes appears not to work, it may be that what the person administering it believes is a punishment may be considered by the punished person as a rewarding experience, or he may choose not to change his behaviour because alternative behaviours do not seem to be possible, or they are perhaps met with even stronger punishments.

The trouble with imprisonment as punishment is not that it does not punish, it does in most cases. But it also suffers from the defects of most punishments just mentioned. It is particularly easy to point to undesirable side-effects of imprisonment. It is also a kind of punishment which soon loses its punishing value. The additional evils which it draws with it and which, according to Homans and others (1951), make it effective, always accompany the first sentence, and this effect seems to diminish each time the punishment is repeated. Further prisoners get accustomed and adapt to prison life with resulting negative effects. What research within the field of special prevention has told us about the effects of imprisonment is not directly that it is not effective as a punishment, but that it may be less effective for various reasons than some other punishments and, as has been pointed out by Nigel Walker (1971), that penal measures are to a large extent interchangeable. Besides, we should not forget that rewards are in general more effective than punishments. Unfortunately it is so much easier in our type of society to punish than to reward. These are some of the reasons why policy-makers within the field of crime prevention are on the look-out for alternatives to imprisonment all over the world today. However, such alternatives as have been suggested are all more or less punitive in kind. The resolution no. 10, 1976, by the Committee of Ministers of the Council of Europe is accordingly entitled: 'Alternative *Penal* Measures to Imprisonment' (Council of Europe, 1976).

The belief in the general preventive effect of punishment, including imprisonment, is based on the alleged fact that people conform to laws and other norms not only because they have offended against them and been punished for it in the past, but also because they can see or imagine what would happen if they did not comply, though in fact they do. The image of the likely consequences will then be more important than the actual consequences. It looks as if we could do more or less without prison as we have known it up to now. But we seem to have no idea of how to cope with undesirable behaviour except through punishment. We seem to be afraid that if we do we shall have to follow Skinner beyond freedom and dignity (1971). Or is it mainly because it is emotionally rewarding to punish other people? (Homans, 1974, p. 26).

Still, it must be possible to conceive of better ways to control behaviour, including the behaviour of our controllers. We must concern ourselves more with the consequences of what we actually do to each other, not just the immediate consequences but also the so-called deferred consequences. As Harvey Wheeler once put it: 'We need methods for presenting future consequences as part of the present environment' (1973).

References

Andenæs, J. (1973), *Fremtidsperspektiver på strafferetten* (Future Perspectives in Criminal Law), Oslo, Lov og Rett.

Andenæs, J. (1975), 'General Prevention Revisited: Research and Policy Implications', *The Journal of Criminal Law & Criminology*, vol. 66, no. 3.

Bailey, W. C. (1966), 'Correctional Outcome', *Journal of Crim. Law & Criminology*, vol. 57.

Berntsen, Karen & Christiansen, K. O. (1965), 'A Resocialization Experiment with Short-Term Offenders', *Scandinavian Studies in Criminology*, vol. 1, Oslo, Universitetsforlaget.

Bishop, Norman (1975), 'Beware of Treatment' in Erland Aspelin *et al.: Some Developments in Nordic Criminal Policy and Criminology*, Stockholm, Scandinavian Research Council for Criminology.

Bondeson, Ulla (1968), 'Argot Knowledge as an Indicator of Criminal Socialization' in *Scandinavian Studies in Criminology*, vol. 2, Oslo, Universitetsforlaget.

Bondeson, Ulla (1974), *Fången i fångsamhället* (The Prisoner in Prison Society). Stockholm, Norstedts.

Bondeson, Ulla (1977), *Kriminalvård i frihet* (Care of the Criminal in Freedom), Stockholm, Liber Förlag.

Christie, Nils (1971), 'Scandinavian criminology facing the 1970s' in *Scandinavian Studies in Criminology*, vol. 3, Oslo, Universitetsforlaget.

Christie, Nils (1972), 'Om forskningens avmytologisering—individualprevensjon og almenprevensjon' (Demythologization of the research—special prevention and general prevention) in Aslak Syse (ed.), *Kan fengsel forsvares?* (Are Prisons Justified?), Oslo, Pax Forlag.

Collins, Philip (1968), *Dickens and Crime*, Indiana University Press, Bloomington/London, Midland Books.

Council of Europe (1976), *Alternative Penal Measures to Imprisonment*. Strasbourg, Council of Europe.

Goffman, E. (1961), *Asylums*, New York, Doubleday Anchor Books.

Homans, G. C. (1951), *The Human Group*, London, Routledge and Kegan Paul.

Homans, G. C. (1974), *Social Behavior; Its Elementary Forms*. 2nd ed., New York, Harcourt Brace, Jovanovich.

Kyvsgaard, B. (1977), Undersøgelser over effektiviteten af foranstaltninger over for kriminelle (Researches on the effectiveness of measures against criminals), Nordiska Samarbetsrådet för Kriminologi, Nyborg, Denmark, Stencil.

Lipton, D. *et al.* (1975), *The Effectiveness of Correctional Treatment*, New York, Praeger.

Mathiesen, Th. (1972), 'Fengselsvesenets ideologi 1600–1970' (The ideology of the prison system 1600–1970) in Aslak Syse (ed.), *Kan fengsel forsvares?* (Are Prisons Justified)?, Oslo, Pax Forlag.

Philip, Kjeld (1947), *Staten og Fattigdommen* (The State and Poverty), Copenhagen, Jul. Gjellerups Forlag.

Seagle, W. (1947), *Men of Law*, New York, The Macmillan Company.

Skinner, B. F. (1973), *Beyond Freedom and Dignity*, Harmondsworth, Penguin Books.

Solomon, R. L. (1964), 'Punishment,' *American Psychologist*, vol. 19, no. 4.

Walker, Nigel (1971), *Crimes, Courts and Figures. An Introduction to criminal statistics*, Harmondsworth, Penguin Books.

Weiss, C. H. (1972), *Evaluation Research*, New Jersey, Prentice Hall.

Wheeler, H. (1973), Beyond the Punitive Society. W. H. Freeman and Company. San Francisco.

Wilkins, L. T. (1969), *Evaluation of Penal Measures*, New York, Random House.

Wolf, Preben (1971), 'Nye veje i kriminalpolitikken' (New Ways in Crime Policy) in Erik Manniche (ed.), *Sociale Problemer* (Social Problems), Copenhagen, Fremads Fokusbøger.

Wolf, P. (1972), 'Udgangspunkt' (Point of Departure) in Bertil Sundin, *Individ, institution, ideologi* (Individual, Institution, Ideology), Danish ed. Copenhagen, Munksgaard.

Wolf, P. (1977), 'Apparent tendencies in Scandinavian criminology during recent years', *Annales internationales de criminologie*, Paris. Forthcoming.

11

THE CASE FOR PRISONERS' RIGHTS

Graham Zellick

I

No volume on *The State of the Prisons* would have been thought complete had the subject of prisoners' rights found no place in its contents. That in itself is significant, for if this bicentenary had fallen a decade ago, the organizers would certainly not have thought fit to include such a topic; and even five years ago they might have been forgiven if pressure on space had forced them to omit so tentative and tendentious a subject!

A book of this kind presents an excellent opportunity to deal generally with the subject of prisoners' rights, in particular to attempt a definition, or rather description, of the term; to argue the case for their recognition; to indicate what form this might take; to consider the objections and reservations to the argument; and to speculate on future developments. The result should be a blend of theory and practice. Many of my references will inevitably be to the English experience, with which I am more familiar, but I hope that my observations will nonetheless have a wider application.

II

A jurisprudential analysis of the word 'rights' in this context will not take us very far, since the word is used even more loosely than it commonly is.[1a] 'Prisoners' rights' is no more than a compendious or generic expression which usefully denotes a different dimension to penal policy, of which the focus is the prisoner's status: it has variously been termed the 'justice model', 'the due process model' or the legal approach. It is not merely or even mainly a question of listing a number of rights which the prisoner may assume to be inviolable, but rather of fashioning the requirements of penal policy and the overall treatment of prisoners in such a way that they conform to these precepts of 'justice', 'due process' or the Rule of Law. A penal policy or régime based on prisoners' rights is one which respects the prisoner's inherent dignity as a person, recognizes that he does not surrender the law's protection on being imprisoned, and accords procedures and facilities for ensuring that his treatment is at all times just, fair and humane. Certainly, it rejects expediency, administrative convenience and especially benign paternalism (in whose service much that is grotesque has been perpetrated) as the dominant forces, and substitutes a régime which satisfies other criteria. Admittedly, these are notoriously elusive concepts. What, then, do they imply?

I start with two axioms. I take it as axiomatic that the powers of any authority exercised over individuals must be subject to limits. The only questions then are *where* and *how* these limits should be set. It has been recognized for over a century and a half in England that the powers of the prison authorities must be explicitly controlled by legislation;[1] but even before that the common law (in theory at least) set limits to the coercive powers of the authorities and protected the physical integrity of prisoners against unlawful action.[2]

I also take it as axiomatic that imprisonment no longer involves (as once it did)[3] the extinction of a prisoner's legal personality or his formal degradation and that, accordingly, he should surrender only such rights and freedoms of action which the citizen ordinarily enjoys as are necessarily and inevitably lost by virtue of the fact of imprisonment itself. The gratuitous denial of such rights and freedoms cannot be regarded as a natural or normal incident of imprisonment, and would need special justification.

But these axioms alone are only rough guides. We need to look more closely at the justifications for the recognition of prisoners' rights in order to see how penal policy should be shaped.

Firstly, there is a level below which we cannot go in the treatment of prisoners, or indeed of anyone else. This is the fundamental human rights argument, which outlaws torture and other cruel and degrading punishments, whether aimed at the body or the mind, and allows no distinction in respect of suspects, prisoners, terrorists, or the mentally ill. There are those who call for prison conditions so harsh and unbearable that they would provide a real and unique deterrent, oblivious to the fact that experience of such methods in the past lends no support to their thesis. It should not be necessary to labour the point that even prisoners do not forfeit these basic protections, though I fear that there are some who would not accept it. This justification for prisoners' rights constrains the authorities to eschew torture in all its hideous forms, and to ensure that accommodation, food, medical attention, hygiene and safety all attain a satisfactory standard, and that punishments for disciplinary offences are likewise acceptable, and do not include deprivation of food, removal of clothes, use of dark or cold cells, corporal punishment, and techniques of sensory deprivation.

Opinions may of course differ as to what constitutes torture or inhuman treatment. After what period does solitary confinement become unconscionable? One American judge,[4] later overruled,[5] thought the maximum permitted period was 15 days, after which it became a 'cruel and unusual punishment'. In England, the maximum period is 56 days,[6] but it is not unknown for prisoners charged with several disciplinary offences on one occasion to be awarded two or even more 56-day periods of cellular confinement. Even allowing for the required approval of the medical officer,[7] these periods might be regarded as excessive.

Another illustration of conflicting opinions arose in connection with the interrogation practices employed by the British security forces in Northern Ireland in 1971. Detainees were hooded, subjected to continuous noise, made to lean with hands raised against a wall, legs apart, and deprived of sleep and food. The Government denied that these practices or 'techniques', which had been employed in all emergencies in which Britain had been involved in recent years, contained any element of cruelty or brutality. A committee under the chairmanship of a former Ombudsman, appointed by the Government to investigate the matter, drew a nice distinction between physical brutality, which these methods did not constitute, and physical ill-treatment and hardship, which they did.[8] A second committee was then established consisting of three Privy Councillors with the task of reviewing the procedures and methods employed in interrogating those suspected of terrorist activities and offering advice and guidance.[9] The chairman, a former Lord Chief Justice of England, and one of the Privy Councillors—a former Conservative minister—concluded that these methods were acceptable in extreme circumstances, including Northern Ireland at that time, notwithstanding that some of the techniques amounted to criminal assaults under English law. In a minority report, the third member of the Committee—a former Lord Chancellor in a Labour Government—judged that these techniques were unlawful and morally objectionable, and this view prevailed on the Government, which announced that such methods would no longer be employed.[10] A case brought by the Republic of Ireland against the United Kingdom under the European Convention on Human Rights led both the Commission and the Court to denounce the practices as being contrary to Article 3, which prohibits torture and inhuman or degrading treatment.[11] This unhappy episode illustrates all too clearly how widely differing views may be entertained. But difficulty in securing agreement on what constitutes improper treatment is no reason for tolerating or acquiescing in conditions or methods felt to fall below minimum standards.

Secondly, it is necessary to equip prison administrators with the best tools for the job. Chief among these tools are procedures designed to reach the best possible decisions. This may be called the natural justice argument. The most striking feature of the English Prison Rules, in common with most others, is the enormous discretion they confer on the prison authorities, which means that much of the administrator's job is to exercise his discretion in particular cases: which categorization? which job? which prison? whether to order administrative segregation, to recommend parole, to grant home leave, to punish. Whatever decision the administrator faces, he should ensure that he is possessed of all the relevant information and this includes information supplied by the prisoner himself. That he should have ample opportunity to state his own case is one of the most fundamental ingredients of prisoners' rights, and it applies far more widely than may be supposed. The prisoner may furnish a quite different and cogent explanation. It cannot be stressed too heavily that an incorporation of correct procedures, formal and informal, is crucial to the development of a sound penal policy. It implies, too, that prisoners should be entitled to assistance—from lawyers and others—the better to enable them to put their case.

All too often the use of the hearing is regarded as an unnecessary luxury, not only with regard to prisons but in connection with administration generally. In the penal field, the English parole system affords the leading example.[12] This vital decision is taken on the basis of copious papers, but the inmate's own contribution is limited to a brief interview with a single member of the local review committee,[13] plus anything he submits in writing, for which he is not allowed legal assistance. The reason for requiring the prisoner to be given adequate opportunities is, not to alter the fundamental nature of the process in question, but to improve the quality of decision-making. Unless this is done, we cannot be confident that the decision reached is the best in the circumstances. Perhaps the greatest contribution which the common law has made to the conduct of affairs is the rules of natural justice, one of which, *audi alteram partem*, is the foundation of the judicial approach, long since extended in certain circumstances into the administrative forum.[14] It so happens that such procedures also serve another purpose, which is the *third* rationale for prisoners' rights.

A feeling on the part of prisoners that they are being treated fairly, that they have a say in their disposition within the penal system, that their dignity is not needlessly undermined, and that their personality and responsibility are respected, is more likely to conduce in due course to a respect for society and its laws than treatment which is harsh and unthinking. Too many penal systems regard and treat inmates as objects. So far from promoting a man's rehabilitation, it is an almost certain prescription for engendering bitterness and antipathy towards society. There must, therefore, be a sound complaints machinery, which is independent of the prison administration, sufficiently speedy and which does not automatically expose the prisoner to disciplinary action if his complaint is rejected. There must be ready access to the courts and to lawyers for redress, which is surely the hallmark of any society claiming to live under the Rule of Law. There must be continued contact with the world outside, without unnecessary censorship and visiting restrictions. There should be adequate arrangements for prisoners, at least within each institution, to express a collective view. And rules and regulations should be readily available to the prisoner, including internal documentation which directs the prison staff as to their implementation, without which he cannot know whether or not his treatment complies with those rules.

A prison policy along these lines accomplishes a *fourth* objective, too, which no prison administrator should underestimate, namely, the reduction of tension within institutions, which, with overcrowding and staff shortages in our prisons, is no small benefit. By easing frustrations and reducing confrontations, the atmosphere in prisons would become less volatile and they could be more easily managed.

III

One caveat should be mentioned at this stage. You may construct the most advanced regimen of prisoners' rights to be found anywhere, but what chance do you give those plans if you have a prison staff that is disaffected, unsympathetic or hostile? Without 'rights' for *prison officers*, there is no hope at all for *prisoners'* rights. A prison staff to whom prisoners' rights are anathema can make nonsense of it all.

The staff of prisons must be selected with care, for they have a responsible job with considerable power over other people; they must be well trained, including instruction in penal philosophies and trends; they must be paid and housed reasonably well, and accorded tolerable working conditions. Prison staff frequently face danger and in many respects have an unenviable task, but one which is crucial in our society. The quality of the staff of prisons, at all levels, is probably the single most important factor in determining the success of any enlightened penal policy—which the penal reformer ignores to his cost. Nor should the uniformed officer be pushed to the periphery and demoted to a mere custodian, while all the constructive work is undertaken by specialists—welfare and probation officers, psychiatrists, psychologists and so forth—for his interest and support cannot then be engaged and sustained.

There must, therefore, be a high quality and sympathetic prison staff if prisoners' rights are to become a reality. But what would be the likely effect on recruitment if such policies were to be introduced? On one view, the result would be disastrous, for good candidates would be deterred from joining, leaving either an undermanned service or one wanting in ability, both of which would arrest progress towards prisoners' rights. According to the Chief Inspector of the English Prison Service, writing in 1976: 'The widely held view within the Prison Service is that if the present trend towards the greater liberalisation of prison life continues it will become increasingly difficult to attract men and women of the right calibre into the Service (and it is fortunate in the staff it has now) who will be prepared to make a career for life in an environment in which every lawful order is under challenge and the officer's status is gradually undermined . . .'[15]

On the other hand, it may be that a more liberal prison régime would attract high calibre candidates of a less authoritarian disposition who are at present deterred from joining, while some of those currently drawn by the power and authority associated with the job might usefully be discouraged. In any case, the Chief Inspector displays his own attitudes conspicuously when he equates 'greater liberalisation' with an environment in which every lawful order is challenged and the officer's status is undermined, which is a caricature of what is proposed. So far from the officer's status being under-mined, it might even be enhanced. His job would certainly be more sensitive and demanding. I cannot venture to dispute the Chief Inspector's diagnosis of the common view of the service, but I suspect that it may be ascribed as much to the general malaise in the service at the present time, as to a sincere opinion that more liberal policies are intrinsically undesirable. Perhaps prison officers do feel, as the Chief Inspector observes, that they are 'not reinforced where necessary by the weight of well-informed public opinion' which 'is unfairly weighted at the moment in favour of the prisoner',[16] but the penal reformer does not perceive it so, as he continues to battle against society's indiscriminately hostile attitude towards all offenders in order to secure the most modest reforms.

IV

Let me now delineate the substance of prisoners' rights with some particularity by selecting three central areas for the purpose: access to the law; disciplinary offences and procedures; and grievance mechanisms.

(i) *Access to the Law*

A prisoner's legal problems will generally fall into three broad categories: domestic matters, such as landlord and tenant, hire purchase, matrimonial and child custody; matters arising in connection with his conviction and

selected;
the same
criminal

(iii) *Grie*
   It is n
machine:
those pl
public o
be chann
and enjc
impressi
   Prison
within tl
will also
have a ri
for this p
in a pris
the adm
question
to the re
That au
acknowl
decisions
through
the ultin
it is sug
the auth
where p
governo
   There
English l
attached
presence
out their
investiga
administ
although
confuses
ment, ar
pointed

sentence, including petitions to the Home Secretary seeking a reference to the Court of Appeal or the exercise of the prerogative of mercy; and matters arising from imprisonment itself, where the conflict will be with the prison authorities.

In connection with all these matters, prisoners should enjoy untrammelled ability to make contact and have confidential meetings with lawyers and to approach the courts. So far as civil proceedings go, this is guaranteed by Article 6 of the European Convention on Human Rights. In practice, of course, prisoners will experience difficulties in securing legal assistance even if the prison authorities dismantle formal barriers. Their geographical location, often in remote areas, is a real obstacle to be overcome, since solicitors will not eagerly make the trip. Hence, regular visits to prisons by lawyers to hold 'surgeries' should be permitted by the prison authorities and organized by the legal profession or interested groups.[17] It is, of course, imperative for an adequate legal aid system to be made available, and essential for an adequate supply of basic legal texts to be on hand in every prison.

Whatever valuable work may be performed in prisons by welfare officers or others, this cannot be a satisfactory substitute for skilled legal advice where that is necessary. No one is suggesting that a prisoner should be forced to take such advice, but only that it should be available if he wishes to take advantage of it.

(ii) *Disciplinary Offences and Procedures*

The internal legal system of the prison is a critical and usually infallible yardstick by which to measure the extent of prisoners' rights. The natural justice argument applies, since without proper and fair procedures, justice is inclined to miscarry; and the system for dealing with disciplinary infractions will go far in determining whether inmates feel they are being treated justly, which will in turn affect the whole ethos of the institution.

Serious breaches of discipline which constitute criminal offences ought wherever possible to be removed to the ordinary courts for trial, even though this will expose the prisoner to severer penalties than an internal tribunal can impose. While minor breaches of discipline may properly be heard by the institutional head, observing due process none the less, an independent tribunal for more serious matters is essential. Few penal systems satisfy this requirement. Some familiarity with judicial proceedings is necessary for members of this tribunal, though they need not be lawyers. Lay magistrates, for example, would suffice; but where the board is not chaired by someone who is legally qualified, its clerk should be a lawyer, ideally with experience of courts.

The procedure should approach that which obtains in an inferior criminal

An Ombudsman for prisons, even though without executive power, is a valuable safeguard.[25] It is preferable to appoint a separate Ombudsman for prisons, who can then acquire considerable expertise and deal promptly with the large number of complaints he can expect to receive. His jurisdiction should extend beyond maladministration to decisions where discretion has been exercised without maladministration but which are nevertheless devoid of merit. He should also be able to question policies, rules and legislation. Access to the Ombudsman should be direct and uncensored. An increasing number of jurisdictions is appointing special correctional Ombudsmen, but not always with sufficient independence, staff or power. The Ombudsman must be authorized to visit prisons, interview staff and call for papers. His reports would be published.

There is much to be said, too, for a fully independent inspectorate of prisons—independent, that is, of the prison authority itself. This body could undertake not only regular, routine inspections, but also *ad hoc* inquiries at the request of the Ombudsman or otherwise. Some, but by no means all, of its personnel should be former members of the prison service.

Elaborate safeguards of this kind must not be rendered nugatory by the threat of disciplinary proceedings if the allegation is found to be false or malicious. To expose a prisoner to that peril is bound to discourage the expression of even genuine grievances.

So far as unofficial complaints are concerned, prisoners should be allowed to write to Members of Parliament, organizations concerned with prisoners' welfare, penal reform and civil liberties, and the press. The press is regarded as the ultimate protection in a free society and to cut prisoners off from this essential apparatus of the democratic state is improper. In any case, unfounded and scurrilous allegations would attact no interest from editors who would soon learn to distinguish letters of some merit from others, if only because no editor would be disposed to print or give publicity to every letter from a prisoner which he received. Moreover, the law of libel will normally dissuade editors from pursuing a reckless course. In England, prisoners may not correspond with anyone about their treatment or conditions in prison, other than a Member of Parliament, and then only after an internal complaint has been investigated.

V

The English penal system is not without some laudable attributes judged by these standards; notable is the exercise of adjudicatory functions by an independent body, the board of visitors, although criticisms may be made of their detailed working.[26] There have also been several limited reforms in recent years: for example, censorship has been largely abandoned in open prisons;[27] corporal[28] and bread-and-water[29] punishments have been abolished; remission once forfeited can be restored;[30] the forcible feeding of hunger-striking prisoners is officially discouraged;[31] the rules governing access to lawyers have been slightly relaxed;[32] the minimum number of visits has been increased to one a month from one every two months;[33] time spent in custody before conviction counts for the purpose of calculating the one-third remission of sentence;[34] convicted but unsentenced prisoners are not required to have their hair cut or beard shaved;[35] the disabilities attaching to conviction for felony have been repealed;[36] and prison administration is subject to investigation by the Ombudsman.[37] There is also the review of prison standing orders, initiated by Mr. Jenkins when Home Secretary in 1976, because prisons 'had failed to keep pace with our changing society',[38] although nothing has so far emerged from this and it may be doubted whether anything will.[39]

But these changes do not emanate from any coherent conception of imprisonment, let alone of prisoners' rights. Pragmatism is the prevailing ideology in the British Home Office. The new rules on access to lawyers when in contemplation of litigation were imposed on a reluctant government by the European Court of Human Rights and even then were framed as narrowly as possible, both as regards access to lawyers and censorship, the latter of which the Government claimed to be wholly unaffected by the judgement.[40] Other advances were paralleled by changes, or involved features, which contradicted any discernible trend towards liberalization. For example, remand prisoners while earning remission may also forfeit remission for indiscipline in anticipation of the sentence they may receive on conviction;[41] the special visiting privileges for appellants have been abrogated;[42] uncertainty surrounds the restoration of remission once lost;[43] routine censorship in open prisons may have gone but the extensive restrictions on what may be written survive intact; the disability attached to those convicted of felony lapsed automatically when the category of felony was abolished,[44] although Parliament soon restored the restriction on voting and applied it to *all* convicted prisoners;[45] and the control units, eventually withdrawn in the face of fierce opposition, seemed a regression to an earlier penal era. Many of the remaining reforms came about in response to particular incidents, such as the protracted hunger-strikes by young IRA prisoners;[46] the hair-cutting of the defendants remanded for sentence in the *Oz* obscenity trial; and the general campaign which gathered force in the 1960s for an Ombudsman to deal with maladministration generally in central government, without any special attention being given to prisons,[47] other than to exclude from his remit the Home Secretary's powers in regard to the royal prerogative of mercy and references to the Court of Appeal.[48]

It is thus impossible to avoid the conclusion that prisoners' rights are accorded grossly inadequate recognition in England,[49] and there remains a long way to travel before we can feel that a true appreciation of prisoners' rights has arrived in the Home Office—and I daresay the same may be said of most prison administrations elsewhere.

Why is there this reluctance? One powerful factor is public opinion. Penal reformers experience difficulties at the best of times; and these can hardly be described as the best of times. Increased crime rates, hard-pressed policemen and prison officers, and what the public erroneously takes to be undue leniency towards offenders have not produced the background against which the penal reformer's message is likely to be warmly received, especially when that message additionally takes the form of a demand for prisoners' rights. This reaction is important, because those with power in the penal system, administrators as well as politicians, pay considerable respect to these views, particularly as articulated in the popular press. Whether that is to be characterized as timidity or as a healthy regard for the views of the people, I prefer not to say; but it must be clear that such a response cannot be ignored. Without conjecturing how far the climate of opinion is susceptible to change, the fact is that there are rational arguments to be deployed and, although many will remain unpersuaded, there is much prejudice and ignorance to be dispelled.

A second factor, closely allied to the first, is the collective hostility of prison officers, angry as never before over their pay and conditions and incensed over what they see as the preferential treatment given to prisoners. The Home Office is in no mind to exacerbate its difficulties with prison officers by yielding to demands for prisoners' rights. Prison officers have 'a difficult, distasteful and sometimes dangerous'[50] job and an accommodation with the Government is to be hoped for. But as a general principle I cannot accept that it is legitimate for penal reform to go only so far or so fast as prison officers will allow. Nor am I persuaded that all the resistance in the Home Office which is attributed to this factor is in reality its product.

There is, I fancy, a more basic reason. Administrators prefer simple, smooth administration; and this is readily understandable in a system managing some 42,000 prisoners in inadequate conditions and with inadequate resources. Lawyers, courts, complaints, hearings, reasons for decisions, letters, visits all intensify the problems of administration. Delay, caution on the part of officials and general inefficiency, as well as increased costs, are feared. However, it is easy to exaggerate administrative difficulties. The truth is often otherwise. In the first place, the administrator benefits enormously by having the temperature in institutions reduced—the diminution in tension to which I have already referred. A single prison riot may cause damage approaching a million pounds. Secondly, the intervention of lawyers and others from outside will often convince a prisoner that he has not been wronged, or at all events cannot hope to secure redress for one reason or another. The professional complainer may be stopped in his tracks or at least be content with independent advice. It happens often, to the prison authorities' considerable advantage. Thirdly, the anticipated chaos will often not materialize for other reasons. Take access to lawyers, where it is envisaged that the Home Office would be inundated with writs. How many prisoners would be able to finance their own litigation? Virtually every prospective plaintiff would need legal aid, and the legal aid committee would assess the application in the ordinary way. If a certificate were then granted, can anyone seriously argue that the case ought not to come to court on account of the burden this would place on the Home Office? Fourthly, there are some changes which would directly reduce the burden on prison staff. The abolition of censorship, for example, would save the time of hundreds of prison officers. Scarcely anyone occupying a senior position in the English prison administration defends censorship of letters on its merits: it survives only in deference to the views of prison officers.

A final reason for doubting the wisdom of more rights for prisoners among prison staff and administrators, apart from the implications for recruitment already considered, is the fear of a loss of control. While it is true that the retention of control in institutions is of the first importance, I hope I have said enough already to indicate that these fears seem largely groundless. Control and discipline are not destroyed merely because rights are accorded to prisoners.

Some, mostly in the United States, have also strongly objected to this so-called justice model on the ground that it militates against a rehabilitative régime and is therefore inimical to the true purpose of imprisonment, or at any rate frustrates that purpose. In other words, 'humane containment' is not the function of imprisonment. The rights adumbrated here may, it is true, impose limits on what the prison authorities may do. But within the framework of these minimum standards, treatment opportunities may be provided and rehabilitation facilitated. Indeed, the third justification advanced above for prisoners' rights was that they magnified the prospect of rehabilitation, where earlier methods positively derogated from it. Applied sensibly, a programme of prisoners' rights need not diminish the potential for treatment of inmates. If some rehabilitative measures did collide with an inmate's rights, the latter should prevail. But those intent on reforming inmates need have no fears unless their methods take little account of the integrity or dignity of the individual. While humane containment may not be prisons' main business, any containment which is not humane is *a fortiori* not their business either.

VI

How are things likely to develop in England? The agitation for prisoners' rights will certainly continue, but an embracing of the doctrine by the Home Office in the near future cannot be expected. Reforms will be *ad hoc,* sometimes wrested from a resisting administration, as by victory under the European Convention, sometimes more willingly proffered after argument, discussion and consideration. At this stage we can only speculate on the rôle to be played by the courts, but I do not myself entertain much hope. I certainly hope to see before long a repudiation of the unwarranted and dubious authority that a breach of the Prison Act or Rules is not justiciable,[51] which is incompatible with the whole tenor of post-war administrative law. Lord Justice Goddard went out of his way to lay down the rule that a breach of the Act or Rules gave rise to no cause of action but only to internal redress, distinguishing earlier authorities to do so, when all he was in fact called upon to decide was whether such infringement amounted to a breach of statutory duty for which damages were recoverable. In any case, such is the nature of the Prison Rules that relatively few causes of action would arise even if this change did come about. The courts generally evince no great sympathy for the prisoner: his remission is entirely a matter of apparently unreviewable discretion,[52] he has no right to legal representation at a disciplinary hearing,[53] which is not subject to review by the courts,[53a] and the rules of natural justice have no application to his categorization.[54] The absence of a written Bill of Rights forces us to look to other authority than the domestic courts for most of the reforms we wish to see. The European Commission and Court of Human Rights are likely to have some impact but, in my view, confined for the most part to the questions of censorship and access to lawyers, on which several cases are pending, except for relatively minor matters such as the right to marry under Article 12,[54a] or practise one's religion under Article 9 (1).[54b] The principal provision in the Convention bearing on imprisonment is Article 3 which prohibits 'torture or degrading treatment or punishment', but, other than in wholly exceptional circumstances, this is not likely to pose difficulties for this country. I have no doubt, though, that the short-lived control units introduced in 1974 to deal with particularly troublesome prisoners would at the very least have provided an arguable case under Article 3. Most other provisions in the Convention have little if any application to imprisonment.

While little in this country in the way of prisoners' rights may so far have been achieved, a new dimension to penal reform has emerged, of growing interest, and this has happened in a fairly brief time span. I am confident that it will bear fruit in the future, though I am not sanguine about early triumphs. I am also confident that in this especially interesting period, when so many of the problems are intractable, we have much to learn from experience abroad. We must all give our minds to ideas and ideals in the treatment of offenders. Those who advocate prisoners' rights do not claim a monopoly of wisdom; but we do claim that prisoners' rights should form an indispensable element of imprisonment in the twentieth century, whatever other methods may be tried.

References

1a. An argument based on theory could, however, be made. See esp. Dworkin, *Taking Rights Seriously* (1977).

1. Gaols Act 1823.

2. See *e.g.* R v *Huggins* (1730) 2 Stra. 883; 93 E.R. 915.

3. In England, the private law disabilities (e.g. capacity to sue) were removed by the Criminal Justice Act 1948, s.70(1) and the public law disabilities (e.g. eligibility to sit in Parliament) by the Criminal Law Act 1967, s.10(2) and Sched. 3, Pt. III, which abolished the distinction between felonies and misdemeanours. Since the disabilities attended convictions for felony, they automatically lapsed when the Act abolished the concept. Other jurisdictions explicitly recognized the doctrine of 'civil death'.

4. *Sostre* v. *Rockefeller,* 312 F. Supp. 863 (S.D.N.Y. 1970).

5. *Sostre* v. *McGinnis,* 442 F. 2d 178 (2d Cir. 1971).

6. Prison Rules 1964 (S.I. 1964 No. 388), as amended by the Prison (Amendment) Rules 1974 (S.I. 1974 No. 713), r.51(4)(*e*). References hereafter to the Prison Rules 1964 will be by rule number alone (e.g. 'r.43') and to the various Prison (Amendment) Rules by the Statutory Instrument number (e.g. S.I. 1974 No. 713).

7. r. 53(2).

8. *Report of the Enquiry into allegations against the Security Forces of Physical Brutality in Northern Ireland. Arising out of events on 9 August 1971* (Cmnd. 4823, 1971).

9. *Report of the Committee of Privy Counsellors Appointed to Consider Authorized Procedures for the Interrogation of Persons suspected of Terrorism* (Cmnd. 4901, 1972).

10. 832 H.C. Debs., c. 743 (2 March 1972).

11. *Ireland* v. *U.K.,* Application No. 5310/71, Report of the Commission, 25 January 1976. Judgement of the Court, 18 January 1978 (*The Times*, January 19, 1978, pp. 1 and 5). The Commission took the view that the practices amounted to torture while the Court concluded that they were not torture but did constitute inhuman and degrading treatment.

12. See e.g. Hall Williams, 'Natural Justice and Parole' (1975) *Criminal Law Review* 82, 88–90 and 222; Hawkins, 'Parole Procedure: An Alternative Approach' (1973)13 *British Journal of Criminology* 6; and Shea, 'Parole Philosophy in England and America' in West (ed.), *The Future of Parole* (Duckworth, London, 1972).

13. Criminal Justice Act 1967, s. 59(6)(*b*) and the Local Review Committee Rules 1967 (S.I. 1967 No. 1462), rr. 3–4.

14. See e.g. Jackson, *Natural Justice* (Sweet & Maxwell, London, 1973); De Smith,

Constitutional and Administrative Law (3rd ed., Penguin, 1977), pp. 564–74; and *Judicial Review of Administrative Action* (3rd ed., Stevens, London, 1977), Chap. 4.

15. *Report of an Inquiry by the Chief Inspector of the Prison Service into the cause and circumstances of the events at H.M. Prison Hull during the period 31 August to 3 September 1976* (H.C. 453, 13 July 1977), para. 257.

16. Ibid.

17. See Zellick, 'Legal Services for Convicted Prisoners' (1977)16 *Howard Journal of Penology* 65.

18. r. 47(20).

19. r. 47(13).

20. r. 47(14).

21. r. 47(15)

22. r. 47.

23. See Zellick, 'Lay Involvement in Prison Administration: The British Board of Visitors' (1977) 27 *University of Toronto Law Journal* 105.

24. *Boards of Visitors of Penal Institutions: Report of a Committee set up by JUSTICE, The Howard League for Penal Reform and the National Association for the Care and Resettlement of Offenders* (Chairman: Earl Jellicoe), (Barry Rose, London, 1975), Ch. 6.

25. See e.g. Fitzharris, *The Desirability of a Correctional Ombudsman* (Institute of Governmental Studies, University of California, Berkeley, 1973); Tibbles, 'Ombudsmen for American Prisons' (1972) 48 *North Dakota Law Review* 383; Zellick, 'Why prisoners should have an Ombudsman of their own', *The Times*, 4 October 1976, p. 6; and May, 'Prison Ombudsmen in America', *Corrections Magazine*, vol. 1, Jan./Feb. 1975, p. 45.

26. See Martin, 'Justice in Prisons', *New Society*, 27, 766 (28 March 1974); Home Office, *Report of the Working Party on Adjudication Procedures in Prisons* (1975); Zellick, *loc. cit.*, note 23 *supra*; the literature cited in note 49 *infra*; and the Jellicoe report, note 24 *supra*. See also Professor Morris's lecture in this volume.

27. 897 H. C. Debs., *W. A. c.148* (5 August 1975).

28. Criminal Justice Act 1967, s. 65.

29. S.I. 1974 No. 713, r. 5 & Sched., Pt. II.

30. r. 56(2), inserted by S.I. 1974 No. 713.

31. 877 H. C. Debs., c. 451 (17 July 1974). See Zellick, 'The Forcible Feeding of Prisoners: An Examination of the Legality of Enforced Therapy' (1976) *Public Law* 153; and 'The Hunger-Striking Prisoner' (1977) 127 *New Law Journal* 928.

32. r. 37A (4), inserted by S.I. 1976 No. 503, r. 4. See Zellick, 'The Prison (Amendment) Rules' (1976) *Legal Action Group Bulletin* 138.

33. r. 34 (2)(*b*), as amended by S. I. 1974 No. 713, r. 4.

34. r. 5 (2)(*a*), inserted by S.I. 1968 No. 440, as amended by S.I. 1972 No. 1860, r. 2.

35. r. 26(2), as amended by S.I. 1971 No. 2019, r. 2.

36. See note 3 *supra*.

37. Parliamentary Commissioner Act 1967, s. 4(1) and Sched. 2.

38. *The Times*, 13 July 1976.

39. See Zellick, 'Prison rules and prisoners' rights', *Social Services*, 20 September 1976, p. 12. A review of S.O. 4 on privileges is said to be completed and one on S.O. 7 on religious education, physical education, libraries and welfare was begun: 387 H.L. Deb. 2099 (13 December 1977).

40. *Golder* v. *U.K., Judgement*, 21 February 1975 (Council of Europe, Strasbourg); 897 H.C. Debs., *W.A. c. 148* (5 August 1975). See Zellick, 'The Rights of Prisoners and the European Convention' (1975) 38 *Modern Law Review* 683; 'The tricky task facing the Home Secretary over prisoners' letters', *The Times*, 16 July 1975, p. 14: and Nash, 'A Prisoners' Right to Access to a Solicitor' (1975) *Legal Action Group Bulletin* 175.

41. r. 54, inserted by S.I. 1974 No. 713, r. 5 & Sched., Pt. II.

42. S.I. 1972 No. 1860, r. 4.

43. See Zellick, 'A Bad Code for Good Conduct', *The Sunday Times*, 28 July, 1974, p. 10.

44. Following the Seventh Report of the Criminal Law Revision Committee, *Felonies and Misdemeanours* (Cmnd. 2659, 1965), para. 79.

45. Representation of the People Act 1969, s. 4. See Cmnd. 3550 and 3717 (1968).

46. See Zellick, *loc. cit.*, note 31 *supra*.

47. For an account of the genesis of the office of Parliamentary Commissioner, see Stacey. *The British Ombudsman* (Clarendon Press, Oxford, 1971); and Gregory and Hutchesson, *The Parliamentary Ombudsman: A Study in the Control of Administrative Action* (Allen & Unwin, London, 1975), Chaps. 2 and 3.

48. Parliamentary Commissioner Act 1967, s. 5(3) and Sched. 3, para. 7.

49. See English, 'Prisoners' Rights: *Quis Custodiet Ipsos Custodes?*' In Bridge *et al.* (eds.), *Fundamental Rights* (Sweet & Maxwell, London, 1973): Zellick, 'Prisoners' Rights in England' (1974) 24 *University of Toronto Law Journal* 331, revised as 'Prisoners and the Law' in McConville (ed.), *The Use of Imprisonment: Essays in the Changing State of English Penal Policy* (Routledge & Kegan Paul, London, 1975); 'Lawyers and Prisoners' Rights' (1974) *Legal Action Group Bulletin* 186; and Morris in *Detention: Minimum Standards of Treatment* (Barry Rose, London, 1975), pp. 24–30.

50. *Report of an Inquiry by the Chief Inspector of the Prison Service,* note 15 *supra,* para. 257.

51. *Arbon* v. *Anderson* (1943) 1 K.B. 252; followed in *Silverman* v. *Prison Commissioners* (1955) Crim. L.R. 116 and *Hinds* v. *Home Office, The Times,* 17 January 1962, C.A.

52. *Morriss* v. *Winter* (1929) 1 K.B. 243; R v. *Maguire* (1956) 40 Cr. Appl.R. 92, 94 (C.C.A.); *Hancock* v. *Prison Commissioners* (1960) 1 Q.B. 117; R v. *Governor of Leeds Prison, ex p. Stafford* (1964) 2 Q.B. 625, 630 (D.C.); and *Re Savundra* (1973) 3 All E.R. 406.

53. *Fraser* v. *Mudge* (1975) 1 W.L.R. 1132, C.A.

53a. R v. *Board of Visitors of Hull Prison, Ex p. St. Germain, The Times,* 7 December 1977 (D.C.) (appeal pending).

54. *Payne* v. *Home Office* (1977 unreported), *The Times,* 3 May 1977.

54a. See *Hamer* v. *U.K., No.* 7141/75 (1977), Council of Europe Press Communiqué c (77) 35 (decision on admissibility, 13 October 1977).

54b. See Application No. 7764/77.

12

THE FUTURE OF PAROLE

F. H. McClintock

1. *Introduction*

Firstly, I think it is important to recognize that the future of parole is problematic in the sense of uncertainty whether it will survive at all; it is not just a question of what *form* it will take in the future. Secondly, although this essay deals with the working of penal systems today, it is also strictly pertinent to the future of prisons and other means of deviance control. But perhaps we should not be too conscious of the threefold division into Past, Present and Future; we should remember the wise words of T. S. Eliot: 'Time past and time present are perhaps both together in time future.' Thirdly, I wish to emphasize that, although many of the contributors to this volume are by profession academic criminologists, the administration of prisons and parole licences is a proper subject of interest to politicians, and cannot and should not be divorced from the political context. We are not therefore discussing a technical question, although it broadly embraces a number of technical issues. Prison, and therefore parole, is perhaps in peacetime the largest area over which the *servants of the state* exercise power on a regular basis. The executive side of imprisonment and parole, I suggest, presents one very important aspect of the balance between freedom and authority fundamental to modern societies. Moreover, in relation to the allotment of power into the hands of bureaucracy, we should recall the political truth enunciated by a great English historian, Lord Acton: 'power corrupts and absolute power corrupts absolutely'. Civil servants sometimes betray signs of sensitivity when academics and other citizens stress the need for legality and accountability, in their uneasiness about secrecy and anonymity in our prison affairs. One can only say that it is an essential part of the democratic process. As Sir Winston Churchill said, early in his career when Home Secretary, 'The way in which a country deals with its criminals is a sure index as to the level of its civilization.'

Fourthly, it is important to stress that any consideration of the advantages and disadvantages of parole, and especially its future development, cannot be fruitfully considered in isolation from the substantive criminal law, the powers of the courts, sentencing principles and practice, and the rôle of prisons. If we deal *only* with the business of letting people out of prison, we will deal primarily with technicalities and not with the fundamental issues involved in penal detention: clearly the policy of executive intervention in letting people out of prison is part of the whole question of the soundness of our reasons for putting them into prison in the first place.

Fifthly, I would remind you of Thorsten Sellin's declared opinion in his introduction to G. Rusche and O. Kirchheimer's *Punishment and Social Structure* (1939): 'The character of punishments . . . is inextricably associated with and dependent on the cultural values of the state that employs them.' We should therefore be asking ourselves how it is that the present prison, criminal justice and penal systems have come into existence and what cultural factors will govern their modification or even disappearance. To quote Sellin again, 'The protection of society is the aim of all punishment, or penal treatment, no matter what form it may take. The social values which are given the protection of the law, the rules which are enforced by the political power of the state because they are embodied in the criminal code, are those which are deemed desirable by those social groups within the state who have the power to make law.' We need therefore to recognize and examine the close inter-relationships between forms of punishment and the culture which has produced them. To be unaware of the economic, social and ideological factors associated with penal policy and practice, means that protests on the grounds of inhumanity alone are like protests in the void.

Lastly, the decisions taken as to imprisonment and parole result from assumptions that underlie our accepted *explanations* of criminality. Although many practitioners claim they have no theory of crime, this is to ignore the fact that theory may be either *implicit* or *explicit*, as well as to make a false dichotomy between social actions and social theory.

We cannot, of course, in a short essay explore all these important avenues relating to parole—they would require at least a modest-sized volume if they were to be treated adequately. Elsewhere in this volume the issue of prisoners' rights has been discussed, which of course has many connections with the various models of parole that are in existence.

2. *Origin of term*

The term, I may remind the reader, is borrowed from the French: a person gives his *word* (parole), or is put on his word, not to escape or not to pursue a certain line of conduct, and is thereby granted certain privileges condition-ally. The historian of parole, certainly in so far as it has a place in the British systems, will trace it back to the 'ticket-of-leave' system that mitigated first transportation and later penal servitude. In the former case *conditional* liberty in the penal colony was granted towards the end of a long sentence. Today, it is not without significance that the ticket-of-leave originated as a privilege that was earned, and not as a right that belonged; and that, when transportation was abolished and penal servitude took its place, there was grave public concern that such offenders were to be released on ticket-of-leave into the United Kingdom, as can be seen from the correspondence in *The Times* in the late 1850s.

3. *Basis of parole in Great Britain*

Parole in the United Kingdom had its immediate origins, or at least its justification, in the rehabilitative model. In the 1960s, in the White Paper on the Adult Offender, it was argued that in the course of a long prison sentence an offender's conduct reaches a peak in response to incarceration and training; and when that peak is reached it is the most favourable time to release the offender back into the community if recidivism is to be prevented and further deterioration in his social readjustment is to be avoided. However, it has also been seen as a political trick to reduce the prison population without interfering with the sentencing powers of the judiciary. Clearly, in its origin and legislative enactment, it constitutes a *privilege* granted to the offender to spend part of a custodial sentence in the community under certain conditions. The composition of the Parole Boards, both in England and Scotland, indicated a *mixed approach* of (a) expertise (psychiatrists, social workers and criminologists); (b) principles of criminal justice (judges, sheriffs, retired senior police officers); (c) representation of the general public (the 'healthy, well-informed' citizen). The system was introduced into Great Britain in April 1968, and is therefore about ten years old. In 1969 the Home Office declared that in the application of criteria used by the English Parole Board the factors for consideration were 'the public safety, the nature of the offender's crime, his criminal record, his general social history, including domestic circumstances and work record, and his response in prison'. The list was not an unexpected one, but it gave little indication of the Board's methods of work nor of the importance attached to each of the factors.

Along with that of most other countries the British parole system—or more particularly that of England—came in for serious criticism in the early seventies, which has subsequently developed into a sustained attack on the whole concept of parole. Following the Hood-Walker debate in England, there came in June a NACRO report *Parole, the case for change* (1977). Essentially the authors' argument for change is based upon a criticism of executive discretion as contrasted with judicial process; it also involves an implied criticism of the rehabilitative or treatment model, and dissatisfaction on humanitarian grounds that it is a system that leads to considerable suffering, affecting both the prisoner and his family. Basically it advocates that parole should be a *right* and not a privilege; in the majority of cases, i.e. all those sentenced to imprisonment up to three years, the issue of a licence should be automatic; for those sentenced to more than three years the Parole Board should state reasons openly and they should hear legal argument, with the inevitable sequel of a right of appeal.

4. *Various Parole Board models*

David Thomas in his Cropwood paper (1973) noted, in commenting on the style of our parole system, two other ways in which the Parole Board might have been conceived in relation to the sentencing function of the courts.

1. It could have made up for judicial excess in sentencing, by more or less 'mechanically' releasing prisoners and thus reducing the effective level of sentencing by debasing the judicial currency. Clearly such a course would not have been acceptable: in that crude form it would have been an affront to the judiciary.
2. The second line would have been to limit the Parole Board's function to decision-making based entirely on risk of reconviction, actually or clinically, or in a combination of both. On this basis the Parole Board would not have been concerned with the gravity of the offence or other 'public interest' considerations which influence sentencers, except perhaps a policy of varying the degree of acceptable risk in terms of probability of reconviction in relation to the seriousness of the offence likely to be committed. The review procedure would have many features similar to those of the Mental Health Review Tribunal.

The one actually adopted in Great Britain is a hybrid one lying between a review of the initial sentence and the risk model, which Thomas refers to as the Appellate Parole Model. The decision to recommend the release of a prisoner on this model would appear to depend upon the evaluation of the risk of the offender committing further offences, unless the offences fall within particular categories in respect of which the Board maintains a general policy of withholding or delaying parole in order to emphasize general deterrence or retribution.

I would suggest therefore that what we have in Great Britain is a parole system which is an amalgam of a criminal-justice, or 'just-deserts' model, and the rehabilitative treatment model, related to prediction or risk of subsequent criminality.

I think, in retrospect, it is not surprising that such a curious system came into existence; if we follow the line of reasoning of Rusche and Kirchheimer, we can recognize the way in which the social welfare ideology of a paternalistic state permeated our criminal justice system from the 1930s onwards, and was the foundation and justification of the rehabilitative philosophy in the penal system; and the parole system was the last of a line of innovations based upon that ideology. In many ways the Howard League for Penal Reform is suffering from the mistake of linking humanitarianism too closely with the idea of effectiveness through rehabilitative processes.

5. *Rehabilitation and the present parole system*

It can be suggested that today the serious debates and criticisms that trouble the administration in many of our fellow states about parole, are reflections of the dilemma brought about by the collapse of the rehabilitative ideology, which started some ten or fifteen years ago. If the rehabilitative model were re-established, then a parole system based upon a case-conference approach would be justified and could be developed; failing that, a 'just-deserts' model seems the only model likely to be acceptable. If that be the case, then instead of tinkering with a hybrid system, and modifying it so that it is more judicial, serious consideration should be given to the question of whether a parole system can be justified at all.

6. *New classicism and neo-classicism implications*

Some of those who have been involved in the debate about the future of parole seem to take a rather simplistic view that the only function of the Parole Board has been that of reducing the prison population, and therefore if one curtails the courts' powers of imposing sentences of imprisonment, or *long* sentences of imprisonment, that is all that is required. I would suggest that the situation is much more complex than that, as there is the fundamental principle of maintaining the confidence of the public in the whole of the criminal justice system. In this context, as mentioned at the beginning of this essay, it involves the sentencing process—the use of imprisonment, the rôle of prisons and the method of release from prisons through a Parole Board or by some other means.

Criminological thought has turned *almost* a full circle; from the classical period of the eighteenth century enlightenment of Beccaria, with its emphasis on free-will, a rational basis of social behaviour, and the principle of *limited* retribution based upon the social contract theory of the state; to what some have termed the *new classicism* or neo-classicism in criminology, in which free-will and self-determination are considered the most appropriate assumptions on which to build the criminal justice system. It is also recognized by a growing number of people that as a form of social control the criminal justice system is not a very effective one and alternative ways should be considered. In this connection those who are aware of the Dennis Carroll Memorial Lecture given by Peter Scott in 1977 will remember his apt quotation from

Professor J. N. Morris, who from an epidemiological study of heart disease concluded: 'We appear to have come to the end of the road with our policies of "health" based so predominantly on treatment and medication ... there is now a rapidly growing interest in the possibilities of health and prevention through modifying ways of living and the environment.' The same can, I think, be said for the 'treatment model' in criminal justice, and therefore if it is recognized, with Professor Louk Hulsman, that basically the criminal justice system is a power-system producing suffering, then one group of criminologists suggests that the less we have of the criminal justice system the better it will be for society. On this view, in so far as prisons are held to be necessary, they should be used to a minimum extent; should provide, on a humanitarian basis, facilities for the self-development of the prisoner (and not treatment programmes), and parole should be a right; in Lord Hunt's terms, it would be a built-in conditional-release portion of a custodial sentence, in which it would appear that the Parole Board would have a very modest part to play.

7. *Schools of criminology or deviance, and penal implications*

Not all criminologists, by any means, would regard themselves as adhering to the new classicism in criminology; and the history of criminological thought from the enlightenment classicism to the new classicism has still to be written. Certain stages in that history currently influence the way people explain the phenomenon of crime and consequently the way in which they look at penal intervention, including the activities of the Parole Board. These may be summarized as follows:

	School of Thought	Explanations of Crime	Penal and Social Interventions
1.	Individual positivists	Biological or psychological factors	Psychological treatment Biological manipulation Programmes of behaviour modification Incarceration of the untreatable
2.	Social positivists	Family, school and other neighbourhood factors of a social and economic nature	Probation or social-case work, educational programmes, community projects
3.	Consensus sociologists	Defects of social institutions within the social system	Modification of social institutions as a way to prevent crime

School of Thought	*Explanations of Crime*	*Penal and Social Interventions*
4. Marxists or radical sociologists	Economic and social order seen as pathological	Radical change of society
5. Phenomenological sociologists	Social description and analysis of deviance and control seen as the only function of an academic	Radical *non-intervention*

The concept of a treatment ideology in the penal system, the justification of a parole system, the notion of the rôle of experts, and the ideas of predictive risk, are located in the first and second schools of thought, and are often described as embraced by traditional scientific criminologists. It has to be recognized at present that positivists in criminology are today in a minority, and on sociological and general theoretical grounds alone it seems unlikely that parole—in the forms in which we now know it—has much of a future. The abolition of parole, or its drastic modification, would restore much more responsibility to the judiciary. However, it can be argued that sentencers lack the capacity or professional education to enable them to assume new responsibilities which might involve them in dealing more intimately with complex social and psychological issues. This may be so, and certainly the abolition of the parole system would have to be related to a reappraisal of the selection and training of judges. But it also has to be emphasized that the new classicism claims that the *criminal justice system* should not, and cannot successfully undertake to deal with fundamental issues relating to questions of *social justice* in the modern state.

In this essay I have not dealt directly or in any detail with specific criticism levelled at existing parole systems: the mental suffering caused to prisoners, the very short periods of parole, the failure to give reasons, the lack of right to make an appearance, the kind and reliability of information available, the adequacy of the criteria for parole decisions, the nature of the recall procedure, and various administrative deficiencies. This is not because I do not think they are important to individuals on humanitarian grounds, but because I think that they are subordinate to the central issue of the rôle of imprisonment and the view of the criminal justice system, whether it is seen as a treatment or rehabilitative model or as a just-deserts model.

The early efforts of the Howard League, and its precursors, were directed to reforming the criminal justice system on humanitarian grounds; for some

time it subsequently diverted its energies—within the social-welfare rehabilitative model—to reforming offenders. It is perhaps today finding significance
in its old rôle of emphasizing individual needs for humanitarian treatment
within criminal justice systems which inevitably create suffering whether
through the overt aim of punishment or covertly through pursuing a formal
goal of rehabilitation. A 'just-deserts' model of criminal justice combined
with humane containment or control is likely to be a precariously balanced
system and will need all the vigilance of the Howard League for Penal
Reform, and similar organizations, if a new barbarism in criminal justice is to
be avoided.

13

CLASSIFICATION FOR RISK AND SUPERVISION—
A Preliminary Conceptualization

Edith Elisabeth Flynn

Today, the American criminal justice system is buffeted by strong winds of public discontent and is in great turmoil concerning its purposes, objectives and methods. Changes in crime control policy are now being advocated which distinctively reflect a 'hard-line' philosophy as far as societal response to the offender is concerned (van den Haag, 1975).* There are calls for increased police effectiveness, in view of the fact that the majority of offenders who commit crimes against persons and property escape apprehension. There are efforts to reform the judiciary through the imposition of mandatory sentencing and the reduction or removal of the judges' discretionary powers by means of legislative fiat. Concomitantly, there is a drive to reduce the use of alternatives to incarceration, such as probation or the imposition of fines, in favour of prison sentences designed to lock more offenders away than ever before and for longer periods of time.

The impact of these efforts and changes has been to reverse a trend in criminal justice during which a greater selectivity and sophistication in the use of crime control and correctional methods was advocated. This trend probably reached its zenith with the publication of the report of the National Advisory Commission on Criminal Justice Standards and Goals (1973) which stressed that the great powers of the criminal justice system should be reserved for controlling those persons who seriously threaten the safety of others, and which viewed the criminal justice system as the agency of last resort for social problems and the correctional institution as the last resort of correctional problems. Since the publication of that report, many court systems in the United States have assumed a more standardized and punitive function, judicial discretion has frequently been subjected to restraints and the widespread use of alternatives to incarceration of the past has been supplanted by extended prison and gaol terms. 1978 saw the highest prison population in the history of this country. The growth of prison and gaol

* The References for this chapter are listed at the end (pp. 148–9) in alphabetical order.

populations has now reached crisis proportion and states are reopening old institutions that had been deemed unsuitable for human habitation at an earlier day. Tents, trailers, airport hangars and even old battleships are now being used to accommodate the fast-rising numbers of prisoners. Across the nation, inmates are reported to be crammed into every conceivable space and prison conditions are deteriorating fast.

The reasons for this far-reaching trend reversal are many: philosophically, the return to the simplicities of punitive action against the criminal is politically attractive and has been hastened by the writings of such conservative academicians as James Q. Wilson (1975) and Ernest van den Haag (1975). There are many within the criminal justice system and without who prefer the uncomplicated processes of retribution to the discretionary latitude of social welfare-oriented decisions. From a practical perspective, it is incontestable that the criminal justice system has been incapable of stemming the spiralling crime rate. Recidivism rates—the rates at which prisoners return to institutions because of new convictions—are unacceptably and notoriously high. There is widespread disenchantment with the rehabilitation model used by most correctional institutions because of its inherent coercive nature and its failure to achieve an acceptable degree of success. As a result, such liberals as David Fogel (1975), Robert Martinson (1974) and Andrew von Hirsch (1976) have joined in the call for the swift and certain punishment of criminals to deter crime and for viewing punishment itself as intrinsically just and beneficial.

What lies behind the failure of criminal justice and this general state of discontent? Unquestionably, the inability of criminal justice to reduce crime and the failure of corrections to correct, have been due in part to public neglect in providing the system with sufficient financial and manpower resources. But more significant in inhibiting change towards greater effectiveness has been the way criminal justice has perceived its task and mission. The definition of corrections as society's official reaction to convicted adult and adjudicated juvenile offenders, neither states nor implies what corrections should try to achieve. This is critical if realism is to replace current ideology and rhetoric in this troubled field. Corrections have many purposes, of which rehabilitation is only one. It could be argued that if correctional processes were truly rehabilitative, they should be extended to all who need them and not be restricted to the convicted adult or adjudicated juvenile. Corrections are limited to the convicted and adjudicated offender because there are other justifications for coercively intervening in their lives in addition to helping them. Among these justifications are the protection of the community from the depredations of those who cannot otherwise be controlled, special and general deterrence, the upholding and confirmation of the validity of society's laws, and the punishment of offenders who deliberately break the law. Clearly, correctional purposes must differ for various types of offenders. When a person is sentenced for murder, correction serves a punitive and deterrent function. When a socially deprived, under-educated, vocationally incompetent youth is adjudicated delinquent, corrections should seek to rehabilitate and reintegrate that youngster into the mainstream of society.

There is no doubt that correction can contribute more than it does to the reduction of crime. To the extent that recidivist crime contributes significantly to all crime, corrections should be able to reduce crime. But it should be abundantly clear at this point that the pursuit of a single purpose for corrections—whether it be rehabilitation or punishment—is doomed to failure. Yesteryear's exclusive focus on the rehabilitation of offenders has failed incontestably. Insofar as the word 'rehabilitation' suggests compulsory treatment or coercive programmes, there is a growing body of opinion in criminal justice, supported by an impressive amount of scholarly reserach, that such a purpose is a mistake. Human beings inherently resist coercion and correctional coercion elicits failure more often than success. But the current return in corrections to neo-classical concepts of punishment and 'just deserts for evil deeds' will also fail. Despite the intuitive attraction and appealing simplicity of these concepts, it must be recognized that they too are built on faulty premises which deny the complexity of human behaviour and ignore the multiplicity of purposes served by criminal justice and corrections. Most importantly, the advocates of greater punitiveness towards offenders and of higher rates of incarceration, fail to consider the social and political costs of their recommendations. Rising gaol and prison populations have exacerbated conditions under which inmates must live to intolerable levels. Conditions such as these have long been identified as a major cause of collective outbursts, prison violence and the tragic loss of life. The need is great to reassess the use of prisons and gaols and to find ways to reduce their burgeoning populations in ways consistent with public safety. Criteria need to be established on the basis of which a process of de-institutionalization (or at least substantial population reduction) can be implemented at state and local institutions. There is tragic irony in the fact that these needs were clearly identified by the National Advisory Commission on Criminal Justice Standards and Goals in 1973, that they were not heeded, and that a trend diametrically opposed to the Commission's recommendations may finally force the development and implementation of plans for prison population reduction and for de-institutionalization.

Whenever institutional populations are burgeoning and traditional responses such as construction programmes lag because of the time it takes to build new prisons and gaols, the search is on for new techniques designed to reassess the use of corrections and detention institutions and to find ways to reduce the populations in a manner consistent with public safety. At this point in time, a new concept is emerging in corrections, which is concerned with the classification for risk and with the concomitant development of criteria on the basis of which a process of de-institutionalization—or at least a substantial population reduction—can be implemented at state and local institutions.

For the purpose of this discussion it is useful to differentiate between two basic kinds of classification systems in terms of the purposes they serve. First, there are classification systems geared to the resocialization of offenders and their reintegration into society. Such systems provide for the evaluation of offenders (i.e. diagnostic procedures) and are primarily designed to furnish the basis for disposition and treatment interventions. Second, there are classification systems designed to serve administrative and management purposes. The term 'management' implies effective client control: client safety and avoidance of further law violations, at least while the client is under an agency's charge. At the very minimum, such a classification system should provide for the physical safety of inmates and law-abiding behaviour while nmates are in custody. The term 'resocialization' in contrast refers to attempts to alter an individual's values, attitudes and abilities, as the result of outside intervention. Such a process usually involves attempts to change the individual offender or aspects of his or her environment to assure long-term law-abiding behaviour which lasts beyond the period of direct agency supervision.

Ideally, classification systems should combine theoretical and managerial considerations, which would facilitate the provision of planned specified programmes for different types of offenders in ways that would allow for programme evaluation. In view of the current hard line in criminal justice and the serious attacks which are being levelled against the concepts of rehabilitation and resocialization, there is today a critical need for corrections to find the answers to the question of differential effects. What we must know specifically, is which distinctions among offenders make a difference in combinations of interventions, and which combinations of intervention processes will lead to what changes affecting categories of offenders. Unfortunately, the state of the art of classification does not yet provide adequate guidelines for the development of such a comprehensive, differential-effects treatment system. Instead, most (if not all) classification schemes in use today are geared to assessing risk and facilitating the management of offenders.

Even though such systems fall short of the ideal, they should not be considered as being without value or potential. The National Advisory Commission on Criminal Justice Standards and Goals (*Corrections,* 1973: 203) considered the development of a scheme or system that would effectively differentiate among offenders as to their risk of recidivism or their potential dangerousness to others as perhaps the greatest contribution to corrections today. It is the purpose of this essay to (1) explore the potential purposes of a classification system based on risk and levels of supervision; (2) determine the principal characteristics, components, and critical predictor variables of such a system; (3) identify some of the essential system qualities and key criteria for the evaluation of a classification for risk system; and (4) present a description of a classification for risk and supervision system that would meet most of the criteria developed in this discussion.

Purposes and Parameters of a Classification for Risk System

Before identifying the major goals of a classification for risk system, it is necessary to discuss briefly some major philosophical premises and to delineate the parameters within which such a system would operate.

Principally, system design and system implementation should be based on the following considerations: (1) the preservation of equity and justice in criminal justice; (2) the protection of individual liberties; and (3) the recognition for the need to protect members of society from crime and violence, and for the reduction of recidivism. An adequate design would consider each of these concerns equally and compromise none.

Additional premises should include the following: (1) the ability of the criminal justice (or correctional) system clearly to identify groups of offenders who represent unusually high risks in terms of recidivism or potential dangerousness, and obversely, the ability of the system to identify groups of offenders who represent unusually low risks as far as recidivism and dangerousness are concerned; (2) the 'risk behaviour' at issue should demonstrably represent an actual threat and clear and present danger to members of society. As a result, the classification process should seek to identify those offenders who commit serious predatory crimes and violence, in order to separate them from offenders who do not represent any serious risk to the safety of the public; (3) de-institutionalization and population reduction should be a major goal of the classification system. System design and planning should therefore include statements concerning anticipated population reductions (e.g. closing of institutions), the achievement of which should be periodically assessed; and (4) the disposition of the offender (in terms of time and type of sentence served) *should never exceed* the maximum statutory term of punishment prescribed for the offence of which he or she has been convicted.

This final point is critical. It clearly dissociates the classification system under discussion from any model advocating preventive confinement of alleged or convicted offenders. It is felt that the preservation of the integrity of our system of justice demands that persons may only be deprived of their liberty on the basis of a determination of guilt for past offences and not on the basis of their assessed potential for future criminal behaviour.

System Decisions

Even though the model proposed here rules out offender dispositions based on predicted behaviour which would extend the terms of imprisonment beyond the maximum prescribed by law for the offence of which the person has been committed, it would permit the following actions and decisions: (1) the minimization of offender penetration into the criminal justice system, if it is clearly ascertained that they present a minimal risk in terms of recidivism and especially of dangerousness to society. In this sense, the classification for risk system would provide a decision-making structure, which would facilitate the 'classifying out' of the criminal justice system of many offenders who probably would not commit further criminal acts and who would benefit from minimal involvement with the system. Among the disposition options available under the concept of minimized penetration, would be every conceivable form of alternative to incarceration: deferred prosecution, suspended sentence, fines, probation, community service, restitution, residential counselling, etc.; (2) the minimization of supervision for probationers and parolees, and those offenders who have been assigned to community-based programmes, if it is determined that they represent a minimal risk to the community at large. Implementation of a risk classification system would assess each individual for his or her supervision needs and assign that person to that level of supervision which can best meet those needs. The impact of such a system would free agency resources to concentrate on those offenders who pose the greatest danger to society, and for whom at present no effective programme exists; (3) the assignment of offenders to pre-release, work- or study-release, furlough programmes and to minimum security status, whenever it is determined that they are low-risk cases, who would be unlikely to engage in serious criminal conduct. The implementation of this option would have the immediate effect of reducing current overcrowding of facilities. It would also save scarce resources, which in turn could be applied to develop, implement and expand alternative programme options; and (4) the granting of early release into residential and non-residential community-based programmes of offenders with low-risk assessments, as well as the granting of early parole of persons who present no danger to the community at large.

Inversely, the classification for risk system would equally facilitate the following actions and decisions: (1) the retention of offenders in correctional institutions up to the limit prescribed by law for their current offence, if it can be proved that they represent a high risk in terms of recidivism and dangerousness. Again, at no time should the period of incarceration exceed the time limit determined by statute, nor should the conditions of incarceration be any more severe than prescribed by law. Subsumed under this category is the possible denial of work- and study-release, furloughs, or the assignment to minimum security custody, should the evidence warrant such stark measures. It is necessary, however, to recommend great caution in this respect. Gradual release programmes, such as pre-release activities, work release and furloughs have long been regarded as vital and integral components of progressive correctional programmes and constitute prudent correctional practice. Substantial evidence exists for the need to facilitate a smooth transition for offenders from correctional institutions into the community. Trial runs (in the form of graduated release), assistance in finding a job and a place to live, as well as opportunities to re-establish community ties are all deemed essential, if an offender is expected to refrain from further law violations; (2) the denial of parole, whenever the classification for risk system determines a high probability that an offender would engage in serious or dangerous criminal conduct. It must be recognized that parole systems (and especially parole boards) have come increasingly under serious criticism, much of which is well deserved. A discussion of this issue is beyond the scope of this essay. Suffice it to say here that the current system of justice regards parole essentially as a privilege and not as an automatic offender right. As such, considerations of community protection could conceivably outweigh concerns for early release, as long as the evidence warrants it. Also, parole boards (well known for their arbitrary, subjective decisions) could possibly be replaced (or augmented) by sentencing boards, sentencing review boards and sentencing councils, etc., while traditional parole activities could be transformed into a wide range of after-care and brokerage services (National Advisory Commission on Criminal Justice Standards and Goals, *Corrections,* 1973 : 430); (3) the maximization of supervision of offenders deemed significant risks to community safety. Once the classification system identifies an offender as a high risk, he or she would be supervised on smaller caseloads and would receive the full attention of the supervising agency in an effort to reduce further involvement of offenders in criminal activities; and (4) the option of sentencing an offender to a correctional institution should be utilized by the judiciary only if (a) incarceration is clearly prescribed by statute as punishment for the current offence and (b) if the classification for risk system indicates that the offender represents a severe risk to the safety of the public. Consistent with the earlier discussion, item (b) by itself, should never be sufficient to warrant incarceration.

For all practical purposes, most judicial systems operate under these precepts. However, they do so in a highly subjective and arbitrary manner. Sentence disparities and other inequities are well documented and have given rise to many calls for reform. The introduction of a risk evaluation system (and related recommendations for judicial decision-making) would therefore not only enhance sentencing equity and uniformity, but would also bring rationality into a system too long characterized by irrationality and subjectivity.

Principal Characteristics, Critical Components, and Critical Predictor Variables of a Classification for Risk System

The foundation of a comprehensive classification for risk system should be built on the cumulative knowledge of past research findings in criminal justice and corrections. As such, it should include such items as (1) scales and interviews presently being used for screening new arrestees and for release on recognizance decisions, etc.; (2) uniform pre-sentence investigations used to aid dispositional decision-making; (3) prediction and base expectancy studies, which have been available to correctional decision-makers for a number of years; and (4) decision guides currently being used for work- and study-release and furlough programmes. These, along with classification schemes for probation, parole and other community-release supervision would constitute the skeleton of a comprehensive system oriented towards risk-classification and minimizing criminal processing for most offenders.

Subsequent to implementation, experimentation and comparison group analysis would provide the necessary feedback for improvement, streamlining and increased sophistication of the system. Recent research on actuarial prediction has begun to address itself to such questions as whether offenders represent better or worse risks after longer or shorter periods of confinement (Jaman and Dickover, 1969; Babst *et al.,* 1971). Future tasks of considerable significance for the purpose at hand would entail the preparation of actuarial tables which would indicate the risks of different kinds of recidivism, such as the commission of violent crimes as opposed to relatively harmless offences.

When implementing the classification for risk system, which would heavily rely on a combination of predictive devices outlined above, it would be important to remember that such a system would function primarily as an 'advisory device', and not as an 'unalterable basis' for decisions. Past experience has shown a tremendous resistance to actuarial prediction tables as a source of advice on risks of recidivism among parole board members (Glaser, 1973). Similar resistance is being encountered from the judiciary when faced with release recommendations obtained from scales and intake interviews.* These findings persist, in spite of the fact that predictive devices can significantly improve the demonstrably less accurate case studies which judges, parole boards and correction officials now use to help them assess (or guess) the degrees of risk involved, whenever alleged or convicted offenders are to be released (Mannheim and Wilkins, 1955: 158–60, 170, Appendix V; Postman, 1962, Ch. 9; Glaser, 1962: 242–5).

In the light of the above, a change in attitude and perception among decision-makers concerning predictive devices will be slow in coming. Also, since sentencing and disposition decisions are never made solely on the basis of risk or the desire to protect others, decision-makers would be optimally guided by a combination of the following considerations: (1) risk assessment, as provided by the classification system; (2) humanitarian concerns, in view of the fact that most offenders have some unique positive (and negative) features, which would serve as mitigating or aggravating factors; and (3) concerns for individual and general deterrence, which would include the consideration of punishment and 'just deserts'. There can be no question, however, that the perusal and application of predictive devices in the decision-making process could greatly enhance its accuracy, objectivity, clarity, cost-effectiveness, dispositional effectiveness and, ultimately, could serve to increase the safety of the community.

Among the more promising methods for the computation of statistical risk estimations today are the 'manifold classification' techniques developed by Glaser (1964) and the configurational analysis procedures developed by Wilkins and MacNaughton-Smith (1964) and Newman's configurational analysis applied to corrections in 1972. Manifold classification utilizes a small number of salient variables to classify all cases under analysis. A process of consecutive subdivisions creates a fertile number of groupings which permit the typing of offenders in terms of several categories of recidivism or violence risk. Configuration analysis (and an Automatic Interaction Detector computer programme developed by Sonquist and Morgan in 1964) facilitates searches for tree-like configuration of attributes that have maximum predictive power.

At this point in time, the following classification-aids have been identified as useful in determining risk and/or levels of supervision: (1) the Manhattan Summons Interview used for screening new arrestees and the Manhattan Bail Interview used for Release on Recognizance decisions. Both instruments have undergone considerable replication and testing throughout the United

* *See* for example Glaser, Daniel (1962), 'Prediction tables as accounting devices for judges and parole boards'. *Crime and Delinquency*, 8: pp. 239–58. Also, verbal communication with many judges during many planning projects showed a significant reluctance to use actuarial devices in their decision-making processes.

States; (2) a number of pre-sentence investigations and probation and parole classification schemes used to aid in dispositional decision-making by a number of states (e.g. California, Illinois, Maryland, North Carolina and Oregon), to be discussed in more detail later on; (3) base expectancy scales, as discussed above; and (4) certain personality inventories, such as the Minnesota Multiphasic Personality Inventory (MMPI), the Jesness Inventory (Jesness, 1962), the Interpersonal Maturity Level Classification system developed by Grant-Warren (1966); and the California Psychological Inventory (CPI) (Gough, 1957).

Two recent research efforts have brought some promising results. The first effort attempted to assess optimal intensity of supervision by means of an actuarial approach and predictions from personality inventories (MMPI and CPI). The study corroborated previous findings to the extent that caseload size and intensity of supervision do not, in and of themselves, work to reduce recidivism rates when clients are randomly assigned to different levels of supervision (Robison, 1969). However, the selection of offenders on the basis of a four-factor classification system (which places all cases on a continuum from lowest to highest risk of recidivism) may indeed produce positive results. The second effort is a classification for risk study conducted by the Michigan Department of Corrections (Johnson and Kime, 1976). It is an ongoing project which seeks to identify groups of parolees with unusually high potential for violence (while on parole) and other groups with unusually low potential for violence. Preliminary analysis of the study findings revealed six variables, which, in various combinations of two or three, identify high and low risk groups. Base rate tabulations for the total sample of 2,033 parolees revealed an 'average probability' of violent crime on parole of ten and one-half per cent (i.e. just over 10 of every 100 parolees were detected as likely to be involved in an offence that would constitute a violent felony while on parole). Cross-tabulations along the critical variables identified about six to seven per cent of the institutionalized population which could be classified as having three and one-half times (or more) the potential for violence than the average parolee. In addition, the analysis identified nearly one third-of the inmate population as having less than half the risk of violence of the population as a whole. About one-fifth of the population has less than one-tenth the violence potential of the entire population. Michigan is now in the process of incorporating these preliminary research findings in their classification and parole decision-making processes. The results should be beneficial not only in terms of relieving population pressures but also in terms of enhanced public safety.

Critical Predictor Variables

Even though most of the classification for risk systems discussed above differ substantially from one another in terms of their most differentiating predictors, some consistencies do emerge. The following listing is but a preliminary attempt to present some of the recurrent critical variables, as they appear in the literature. The culling of critical variables from the plethora of existing study findings, their refinement and testing would require substantial effort but would promise a significant pay-off in terms of developing effective classification for risk schemes.

Age appears consistently in most risk assessments. For example, the earlier the age at which offenders become involved with the criminal (or juvenile) justice system (e.g. age of first arrest), the greater the probability that the offender will recidivate or commit a subsequent violent act. Inversely, the older an offender is at time of arrest, incarceration or release from the correctional system, the better the chance that he will not recidivate or commit another act of violence.

Prior institutional commitment appears to be a major differentiating predictor in the expected direction: offenders with no prior institutional commitment (reform school, gaol, or prisons) have a better success rate than those who do have one. In case of juveniles, the delinquent behaviour at issue must involve actual delinquency, not status offences.

Institutional adjustment measurable by disciplinary records (e.g. time spent in involuntary segregation, reprimands, etc.) also appears to be a good predictor in the expected direction. Unsatisfactory adjustment and substantial time spent in segregation predicts failure.

Marital status is a consistent critical variable. Being single (or widowed or divorced) either at the time of the commission of the offence or never having been married predicts failure in terms of recidivism or subsequent violence.

Type of current offence is predictive of future criminal behaviour. It is important for the success of the prediction to utilize 'actual behaviour' before plea bargaining (rather than the legal category under which an offender may have been convicted) for the analysis. For example, violent and assaultive offences are good predictors of further violent criminal activity.

Prior record. Offenders with no prior record (or traffic offences only) tend to be more successful than those with misdemeanour convictions and juvenile arrests without commitments. Offenders with prior felony arrests, convictions, or parole violations (from reform schools, or prisons) and those with juvenile arrests and commitment will be least successful in terms of subsequent involvement in criminal behaviour.

Employment record is predictive in terms of recidivism and future involvement in criminal behaviour. Unemployment and drifting from job to job predict failure. Inversely, the longer a person holds (or had held) a job, the better the chance of his success.

Family ties appear predictive of success or failure in a number of ways. The existence of close family ties (in terms of contact, or living with family members) is positively related to the appearance for trial of an offender on pre-trial release and to successful re-integration after an offender returns to the community from an incarcerative setting.

Community ties are similarly predictive. Length of residence or similar indicators of close community ties predict success. Absence of community ties enhances the chance of recidivism.

Personality traits and characteristics have had mixed success in predicting recidivism or violence. Among those which have demonstrated empirical validity are the MMPI, the CPI (discussed above) and the Environmental Deprivation Scale (EDS) developed by the Rehabilitation Research Foundation in Montgomery, Alabama.

Essential System Qualities and Key Criteria for the Evaluation of the Classification for Risk System

To facilitate evaluation, the classification for risk system should possess the following characteristics: (1) the system should have clarity and objectivity. The characteristics or variables used for the purpose of identifying high and low risk offenders must be clear and specific. Different observers should be able to utilize the classification system and should be able to make reliable assignments of specific persons to the categories in the system; (2) the types of categories used in the classification scheme should be mutually exclusive. That is, actual offenders should fit into one and only one category within the system; (3) the classification system should be comprehensive, i.e. the system should be able to accommodate most (if not all) offenders within the available categories; (4) the scheme should be characterized by parsimony. Even though it may be difficult to determine *a priori* the numerical limits of an effective classification system, the categories it entails should be few to enhance system manageability; (5) system goals and subgoals should be clearly stated and ranked in terms of importance and utility. Methods of measuring goals and subgoal attainment should be precise, reliable and valid; and (6) system evaluation should always be conducted by independent researchers and never by agency staff which conducts the programme.

Turning now to a discussion of the criteria for evaluation, it should be recognized that it is clearly a major goal of a classification for risk and supervision system to reduce recidivism among the population undergoing the classification (and subsequent disposition) process. This assumption is based on the consideration that high risk offenders would be placed into differential treatment programmes, which would facilitate the concentration of scarce resources on those offenders who represent the greatest threat and liability to the community. At the same time, low risk offenders can be placed into more benign (and less damaging) programmes, which in turn should keep recidivism down.

System effectiveness should be measured by the subsequent behaviour of offenders who passed through the classification scheme and its programmes. The *sine qua non* criterion of effectiveness would be the objective measurement of the post-classification (and treatment) criminal or law-abiding behaviour of the system's clients. Recidivism, however, should not be measured in all-or-none terms. It should be measured instead along a number of subcategories, such as re-arrest, reconviction, and re-imprisonment. Further, it should always be separated from technical violations. Other criteria would involve the assessment of such factors as immediacy, and the extent and seriousness of criminal behaviour. In addition, supplementary variables should address themselves to the degree to which offenders become re-integrated into society (e.g. economic self-sufficiency, re-establishing of community, family ties, etc.). Measures of this kind would unquestionably improve the sensitivity of the assessment process and provide the necessary feedback for improving the classification scheme and thereby improve the guidance of criminal justice policy. Evaluators should strive to obtain a representative sample of the population at risk and scrupulously abstain from using subjective data, such as personal judgements about the relative worth of the scheme made by agency staff, client population, or outside observers.

Additional criteria for assessing system effectiveness would involve testing for the attainment of a number of important subgoals: (1) assuming that the classification system is applied at the time of sentencing, the system should in fact divert a substantial proportion of the population from the criminal justice system. That is, the rate of the clients coming under the jurisdiction of a particular court system should decline; (2) pre-trial investigations (assessment, evaluations and recommendations) to the courts should be accurate in terms of risk assessments and supervision for screening, and be measurable in terms of reduced recidivism. Conceivably, a reduction of specific (e.g. violent) crime could be obtained. Further, the reports should have a significant impact on sentencing decisions, which would be measurable by the number of times judges concur with the recommendations; (3) since the system would identify high and low risk offenders, the total burden of the criminal justice system should be reduced by means of referring low risk candidates (e.g. socio-medical problem cases) to community-based agencies; (4) prison and gaol populations should decline measurably since low risk offenders would be accommodated in community-based residential and non-residential programmes; (5) assuming that the classification system is applied at the corrections system level, prison populations should decline measurably, since low risk offenders would be given minimum security assignments, pre-release, work-, and study-release, furloughs or similar community status, or early parole. Additional benefits should accrue through the retention of high risk offenders in terms of a measurable reduction of recidivism and possibly, a reduction of specific (e.g. violent) crime. The assessment of this last factor may be possible only in terms of approximations in view of many well-known intervening (and largely uncontrollable) variables, such as offenders leaving jurisdictions or the 'dark figure' of crime: and (6) the duration of offender confinement and the severity of disposition should never exceed the sanctions prescribed by law for their current offences. The assessment and tracking of this consideration has been previously identified as a critical point and should be built into the classification scheme as a basic system component.

Probably the most sensitive criterion of the effectiveness of correctional classification and treatment schemes, seems to be the average percentage of time offenders are confined during a follow-up period (Glaser, 1973:23). This percentage is generally calculated from the number of days, weeks, or months offenders are incarcerated for new law violations in a given number of years after the classification and treatment experience and has the advantage of reflecting the frequency, duration, and interval between subsequent incarcerations of groups of released offenders. A suitable time span within which recidivism is measured is three years (National Advisory Commission on Criminal Justice Standards and Goals, *Corrections*, 1972:528).

Finally, a cost-benefit analysis should be conducted through which a variety of direct and indirect costs of the classification scheme can be balanced against the financial gains produced by lowered recidivism, the reduction of specific criminal behaviour, and the attainment of the many subgoals outlined above.

Description of a Prototype Evaluation for Risk and Supervision System

At this point in time, there exists no screening system which meets the criteria outlined above. However, this writer has authored and developed a comprehensive assessment and evaluation system under the generic name of Intake Service Center (in conjunction with co-authoring a comprehensive state-wide correctional master plan), which encompasses risk and supervision considerations (State of Hawaii Correctional Master Plan, 1972). The following is a brief description of the principal characteristics and functions of an Intake Service Center (ISC). The ISC is a public agency established to receive and screen alleged offenders referred to it by the police. In the case of juveniles, public and private agencies, parents and other sources can also make referrals. The exemplary ISC would be operated by the state government under the auspices of a blanket state agency, such as a Department of Health and Rehabilitative Services, Department of Human Services, etc. Selection of particular departments is less important than the fact that the ISC be free from the stigma which is usually attached to Departments of Corrections or gaols, as well as free from the influence of the judiciary and the probation system, since persons referred to the agency have yet to be screened for diversion into programmes outside the criminal justice system and prior to the adjudication process.

Ideally, the Center replaces traditional operations such as gaols or juvenile court intake and detention, and expands the scope of the response to crime problems beyond the traditional limits of corrections by facilitating an effective relationship between law enforcement, the courts, corrections and other social service agencies. Three prototypes of ISC's can be distinguished: (1) the non-residential, community-based centre; (2) the community-based residential centre; and (3) a combination of (1) and (2), featuring non-residential as well as residential services. ISCs should be available on a local or regional basis, depending on population distribution and service needs. Among the many inter-related functions of a fully operational ISC are the following: (1) short-term intake screening that emphasizes the diversion of an individual to alternatives to incarceration; (2) development of pre-sentence investigations and subsequent recommendations to the courts; (3) screening for risk and supervision and providing assessment and evaluative services that relate to voluntary pre-trial programmes, pre-sentence investigations, and correctional programmes for sentenced offenders; (4) ongoing evaluation and assessment of an offender's adjustment to given programmes; and (5) co-ordination and referral services related to in-house and community-based services. In summary, the ISC is responsible for the systematic co-ordination of the criminal justice system, including alternatives to incarceration and after-care programmes for those offenders who receive the services of a correctional system in a particular jurisdiction.*

Even though the National Advisory Commission recommended in 1973 that states adopt and implement the ISC concept and incorporate pre- and post-conviction correctional functions within their State systems by 1982

* For more detailed information, *see* the *State of Hawaii Correctional Master Plan,* Summary, 1972: pp. 27–32.

(National Advisory Commission on Criminal Justice Standards and Goals, *Corrections*, 1973:292), it was unlikely that many states would opt for the swift implementation of such dramatic change as described above. Given the state of the art in criminal justice (e.g. system fragmentation, local autonomy, scarce resources, etc.) the adoption of modified models—if any—(e.g. ISCs functioning in lieu of gaols or as auxiliary programmes to gaols) was much more probable. This is in fact what has occurred. Since 1973, only Hawaii has opted for a state-wide, unified, comprehensive criminal justice system, in which the ISC functions as the central intake, diversion, referral and monitoring agency. Substantially more progress has been made with modified ISC models on the local level. A good example is the Kane County Diagnostic Center, which functions (despite the medical model label) under a philosophy of total system planning for local criminal justice efforts.* The Center provides diagnostic information, diversion programming and corrections planning for individual clients within the local adult and juvenile offender population in a county with about 260,000 people. It also evaluates (on request) county criminal justice operations and goals in order to provide the necessary feedback for system improvement. In the area of juvenile planning, the Kane County Diagnostic Center developed and implemented the following plan: (1) the screening and diversion of status offenders (i.e. the elimination of low risk juveniles from the juvenile justice system); (2) the establishing of limits to detention; (3) the training and monitoring of emergency foster parent placements, and long-term, intensive foster parent placement; (4) the screening, diagnosing and monitoring of all juveniles on probation, and (5) the feeding back of results to county government and the community.

Preliminary findings revealed the following encouraging findings: (1) no increase in the rate of serious crime committed by juveniles managed in their home communities who previously had been sent to institutional settings; (2) the use of local alternatives has appreciably shortened the average length of time a youngster stays on probation; (3) the amount of probation officer contact with status offenders seems unrelated to a youngster's success or failure. But the amount of contact with juveniles is strongly related to that youth's eventual success; and (4) the county registered a total cost-saving (in juvenile justice operations) of $519,000 between 1973 and 1975, which included moneys saved when a new juvenile detention home did not have to be built.

Another example of a modified Intake Service Center exists at the St. Louis County Intake Service Center in Clayton, Missouri, where all alleged adult

* Unpublished Report on 'The role of the intake service centre in bringing about local change: A case study of juvenile system intervention', by Robin C. Ford, 1976.

offenders arrested by the police are processed in lieu of undergoing the traditional gaol experience. The Center offers a pleasant environment, in which civilian county employees evaluate, assess, screen, fingerprint, photograph and otherwise process all persons. A host of pre-trial programmes (e.g. bail, release on own recognizance, third-person custody) divert suitable low risk persons into alternatives to incarceration. The Center also provides a number of community services by means of referral. The Clayton Missouri operation shows considerable success in terms of reduced incarceration rates (pre- and post-trial), cost-savings, and apparently has not resulted in any increase in the rate of serious crime.*

It is self-evident from the preceding discussion that the prototype and the variants of the ISC model go beyond the tide-marks of risk and supervision assessment. In the original design, the ISC intends no less than a co-ordinated approach to criminal justice. It focuses on the inter-relationships between the various components of the criminal justice system and those of the community. By applying the scheme before and at the time of sentencing, it stresses optimal offender dispositions, cost-effectiveness and overall improvement in system rationality and effectiveness. But it should be equally evident that the differentiation among offenders in terms of their risk or recidivism and potential dangerousness to the community is at the core of the system's concerns. Without an effective differentiation of high risk offenders from those of low risk, the community would be ill served and the model would justifiably be doomed.

In conclusion, it should be pointed out that a basic requirement for the implementation of a classification for risk system is concerned with the criminal justice system's ability to implement the system's recommendations. By definition, this requires flexibility in the disposition of accused and convicted offenders. Yet the trend in criminal justice today is away from discretion and away from flexibility. In our haste to discard the inequities of the rehabilitation model, the indeterminate sentence, and parole, we may well be pointing ourselves into the proverbial corner. If community-based corrections are to have a future, and if classification for risk is to have a fair trial, we need more flexibility over dispositions, not less. At this point in time, corrections in the United States are at a watershed. Decision-makers have essentially two options: they may opt for collective incapacitation of offenders and incarcerate all who are convicted of sufficiently serious crimes, irrespective of the

---

* A preliminary report on the St. Louis County Intake Service Center was presented by Leo G. Plante, Superintendent of the St. Louis ISC on 16 April 1976, at the Third National Symposium on Criminal Justice Planning: Emerging Concepts and Field Experience, conducted by the National Clearinghouse for Criminal Justice Planning and Architecture, University of Illinois, in New Orleans.

probability of their returning to a life of crime. Or they may opt for selective incapacitation, and incarcerate only those offenders who represent serious risks to the safety of the community. Surely, the social and economic costs of wholesale incarceration represent a sufficiently strong argument to give classification for risk a serious, scientifically controlled try-out?

References

Babst, Dean V., Gottfredson, Don M. and Ballard, Jr., Kelly B., 'Comparison of multiple regression and configuration analysis techniques for developing base expectancy tables', *Journal of Research in Crime and Delinquency*, January 1968, 5: pp. 72–80.

Babst, Dean V., Inciardi, James A. and Jaman, Dorothy R., 'The uses of configurational analysis in parole prediction research', *Canadian Journal of Criminology and Corrections*, July 1971, 13: pp. 1–9.

Fogel, David (1975), *We are the Living Proof*, Cincinnati, The W. H. Anderson Co.

Glaser, Daniel (1973), *Routinizing Evaluation*, Rockville, Maryland, National Institute of Mental Health.

Glaser, Daniel, 'Prediction tables as accounting devices for judges and parole boards', *Crime and Delinquency*, July 1962, 8: 239–58.

Glaser, Daniel (1964), *The Effectiveness of a Prison Parole System*, Indianapolis, Bobbs-Merrill.

Gough, H. G. (1957), *Manual for the California Psychological Inventory*, Palo Alto, Cal., Consulting Psychologists Press.

Gough, Harrison G., Wenk, Ernest A., and Rozynko Vitali V., 'Parole Outcome as Predicted from the CPI, the MMPI, and a Base Expectancy Table', *Journal of Abnormal Psychology*, 1965, 70, No. 6: 432–41.

Jaman, Dorothy R., and Dickover, Robert N. (1969), *A Study of Parole Outcomes as a Function of Time Served*, Research Report No. 35, Sacramento, Cal., Department of Corrections.

Jesness, Carl F. (1962), *The Jesness Inventory: Development and Validation*, Research Report No. 29, Sacramento, Cal., Department of Corrections.

Jesness, Carl F. 'The Preston Typology Study: An experiment with differential treatment in an institution', *Journal of Research in Crime and Delinquency*, January 1971, 8: pp. 38–52.

Johnson, Perry M. and Kime, William L., 'Risk Prediction Classification and Parole Decision', unpublished Report, June 1976, Department of Corrections of the State of Michigan.

Mannheim, Hermann and Wilkins, Leslie T. (1955), *Prediction Methods in Relation to Borstal Training*, London, Her Majesty's Stationery Office.

Martinson, Robert, 'What Works?—Questions and Answers about Prison Reform', *The Public Interest*, Spring 1974.

National Advisory Commission on Criminal Justice Standards and Goals, *Corrections*, Washington, D.C., U.S. Government Printing Office, 1973.

Newman, J. Robert (1972), *The Prediction of Recidivism for Misdemeanant Offenders Released from the Los Angeles County Jail*, Los Angeles, Public Systems Research Institute, University of Southern California.

Postman, J. (1962), *Psychology in the Making*, New York, Knopf.

Robison, J. et al. (1969), *The San Francisco Project*, Final Report, Research Report 14, Sacramento, Cal., Department of Corrections.

Sonquist, John A. and Morgan, J. N. (1964), *The Detection of Interaction Effects: A Report on a Computer Program for the Selection of Optimal Combination of Exploratory Variables*, Monograph No. 35, Ann Arbor, Mich., Institute of Social Research, University of Michigan.

van den Haag, Ernest (1975), *Punishing Criminals*, New York, Basic Books.

von Hirsch, Andrew (1976), *Doing Justice*, New York, Hill and Wang.

Warren, M. Q. (1966), *The Community Treatment Project After 5 Years*. Sacramento, California: Youth Authority.

Warren, M. Q. et al. (1966), *Interpersonal Maturity Level Classification: Diagnosis and Treatment of Low, Middle and High Maturity Delinquents*, Sacramento, California: CTP Publication.

Wilkins, Leslie T. and MacNaughton-Smith, P., 'New prediction and classification methods in criminology', *Journal of Research in Crime and Delinquency*, January 1964, 1: pp. 19–32.

Wilson, James Q. (1975), *Thinking About Crime*, New York, Basic Books.

Part III

14

THE JUSTICE MODEL FOR CORRECTIONS

David Fogel

The Justice Perspective in Corrections

There are few enthusiasts left in prisons. The preachers and teachers and treaters have not produced a pay-off to equal their rhetoric. The prisoner-as-plaintiff now looks increasingly to the courts. But not much may be expected in the way of enduring correctional change through the drama of litigation where the central actors are reluctant judges and resistant prison administrators. In any case '... prison reform cannot be made acceptable just by ensuring rights or the comfort of the inmates.'[1]

On the dim horizon one sees a group of the newest enthusiasts clamouring for their place in the tortuously convoluted history of prisons. They are called behaviour modifiers. Though not new, their language is not well known yet because they are just now emerging from animal laboratories and back wards of hospitals for defectives. Their therapeutic arsenal is equipped with positive and negative reinforcements, pills, chemicals, electrodes and neurosurgical instruments. With corrections experiencing an 'end of ideology' and its weary leadership floating in a vacuum, this new wave of enthusiasm based upon behaviour manipulation may become attractive to them. What follows here is an alternative less enthusiastic perhaps but even less manipulative.

Corrections are much too important an issue to be left in the hands of wardens, Clemenceau might have said. But unfortunately that is a fair picture of current American correctional practice which is still insulated and isolated. As a result it remains uninformed by a theory of human behaviour, hence it may be found to be using several simultaneously. It remains uninformed by a theory of the purpose of the criminal law, hence it passively watches itself become an explosive warehouse in response to legislative whim and caprice. Correctional objectives, such as they are, developed aimlessly. Tappan observed (1951):

... In different periods of social evolution certain ones have emerged out of society's particular climate of values and have been more highly prized than others. Yet each, as it has been crystallized in law, custom, and correctional practice, has impressed a persisting influence upon subsequent policy. Moreover, each objective has become encrusted with layers of rationalization to justify and perpetuate the established treatment methods. The ultimate consequence is a *mélange* of purposes, some deeply bedded in the channels of history ... it is not unusual to find correction exerting, in turn, vindictive, deterrent, and rehabilitative measures in relation to the same offender.[2]

As a result of aimlessness and public neglect the prison never acquired a specific correctional purpose, rather it inherited vestiges of the Puritan ethic and added middle-class values of mobility through work and education to it. Packer (1968) called this a 'leap of faith'.

We can use our prisons to educate the illiterate, to teach men a useful trade, and to accomplish similar benevolent purposes. The plain disheartening fact is that we have very little reason to suppose that there is a general connection between these measures and the prevention of future criminal behaviour. What is involved primarily is a leap of faith, by which we suppose that people who have certain social advantages will be less likely to commit certain kinds of crimes. It is hard to make a good argument for restraining a man of his liberty on the assumption that this connection will be operative in his case. It is harder still if he already possesses the advantages that we assume will make people less likely to offend.[3]

We will propose a limited set of objectives for prisons devolved from a series of propositions concerning our view of man and law in the context of justice. Meaningful prison objectives cannot be successfully divorced from a conception of human behaviour and the criminal law.

Much of the criminological theory development has taken us down a primrose path searching for a 'unified theory' of criminality. It has been in the tradition of early demonology, albeit seeking more 'scientific' unifying themes such as physique, mental aberrations, glandular dysfunction, genetic disabilities, atavistic behaviour, social ecology, cyclic variation in the economy or weather, and associational patterns. Theories have tried '. . . to explain criminal behavior itself, but they do not concern themselves with *why* certain acts are defined as crimes' sometimes oblivious to the interconnectedness of 'the acts [themselves] defined in the law as crimes and the forces that impel some people to commit these acts'.[4] In either case the notion of responsibility is frequently downgraded. Corrections, if not criminology, must come to terms with this problem. We can no longer await the refinement of theories before acting to modernize the field. Theorists, unlike convicts, are not quite so desperate but like them have plenty of time. Correctional administrators are not at such leisure.

We are not sure whether the sentence of imprisonment or any other penal sanction really deters (generally or specifically) but we are in agreement with Norval Morris and Gordon Hawkins when they observed of this endless debate, that it seems to have deteriorated since the days of Beccaria '. . . Discussions of this ancient antinomy which have consumed gallons of jurisprudential ink turn out on examination to resemble nothing so much as boxing matches between blindfolded contestants.'[5] However, we do have a substantial guide for future correctional action from work of Walker and Wilkins.

We put forward the following propositions based upon a perspective suggested by Stephen Schafer:

1. Criminal law is the 'command of the sovereign'.*
2. The threat of punishment is necessary to implement the law.
3. The powerful manipulate the chief motivators of human behaviour—fear and hope—through rewards and punishments to retain power.
4. Socialization (the manipulation of fear and hope through rewards and punishments) of individuals, however imperfect, occurs in response to the commands and expectations of the ruling social-political power.
5. Criminal law protects the dominant prescribed morality (a system of rules said to be in the common and best interest of all) reflecting the enforcement aspect 'of the failure of socialization'.†
6. In the absence of an absolute system of justice or a 'natural law', no accurate etiological theory of crime is possible nor is the definition of crime itself stable.
7. Although free will may not exist perfectly the criminal law is largely based upon its presumed vitality and forms the only foundation for penal sanctions.
8. A prison sentence represents a punishment sanctioned by a legislature and meted out through the official legal system within a process of justice, against a person adjudged responsible for his behaviour; although the purpose of punishment may be deterrence it is specifically the deprivation of liberty for a fixed period of time.‡

---

* And as Schafer reminds us this 'may be a gloomy truth whether the origin of the law is traditional or revolutionary', (Stephen Schafer, *The Political Criminal*, p. 47).

† Schafer states: 'Morality is not the product of law; the law exists to enforce morality' (p. 104) and '. . . criminal law is a kind of back-up instrument in the socialization process, and it comes into operation whenever the state of any moral issue so warrants' (Stephen Schafer, *The Political Criminal*, p. 84).

‡ '. . . if punishment is to be considered as the aim of imprisonment, it must be what the Germans termed *Zweckstrafe*, or punishment for a purpose, rather than *Vergeltungsstrafe*, or punishment as retribution' (A.C.A., *Manual of Correctional Standards* as cited in Killinger and Cromwell, *Penology*, p. 76).

9. The entire process of the criminal law must be played out in a milieu of justice. Justice-as-fairness represents the superordinate goal of all agencies of the criminal law.

10. When corrections become mixed in the dismal swamp of preaching, exhorting, and treating ('resocialization') they become dysfunctional as an agency of justice. Correctional agencies should engage prisoners as the law otherwise dictates—as responsible, volitional and aspiring human beings.

11. Justice-as-fairness is not a programme; it is a process which insists that the prisons (and all agencies of the criminal law) perform their assigned tasks with non-law-abiders lawfully and with an even hand. No more should be expected, no less should be tolerated by correctional administrators.

12. William Pitt said: 'where the law ends tyranny begins'—so does the exercise of discretion. Discretion 'may mean either beneficence or tyranny, either justice or injustice, either reasonableness or arbitrariness'.[6] Discretion cannot be eliminated but the justice perspective seeks to narrow, control, and make it reviewable.[7]

Having stated the propositions we now use them as a springboard for examining their rational implementation in correctional institutions. Of the major areas in correctional administration which most vitally affect the operation of prisons three will be discussed; sentencing and parole boards taken together and prison administration. We are interested in how the prison stay is determined, organized, and for most prisoners, ended. Following this analysis we will propose some alternatives. But in preface some thoughts on justice are offered.

On Justice—A Perspective

Philosopher John Rawls identifies justice as 'the first virtue of social institutions, as truth is of systems of thought' and he continues, 'A theory however elegant and economical must be rejected or revised if it is untrue; likewise laws and institutions no matter how efficient and well-arranged must be reformed or abolished if they are unjust.'[8] In order to develop an operational model of justice in corrections we must move from the philosopher's chair to the cell block. Speaking about the student of ethics Hans Reichenback suggested '. . . [he] should not go to the philosopher, he should go where the moral issues are fought out'.[9]

A concept of justice is useful to the scholar but it does not contain the urgency felt by those who must daily test its utility in practice. Great ideas are played out by average men and not, as Edmund Cahn reminds us, by the legally constructed 'reasonable man' who is usually too dull to get into trouble with officials.[10]

Justice in the Consumer Perspective

We are not interested in 'utopian diagrams about abstract justice . . . justice will mean . . . the active process of remedying or preventing what would arouse the "sense of injustice",'[11] so wrote Edmund Cahn.

The correctional model of justice we arrive at is an adaptation of Cahn's 'consumer perspective'. It focuses the official processor of justice on the consumer—on the people caught in the machinery of the agencies of justice—the offender, the guard, the victim, the witness and the taxpayer. Tappan (1951) had long ago brought this to our attention when he called for the protection of the innocent against injustice: 'Three groups require some special consideration. In order of their numbers, they are the taxpayer who bears the costs, the actual or potential victim of the criminal who is most directly injured, and the innocent suspect who may be unjustly convicted and punished.'[12] In relation to the 'War on Poverty' Cahn's son Edgar and his wife Jean called our approach the 'civilian perspective' rather than the 'military perspective',[13] Jonathan Caspar in 'Criminal Justice' identifies it as the 'consumer's perspective'[14] . . . similarly, it is what Philip Selznick refers to when he speaks of the imprisoned in need of 'justice as therapy'.[15] It is a concern for the micro-world of the participants in action not in abstraction.*

The 'consumer perspective' or 'justice perspective' as we shall now refer to it can be distinguished from the 'imperial' or 'official perspective' (Cahn, *see* n. 13, above).

The official perspective has a typical rhetoric which, when expertly manipulated, can seem very persuasive . . . Some of the familiar phrases are: the public interest in getting things finally settled; the duty to abide by established principles and precedents; the necessity of showing respect for expert judgement and administrative convenience; the dominant need for certainty in the law; the obligation to preserve the law's predictability so that men will know how to order their affairs; the danger of opening the floodgates of litigation; the danger of opening the gates of penitentiaries; the danger of inviting collusion, fraud, and perjury; the deference due to other organs of government; the absurdity of heeding mere speculations; the necessity of leaving certain wrongs, however grievous they

---

* There is a parallel stream of thought encompassed in Lawrence Kohlberg's *Just Community* (Harvard University School of Education, 2 vols.) but in the last analysis it turns out to be a form of group therapy using morality as its rationale rather than the psyche. At times the two are indistinguishable. Niantic Women's Prison in Connecticut is the current setting for the correctional demonstration project of Kohlberg *et al.*

may be, to the province of morals; the paramount need to maintain strict procedural regularity; and (by way of solace to a man on his way to the electric chair) the undeniable right to petition for executive clemency.[16]

The justice perspective involves a shift of focus from the processor to the consumer.

> ... but among the various consumers and their diverse interests, it offers no simplistic formula, no *a priori* preference, no lazy hierarchy of values. Some consumers need bread; others need Shakespeare; others need their rightful place in the national society—what they all need is processors of law who will consider the people's needs more significant than administrative convenience ...

> In the consumer perpsective, there is something repulsive about the complacent grin with which we are assured that not many judges have been caught taking bribes, that the third degree is not so common as it used to be, and that not many prosecutors suppress evidence favourable to the defense or, if they do, it is seldom proved. [Or that uncovering convicts' corpses embarrasses legislators and thereby retards correctional reform.]

> How can one expect to solace them by promising that some day the law will awake to needs like theirs? Unless a litigant happens to be an Olympian philosopher or a legal historian, he probably desires justice here and now ... What he cannot understand is inertia and smug indifference.[17]

Corrections have long been cut off from ties with the general field of public administration. Speaking of the courts but with equal validity in corrections, Judge Marvin Frankel states: 'One need not be a revolutionist or an enemy of the judiciary to predict that untrained, untested, unsupervised men armed with great power will perpetuate abuse.'[18] Low visibility and high discretion eventually corrupt. An unhealthy wall of absolute power has kept correctional administrators shut off from the mainstream of the history of ideas, the spirit of open political conflict (other than those of parochial localisms), their constituencies and from general involvement in the public arena. Wardens have long resisted public accountability.

> ... [the] common demand twenty-five years ago for freedom of the administrator to get on with his job free of the harassment of legal imperatives is the same demand made today by those who administer the new penology. A beginning in the correctional area awaits a general recognition that the correctional agency is not *sui generis,* but another administrative agency which requires its own administrative law if it is to make its maximum contributions harmoniously with the values of the general social order in which it functions.[19]

The usual correctional response has been that large dosages of discretion are necessary if correctional administrators are expected to treat (rehabilitate) criminals. But we have also been warned by Justice Brandeis: 'Experience should teach us to be on our guard to protect liberty when the Government's

purposes are beneficient.'[20] George Bernard Shaw, speaking of the ruthless-
ness of the pure of heart said: 'Malice and fear are narrow things, and carry
with them a thousand inhibitions and terrors and scruples. A heart and brain
purified of them gain an enormous freedom . . .' presumably to do anything
in the name of benevolence.[21]

> There is growing recognition that correctional agencies exercise a very significant
> form of governmental power, even more important to the lives of individuals
> than most governmental agencies . . . there is also need to do so in ways that are
> just and that inspire in the offender, as far as possible, and in the community a
> confidence in the justice of the correctional process . . . But the most important
> question is whether corrections should actively be concerned with the fairness
> of its processes beyond conforming to legal standards and participating in the
> creation of new ones. Legislative and judicial standards for the conduct of
> administrative agencies are necessarily minimum standards . . . Reliance must
> be placed upon the administrative agency itself to achieve that goal.[22]

As a matter of plain fact, correctional administrators have for too long
operated with practical immunity in the backwashes of administrative law
unmindful that the processes of justice, more strictly observed by the visible
police and courts in relation to rights due the accused before and through
adjudication, must not stop when the convicted person is sentenced.[23] The
justice perspective demands accountability from all processors even the
'pure of heart'. Properly understood, the justice perspective is not so much
concerned with administration of justice as it is with the justice of
administration.[24]

We now turn, using the justice perspective, to inform our probes into
sentencing, parole and life in the prison.

On Sentencing and Granting Parole

Judge Marvin Frankel wrote a book entitled *Criminal Sentences* (1973) after
reading which one can very clearly understand the *double entendre* intended.
It might have been entitled *The Crime of Sentencing* or more charitably *The
Lawlessness of Sentencing*. It was not, nor is this analysis intended as, an attack
on judges, rather on a sentencing system which is anomic. With few guidelines and many judges we are effectively, in the area of sentencing, a government of men, not laws.[25]

> Experience, and wisdom flowing out of that experience, long ago led to the belief
> that agents of government should not be vested with power and discretion to
> define and punish as criminal past conduct which had not been clearly defined
> as a crime in advance. To this end, at least in part, written laws came into being,
> marking the boundaries of conduct for which public agents could thereafter

impose punishment upon people. In contrast, bad governments either wrote no general rules of conduct at all, leaving that highly important task to the unbridled discretion of government agents at the moment of trial, or sometimes, history tells us, wrote their laws in an unknown tongue so that people could not understand them or else placed their written laws at such inaccessible spots that people could not read them. [*Ginzburg* v. *United States.* 383 U.S. 463, 477 (1966).[26]]

It is of vital interest to administrators of correctional agencies that the people committed to them, because of the usual bitterness they have upon arrival, also have the feeling that the judicial process immediately undergone was fair, just, and that the sentence received was offence-related and appropriate.[27] This is largely not the case at present.

The nation has several different adult sentencing schemes; (1) a system of both maximum (MA) and minimum (MI) terms fixed by the court (each offence has its own upper and lower limits set by law). (2) Both MA and MI (within limits) fixed by court with the MI not to exceed a portion of the MA. (3) MA (within limits set by law) fixed by court and the MI fixed by law. (4) MA fixed by law and MI by court. (5) MA and MI fixed by law for each offence. (6) MA fixed by law but no MI in law, rather the MI is fixed by the parole board. (7) MA fixed by court, no MI. (8) MI is fixed by law and MA by parole board.[28]

In addition to this crazy-quilt system in the nation, there are sentencing disparities within the same jurisdiction. It is too facile to permit the disparities to be explained as individualized justice being meted out by different judges.* Absent sentencing criteria and the individual judge's attitude surfaces as the controlling force. Like others, judges have strong attitudes about sex, mugging, narcotics and other crimes. The difference in the case of judges is that their attitudes, translated into unbridled action produce the longest prison terms in the Western world. Blacks are treated more severely† by prison sentences than their white counterparts for similar crimes.[29] But race is not the only problem as James Bennett has observed—

In one of our institutions, a middle-aged credit union treasurer is serving 117 days for embezzling $24,000 in order to cover his gambling debts. On the other hand, another middle-aged embezzler with a fine family is serving 20 years, with 5 years' probation to follow. At the same institution is a war veteran, a 39 year-old attorney who has never been in trouble before, serving 11 years for

---

* Richard McGee calls our attention to the fact that the 'hanging judge' and 'soft headed judge' (disparities within a jurisdiction) are largely the same product of rulelessness of sentencing systems ('A New Look at Sentencing-Part II', *Federal Probation*, September 1974, unpublished manuscript, p. 7).

† Blacks, in the Federal system in 1969 and 1970 were averaging 88.5 months compared to whites at 75.1 months. *Federal Bureau of Prison Statistical Report* 1969 and 1970 (table A-3A).

illegally importing parrots into this country. Another who is destined for the same institution is a middle-aged tax accountant who on tax fraud charges received 31 years and 31 days in consecutive sentences. In stark contrast, at the same institution last year, an unstable young man served out his 98-day sentence for armed bank robbery.[30]

Indeterminate sentences, said to be a treatment tool, have without exception produced more severe prison terms.[31]

70 per cent of definite sentence prisoners actually serve two years or less; whereas only 57 per cent of the indeterminate sentence prisoners actually serve two years or less ... Clearly, therefore, in practice the indeterminate sentence system serves to keep a substantially greater proportion of men in prison for long terms than the definite sentence system.[32]

The sentencing procedure itself, which presumably represents the apex of the adjudication process (up to this point justice was largely procedural) where the sovereign now 'restores the balance' by meting out justice, is largely lawless. Legislatively-prescribed procedures are practically non-existent. Regardless of what the judge finally selects as a sentence, the process itself, with rare exception, is inscrutable. We do not know, because we do not require an explication of sentence selective norms, what a judge considers in his selection. 'We do not allow each judge to make up the law for himself on other questions. We should not allow it with respect to sentencing,' said Judge Frankel.[33] Continuing he points out:

In deciding where to fix any particular sentence, he will presumably consider a host of factors in the case: the relative seriousness of the particular offence—the degree of danger threatened, cruelty, premeditation; the prior record of the defendant; situational factors—health, family disturbance, drug use; the defendant's work history, skills, potential; etc. In the existing mode ... the judge is under no pressure—and is without guidelines—towards systematic, exhaustive, detailed appraisal of such things one by one. He probably does not list them even for himself.[34]

Even if he did list them it would be unknowable since we have not developed a procedure mandating judges to do so. Even when judges are thoughtful, the information they have before them, upon which to base a consideration, is frequently inadequate, of a bland generalized nature and ... 'is not mitigated by the appending of diagnostic charts and summaries that are sometimes legible, and less often intelligible, to the sentencing judge'.[35] Finally, whatever the sentencing process is, it is not adversarial and is rarely reviewable.

One would think that with such unbridled and unassailable power the judge's sentence would indeed be carried out to the letter. That used to be true but no longer is.

The correlation between courtroom pronouncement and actual outcome has virtually disappeared. The history of penal policy during this interval is in no small measure one of erosion of judicial power and the evolution of a highly complex process of administrative punishment-fixing that directly involves prosecutors, parole boards and the disciplinary committees ... From this functional perspective, judges are doing less and less of the real decision-making, their role being merely one step in a process in which law enforcement, prosecutors, probation officers, parole boards, parole agents or correctional staff may play major roles. [Caleb Foote.[36]]

In the process of erosion, district attorneys at the front end of the criminal justice system, using their bargaining power, make more decisions concerning the sentence than do judges. And at the other end of the system, the parole board governs the outside length of the sentence.* The prisoner . . . 'Kept in the dark about how to behave' in order to minimize his sentence, finds his life in the prison cast in a 'pattern of cryptic taciturnity'.[37]

Parole boards, without a legal mandate to sentence continue to play a larger rôle than judges in sentencing. Caleb Foote comments on parole board decision-making:

The same basic criteria are usually employed whether the arena is a courtroom or some prison parole hearing room, e.g.: (1) a determination of how much time is right for the kind of crime at issue, with the decision-maker's own sense of values and expectations usually (but not always) heavily influenced by the pressures of his environment and what he perceives to be the norms of his colleagues; (2) classification within that crime category of the offender's particular act as mitigated, average or aggravated; (3) his past criminal record (slight, average or aggravated); (4) the extent of his repentence, his attitude towards available 'treatment', and the official prognosis of his reformability; or (5) the anticipated public (usually meaning law enforcement) reaction to a proposed disposition.[38]

Parole boards, through legislation, have inherited much of the sentencing power normally associated with the judiciary.[39]

The parole board decisions too are unreviewable and are not hammered out in an adversarial clash, rather they are five to fifteen-minute sessions frequently with members using a combination of whim, caprice and arbitrariness. And as if to say amen, Maurice Sigler of the US Parole Board, following *Morressey* v. *Brewer* said in a speech (1973) '. . . perhaps it should have been foreseen that eventually parole actions would have to be governed by considerations of due process.'† [40]

* 'When you think about it, parole boards really have more to say about how long a person's liberty must be taken away from him than the courts do.' (Maurice Sigler, Chairman of the U.S. Parole Board, *The Courts and Corrections*, Speech 8/17/73, Kirksville, Mo.).

† 'The U.S. Board of Parole is opening five regional offices to expedite parole actions and insure that decisions are considered in a manner that provides greater fairness to

Compared to the courtroom which is open, the parole board hearing is secret. Only recently have reasons for denial been given to convicts in a systematic manner, but decisions, short of a finding of abuse of discretion, are not successfully appealed.[41]

We find vague the rhetoric of the imperial or official perspective guiding judges and parole boards in their decisions. The justice perspective challenges the lack of clarity and degree of certainty of such expressions as: 'the sound exercise of judicial discretion', 'the consideration of the crime and the criminal', 'the gravity of the deed', 'the guilt of perpetrator'.[42] They are, Caleb Foote points out, no more than slogans, none are law.[43] In the quest for fairness using the justice perspective we seek a justification in the law for the decisions of those who exercise wide discretion. 'The largely unbridled power of judges and prison officials stir questions under the clauses promising that life and liberty will not be denied except by "due process of law".'[44] Justice Stewart once described some sentencing practices as discriminatory, capricious and freakish.[45]

We have made this brief excursion in the realm of ruleless sentencing and parole-granting not for the purpose of extensive analysis, rather to understand better the prisoner as he enters and tries to leave the prison legally. Prison life is largely a product of the anomie of sentencing and paroling. Like both, it too is effectively ruleless. How could it be otherwise with ninety-five per cent of its prisoners unable to calculate when they will be released or even what, with a degree of certainty, is demanded of them for release candidacy by parole authorities. These two processes, uncontrollable by prison officials, have crucial impact on life inside the walls, to which we now turn.

A Restatement of the Purpose of Prison

At one level the problem with prisons is that they have never bitten off a digestible bite. A narrowing of the rhetoric and purpose is necessary. A prisoner who entered with feelings of despair, after having received a sentence he felt improper but unreviewable, now has to settle down to life in a cage. First he must turn his attention to problems of protecting his internal integrity from another sequence of largely lawless events—prison life. This would be a herculean task for most but additionally he learns that still another lawless (in the sense of ruleless) process needs to be undertaken—his pre-

inmates and to the public. Prisoners will be told why paroles are denied and may appeal the decision to the full Board in Washington, D.C. Regional offices are being opened in Philadelphia, Atlanta, Kansas City, Mo.; Dallas, Tex; and Burlingame, California' (LEAA Newsletter, August & September 1974, p. 26).

paration for parole. As a stranger in a zoo-like world he begins to seek out significant others who can speed his process of release. But who can make such judgements in a prison? What appears to be a rational, even tightly drawn military-like prison staff organization is, upon closer examination, chaotic.* Again the question turns on discretion.

Theoretically, the staff of the prison regularly furnishes the parole board with information pointing to prisoner progress, its pace, or absence. Of the myriad events which take place, how can discriminating information be sensibly selected, collected, distilled and reported to the board? After the board has 'studied' it, it now has to make a decision concerning the convict's future crime-free behaviour basing it upon his behaviour in prison—no small task. Unaided by rules, reviewable findings or precedents, the board usually makes its decision using a *mélange* of whim, time served, caprice, the amount of 'noise' created by law enforcement agencies, arbitrariness, and authoritative testaments from clinical and other prison staff concerning the convict's reformative progress. It is in this process that prison staff decision-making fades into unbridled, low visibility discretion. If at first blush, discretion looks like power, in prison it also produces an arena in which indecisiveness, favouritism, racism, suppression and lawlessness are daily played out. The system calls forth such responses from staff and convicts because it gives no direction, has no accountable mission and in the absence of accountability, claims much more than it can produce.

We have to conceive of the period of incarceration and its place in criminal justice in a new way. Consider the problem facing Thomas Edison when he was thinking about a new technology for developing artificial light. The imagery he laboured under at the time was 'candle power' and how to increase its potency. Staring at the candle and acting upon that model he would have simply produced larger and larger candles. Edison needed and produced a flight of imagination to arrive at the electric light bulb. In corrections we are still toying with the candle. The suggestions to follow are based upon a two-pronged strategy (1) the immediate and short range and (2) the middle range.

* 'Seen from outside, the criminal justice and correctional system present the appearance of a virtually omnipotent conspiracy for the organization of human misery. But once having won his way in, the outsider—now a participant—discovers a shocking fact. Except for the universal penchant of bureaucrats to cover their own trails, there is no conspiracy. Indeed, there is hardly any "organization". What appeared at a distance to be a monolithic system turns out to be no system at all—but rather a concatenation of several interest groups, frequently operating at cross purposes or, worse, without reference to each other at all. In the chaos thus propagated, accident, apathy, non-accountability and sheer inertia are fully capable of producing fortuitously what the most efficient, concerted malice might have achieved by design: the almost total debasement of human aspiration.' (Richard B. Korn, 'The Prisoners of Affirmation: Correctional Administrators as Penal Reformers' in *Prisoners' Rights* by Michele Hermann and Marilyn Haft (eds.), p. 441.)

No long range is offered because of the critical urgency to move rapidly, and 'progress' in corrections is usually counted in decades. The distinguishing characteristics between the two strategies are that the short range requires no legislation or new appropriations while the middle range requires both.

Immediate and Short Range

We need to conceptualize imprisonment differently and to narrow our rhetorical claims. A penal sanction should *only* mean a temporary deprivation of liberty. It is the legal cost for the violation of some laws. The prison is responsible for executing the sentence, not rehabilitating the convict.

> In seeking to make criminal justice more redemptive and less punitive, we may have asked too much of institutions that can barely hold their own, let alone develop the competence to be curers of souls. A retreat from rosy hopes may well be inevitable, if only because rehabilitation entails supervision, and ineffective rehabilitation coupled with open-ended control has little to commend it.[46]

The sentence must be seen as a part of the continuum of justice—it must be experienced as just, reasonable and constitutional. It is in the context of justice that a mission arises for the prison and its staff. The mission is fairness. Until sentencing and parole problems can be resolved, discretion must be harnessed by as much voluntary administrative explication of norms as is necessary to produce a sense of fairness for both the keeper and the kept.

The prison sentence should merely represent a deprivation of liberty. All the rights accorded free citizens but consistent with mass living and the execution of a sentence restricting the freedom of movement, should follow a prisoner into prison. The prisoner is volitional and may therefore choose programmes for his benefit. The state cannot with any degree of confidence hire one person to rehabilitate another unless the other senses an inadequacy in himself which he wishes to modify through services he himself seeks. This should be evident from historical experience. Volition is subversive of the foundation of the clinical model, for the offender exercising independence of choice may not select the clinician as his choice of treatment. The person troubled or in trouble has to want something to happen. The best way to engage him is to treat him with dignity. Administrators should immediately begin to slash the budget of all such programme services not voluntarily chosen by inmates.

The postulate of normality, competence, and worth.
If offenders are to be dealt with as human beings, it must be assumed that they are basically like everyone else, only their circumstances are special. Every administrative device that negates this principle, and any therapy that ignores it, must be questioned and, if possible, set aside.[47]

We will shortly elaborate a prison mission of justice for our current fortress prison environment—but the fortress prison system must be ended if we are to expect further rationality in correctional development.

Middle Range

There are three elements which should govern the middle range strategy which will be elaborated later: (1) a return to flat time sentences with procedural rules governing sentence selection; (2) the elimination of both parole boards and parole agencies; (3) the transformation of the fortress prison into institutions for no more than 300 persons, further divisible into sub-units of 30. The institutions will contain people sentenced to similar terms. Release will be determined by a narrow and reviewable system of fixed good-time rules. We turn first to those elements of a short range which can be immediately implemented by administrators.

A Justice Model for the Fortress Prison

The period of incarceration can be conceptualized as a time in which we try to re-orient a prisoner to the lawful use of power. One of the more fruitful ways the prison can teach non-law-abiders to be law-abiding is to treat them in a lawful manner. The entire effort of the prison should be seen as an influence attempt based upon operationalizing justice. This is called the 'justice model'.

It begins by recognizing, not by moralizing, what the prison stay is about. Simply stated, it is an enforced deprivation of liberty. It is a taking of some or all of the days of a person's life and his confinement within an area. When men are confined against their will in the United States, the bottom line of the arrangement of life for both the keeper and kept should be justice-as-fairness. Opportunities for self-improvement should be offered but not made a condition of freedom.

Confinement and compression in a human zoo, of large numbers of men, who in the past have frequently resorted to the use of force, fraud and violence is at best a precarious venture. James Q. Wilson said, 'We have imposed the rehabilitative philosophy in a way that offends simple justice ... when it is possible for one person, by manipulating the system, to go free while another, convicted of the same crime, remains in prison for a long term.'[48] Prison administrators should not now further confuse their staff with a mission either claiming moral or psychologic redemption nor with one which leans on brutality to create orderliness.

Justice-as-fairness provides the keeper and the kept with a rationale and morality for their shared fates in a correctional agency. Considering the failure of most treatment methods within our current operating structure—the fortress prison—the justice model holds some promise, if not to cut recidivism, then more decisively to preclude Atticas. This model purports to turn a prison experience into one which provides opportunities for men to learn to be agents in their own lives, to use legal processes to change thier condition, and to wield lawful power. Men who can negotiate their fates do not have to turn to violence as a method of achieving change.

It is a sad irony in our system of criminal justice that we insist on the full majesty of due process for the accused until he is sentenced to a prison and then justice is said to have been served. Consider that our criminal codes make it mandatory that before a criminal sanction may be imposed, there be a finding beyond stringent levels of doubt that the accused's behaviour was a union of *act* and *intent*—it was volitional. We will reduce degrees of responsibility for the alleged crimes if the behaviour was adjudged non-volitional. We are tough in standards of arrest, most stringent in the finding of guilt. The defendant is protected under the mantle of the presumption of innocence. The state must prove its allegations 'beyond a reasonable doubt'. The defendant can stand mute in court and is protected from conviction out of his own mouth. Anything brought before the court to support a prosecutor's claim may be challenged. We believe that this system is civilized and protects us from star-chamber injustices. We strain to protect the lowliest from the capriciousness of the legally constituted authority. The great irony occurs after a conviction when the judge commits a guilty offender to prison. It takes a great flight of imagination or studied neglect to include the current prison experience in a system of justice. The entire case for a justice model rests upon the need to continue to engage the person in the quest for justice as he moves on the continuum from defendant-to-convict-to-free citizen.

The justice model seeks to engage both the keeper and the kept in a joint venture which insists that the agencies of justice shall operate in a lawful and just manner. It simply means that we believe that the prisoners did not use lawful means to guide themselves outside the prison and should therefore be provided greater (not lesser) opportunities to learn lawful behaviour while in the institution. The staff effort should be turned to teaching a prisoner how to use lawful processes to achieve his ends. This also implies that the convict accepts the legal responsibility for the consequences of his behaviour. In the absence of a continuum of justice in the prison, most ends are reached unlawfully. When unlawful behaviour is detected, it is itself frequently dealt with in the absence of the very standards of due process we insist upon outside the prison. The result is a further indication to the convict that lawful behaviour has little pay-off. He can be dealt with arbitrarily and usually responds by treating others in the same manner.

The justice model insists that, at least during the period of incarceration, the prisoner and the staff, as society's agents, will deal with problems in strict fairness—something we expect of each other outside of prison, Further, it points to a way of engaging both the keeper and kept in a rhetoric-free manageable prison experience.

Operationalizing Justice in the Prison

The model of justice we propose affects several aspects of prison life. It attempts to create a lawful and rational arena for dealing with problems arising from an artificial environment which charges one group of men to restrain the mobility of another against their wills. While this can probably never be voluntarily achieved there are some immediate short range goals which we believe are realizable; (1) a mitigation of harshness, (2) peaceful conflict resolution, (3) and a safer staff work environment that will emerge from the operationalization of fairness in prison life.

The days of hiding behind the wall are effectively over. Correctional administrators can undergo the turmoil of being forced to go public or can take the initiative and voluntarily begin programmes of playing a more open hand. By this we mean a checks-and-balances system of scrutiny not another torrent of slick publications. For those who believe that such a course of action is a new or radical departure in thinking we cite John Howard in his *State of Prisons*, 1777.

> Finally, the care of a prison is too important to be left wholly to a gaoler, paid indeed for his attendance, but often tempted by his passions, or interest, to fail in his duty. For every prison there should be an inspector appointed; either by his colleagues in the magistracy or by Parliament . . . He should speak with every prisoner, hear all complaints, and immediately correct what he finds manifestly wrong:[49]

Discretion is the central problem of corrections affecting their entire structure from the administrator to the convict. Its successful harnessing could go a long way towards giving the feeling of fairness to all concerned. More significantly perhaps it would free the administrator from bondage in the rhetoric of the imperial perspective and permit him to take a position more appropriate for an agent of justice. In this sense freedom for the correctional administrator lies in the direction of voluntarily adopting a simple justice mode for administering his official affairs. How may this be done? Professor Kenneth Culp Davis suggests several ways of structuring discretion.

> The seven instruments that are most useful in the structuring of discretionary power are open plans, open policy statements, open rules, open findings, open

reasons, open precedents, and fair informal procedure. The reason for repeating the word 'open' is a powerful one; openness is the natural enemy of arbitrariness and a natural ally in the fight against injustice.[50]

Properly understood this discussion is limited to the elimination of unnecessary discretion and the structuring of arbitrary discretion. It does not imply the total elimination of discretion, rather a lifting of the veil so that fairness can creep in to protect those affected. We all respond more positively to fair treatment and even to a punitive action when it is accompanied by a precise explanation of a violated norm.

In the context of prison, justice-as-fairness means having clear rules, insuring their promulgation, and a procedure for determining and punishing rule infractions rooted in due process safeguards (for example: statement of the allegation, notice, counsel substitute, a hearing, the chance to rebut, written findings, appeal). Further, it means giving up the foot-dragging which the litigation so vividly bares. Correctional administrators should not have to be brought to court to provide adequate law libraries and access to them, for more than ten sheets of paper nor for punishing, by segregation, those who use their right of access to the court, the press or the public. A justice perspective assures that expressions of racism will be fought. We should be in the forefront of exposing the indignities of poor medical care, inadequate diets, servile labour, the absence of recreational programmes and inhumane segregative facilities. The case materials show that in court we appear to be alibi-ing for the existence of such conditions instead of agreeing to seek remedy. The public and court will permit us reasonable precautions about what may freely enter prisons, but they look askance at the overbroad regulations surrounding mail, publication, and visitors. Administrators need to make a dramatic break with the vestiges of the nineteenth-century 'buried-from-the-world' philosophy. Courts should not have to *force* modern administrators to adopt any of the above procedures—it embarrasses our claim to professionalism.

Specifically, but not exhaustively, the following programme elements would provide minimal levels for a justice perspective in prison operation.

1. Elements of self-governance.
2. A system-wide ombudsman independent of the Department of Corrections.
3. A law library.
4. Civil legal assistance for inmates.
5. A prevailing-rate wage system in the prison industries.
6. Opportunity to provide community service (a form of more restitution).

7. Recognition of, and opportunity for programming for, different ethnic groups.
8. Due procedural safeguards built into internal behaviour management systems.
9. No mail censorship.
10. An extensive furlough programme.
11. A greater degree of certainty about the length of the prison stay.
12. Open access of the correctional system to the press.
13. A system of victim compensation and offender restitution.
14. Conflict resolution machinery built into the prison operation.

An agenda for fairness for guards should include; clearly drawn work assignments, employment standards and salary on par with the state police, hazardous duty and malpractice liability insurance, a dignified but mandatory earlier (age 55) retirement, special benefits for death in the course of duty, the right to organize and bargain collectively, involvement in programme planning, a grievance procedure, freedom from partisan political pressures, merit* procedures for promotion, and mandatory training which is unambiguous about the guards' work-rôle and focuses on procedures of justice-as-fairness in addition to traditional custodial concerns.

In the micro-world of the prison the justice perspective calls upon the maker of rules to share legitimate power with the enforcers and consumers of the rules. It also urges that all rules and rulings be required to stand the test of being the least onerous way of reaching a lawful end.

Sentencing and Parole—Some Alternatives

We have already examined the maze of sentencing patterns which exist in the nation. We have an idea of the disparities which arise as a result of lawlessness in sentencing procedures. In the area of sentencing we are a government of men not law. Prisoners entering our institutions burdened with a sense of injustice, living in its compressed tension, with ruleless procedures for parole, make the entire prison venture unsafe for all. Yet we will need some form of separation of the dangerous for the foreseeable future. But sentencing can be accomplished more sensibly and equitably.

The indeterminate sentence is now experiencing the beginning of its end. Recently a group of informed leaders have begun sounding the death knell

* At Menard prison in 1973 guards talked freely about purchasing and retaining their jobs, and being promoted as a function of routine payments to county party chairmen, ranging from $50.00 to $300.

for the rehabilitation model and its powerful tool the indeterminate sentence.*
Judge Laurence W. Pierce (U.S. District Court) states in relation to the
rehabilitation model: 'I join the chorus of those who are suggesting that this
commitment be reassessed.[51] Judge Frankel finds the indeterminate sentence
is frequently 'evil and unwarranted'.[52] Judge Constance Baker Motley has
suggested a system of graduated sentences of a mandatory nature for the
repetitive offender but no prison for most first offenders.[53] Dr. William E.
Amos, Chairman of the Youth Corrections Division of the U.S. Board of
Parole, took the following position:

(1) We should confine fewer people.
(2) The philosophy of confinement should be deterrence, accountability, and the
    protection of society—*not rehabilitation*.
(3) Adequate training or rehabilitation centres should be operated by other
    agencies to service those offenders whose offences are directly related to
    educational, physical, or psychological deficiencies. These agencies may be
    vocational rehabilitation, welfare, educational, or even private agencies.
(4) Whenever a person is confined he should be provided the protection,
    services, and opportunities that would reflect our belief in the dignity and
    nature of man. I would further propose that a National Inmate Bill of Rights
    be prepared, and all states be urged to adopt and implement it.[54]

Allen Breed, Director of the California Youth Authority has come to the
position that our 'goal may [have] to be to make rehabilitation fit the crime'.[55]

But we should not confuse the public or ourselves on what we are doing. If
we send offenders to prison we do so to punish them, not to rehabilitate them.
Hopefully, we can carry out our punishment in humane and sensible ways—and
long sentences for offenders who are not dangerous can hardly be called sensible.

The method would vary with the offender. Dangerous offenders must be kept
in secure institutions—for the protection of society—for this must remain our
primary consideration. The vast bulk of offenders need not be incarcerated at all,
or for as short a time as possible, and always for periods that are specified in
advance.[56]

The AFSC Task Force also called for the reduction of discretion in sentencing
and an end to reliance on rehabilitation as a goal in corrections.[57] Richard A.
McGee, president of the American Justice Institute, and perhaps the nation's
most prestigious correctional figure, has after over forty years of practice
concluded:

The divergence of views with respect to the purposes of criminal justice administration on the part of police, courts, corrections, legislature, significant citizen

---

* 'Now both the public and the correctional staff expect prisoners to be, at least, no
worse for the correctional experience and, at most, prepared to take their places in society
without further involvement with the law' (National Advisory Commission on Criminal
Justice Standards and Goals, 1973).

groups, politicians and the communication media gives rise to a total picture of confusion, capriciousness, and injustice, if not irrationality. A system needs to be devised and put into operation which will (a) protect the public, (b) preserve the rights of individuals, and (c) satisfy reasonable men that it is fair, consistent, intelligent, and incorruptible. Such a system must be capable of adapting to the advancement of human knowledge and to the changing social and economic needs of the total society. That such a system of criminal justice does not exist in America today except as an unrealized ideal is scarcely open to argument. This void is more apparent in sentence determination than in most other phases of our present 'non-system' . . . The time for change has come. The question in most jurisdictions now is not do we need change but change to what and how to bring it about. Whether to muddle along responding to unsystematic political sharpshooting or to make fresh plans for orderly legislative enactment—that is the choice. Simple logic dictates the latter course. As a point of departure, this writer after years of frustrating experience and informal consultation with numerous practitioners and students of the problem has devised an alternative sentencing system . . .[58]

McGee urges *inter alia* the (1) end of indeterminate sentencing, (2) a return to flat time sentencing, (3) procedural criteria for sentencing, (4) sentencing review procedures, (5) and an end for both parole boards and parole* itself as a separate entity.[59]

It is indeed an important chorus, as Judge Pierce noted, but at least eight additional widely respected reports must be added to the chorus seeking sensible sentencing: (1) The National Council on Crime and Delinquency's *Model Sentencing Act* (1972), (2) The American Law Institutes' *Model Penal Code* (1963), (3) The ABA's *Standards Relating to Sentencing Alternatives and Procedures* (1969) and their *Standards Relating to Appellate Review of Sentences,* (4) The National Advisory Commission on Criminal Justice Standards and Goals' *Report,* (5) *The President's Commission on Law Enforcement and Adminis-tration of Justice,* (6) *The New York State Citizens' Inquiry on Parole and Criminal Justice,* (7) *The Committee for the Study of Incarceration* and (8) The Group for the Advancement of Corrections', *Toward a New Corrections Policy.*†

All have a common thrust in relation to sentencing best described by the ABA in a commentary, 'Perhaps no single process or series of processes in the criminal justice system is more chaotic than the act of sentencing.'[60]

---

* Milton Rector, Executive Director of the NCCD, looking to 'Corrections In 1993' also advances the elimination of parole boards and parole. He also suggests the periodic mandatory release of prisoners with assessments of how the prisoners fare on these furloughs as determinative of readiness-for-release decisions (Harleigh B. Trecker, ed., *Goals for Social Welfare 1973–1993: An Overview of the Next Two Decades,* 1973).

† This consists of 'Two Declarations of Principles': one by correctional administrators, and a second by the Ex-Prisoners Advisory Group (sponsored and published by The Academy for Contemporary Problems, 1501 Neil Avenue, Columbus, Ohio, 1974).

Although each report represents a variation on a similar theme, the emergent consensus seems to be:

1. Sentencing criteria should be required to be stated by statute.
2. Sentencing should be based upon classification of offenders into risk categories.
3. Sentences should be more definite (there are fairly broad variations but indeterminacy is substantially rejected), or fixed and graduated by seriousness of the offence.
4. Sentences should be reviewable.
5. Sentences of imprisonment should be substantially reduced.
6. Sentences of imprisonment should be justified by the state after an exhaustive review fails to yield a satisfactory community-based sanction.

Others have urged Commissions on Sentencing,[61] sentencing review councils,[62] separate sentencing hearings,[63] an end to plea bargaining (because it limits all other sentencing alternatives),[64] statutory authority for non-incarcerative sentences,[65] an end to the capriciously-excessive 'emergency laws' which periodically panic legislatures,[66] for sentencing decisions to be weighted in favour of promoting a concept of individual liberty[67] and sentence equalization courts (automatic review). Thorsten Sellin, speaking of the historical struggle between the egalitarians and the behavioural scientists, observes:

> With the increase of the number and variety of possible dispositions available to the courts the arbitrary power of courts which the egalitarians were desirous of destroying because of their mistrust of these agencies, has been increased, and more and more discretionary power has been transferred to agencies of correctional administration . . . The treatment philosophy has constantly made more inroads, but has not reached the point of diminishing returns.[68]

The current and persistent thrust may be fairly characterized as a *neo-classical consolidation* of penal sanctions. We add the perspective of justice-as-fairness which insists upon tight procedural regularity, hence a narrowing of discretion, for the agencies of the criminal law.

A Return to Flat Time

> All this leaves the problem just where it was. The irresponsible humanitarian citizen may indulge his pity and sympathy to his heart's content, knowing that whenever a criminal passes to his doom there, but for the grace of God, goes he; but those who have to govern find that they must either abdicate, and that promptly, or else take on themselves as best they can many of the attributes of God. They must decide what is good and what evil; they must force men to do certain things and refrain from doing certain other things whether individual consciences approve or not; they must resist evil resolutely and continually, possibly and

preferably without malice or revenge, but certainly with the effect of disarming it, preventing it, stamping it out and creating public opinion against it. In short, they must do all sorts of things which they are manifestly not ideally fit to do, and, let us hope, do with becoming misgiving, but which must be done, all the same, well or ill, somehow and by somebody.

If I were to ignore this, everyone who has had any experience of government would throw these pages aside as those of an inexperienced sentimentalist or an Impossibilist Anarchist. [George Bernard Shaw.[69]]

Richard McGee's alternative for California returns to flat time sentences in a five-degree felony plan ranging from a minimum of three months to three years in the fifth degree, to seven years to life (and death, if lawful) for first-degree felonies. Considerable discretion is left to judges (with a built-in appellate review council) and state parole is collapsed into the existing probation system in the county where the released convict is expected to dwell. The prison therefore receives no discretion other than through the residual good time law which is not eliminated. Our suggestion, although closely paralleling McGee's, calls for a total flat sentence for three types of felonies mitigated by substantial good time credit. Both plans return power to the judiciary, within statutory guidelines and eliminate parole boards entirely. McGee observes:

> The judicial system is uniquely equipped to manage the decision-making process in accordance with law, if an appropriate system were established to control capriciousness in subjective sentencing judgements. If judges are not social scientists, we submit that most parole board members are not either and even where some of them are, there is no evidence that their decisions on balance are more wise and appropriate than those of judges.[70]

We call for a system based upon a finding of *clear and present danger* to be necessary for the imposition of a term of imprisonment. Imprisonment should be the court's last available sanction following an affirmative action by authorities seeking other alternatives. When a finding of clear and present danger is made it *should* require incarceration. At this point we part with McGee, who we believe, leaves too much discretion to the courts (even with the appellate review council, which we support). If we can accomplish procedural regularity in sentencing we believe a system based upon categories of *demonstrated risk* will bring more certainty and fairness to the prisoner.

But the prison needs one other tool to make prison life more rational. We propose that the limit on the flat time sentence be mitigated *only* by good time credit. This puts the discretion closer to the source which can most usefully employ it. It simply says to the prisoner (in category B for example):

> Your stay has been determined to be four years, no more, you can get out in two years but that's up to you. We reduce your sentence one day for every day

of lawful behaviour. You can't get out any faster by making progress in any other aspect of prison life. Lawful behaviour is the pay-off. We trade you a day on the streets for every good one inside. For rule infractions, which may lead to a loss of good time, you will be able to defend yourself at a hearing, safe-guarded by due process. We publish and issue a list of rules and the penalties for their violation. Our internal court does not deal with any actual crimes you may commit. If we have probable cause to suspect you committed a felony during your term with us it becomes a matter for the local district attorney. This may lead to another prison sentence. The law is such that lost good time, over six months, can be restored by a judge and a thorough appellate court procedure.

The basic idea behind each of the leading sentencing revision plans is a search for the classification of dangerous felons. They presuppose tight sentencing procedures and they propose a variety of ways of accounting for the more dangerous.

Consistently with the neo-classical approach taken in this paper, the organization of the justice-as-fairness prison is based upon the principle of maintaining that spark we all seek as validation of manhood (and woman-hood)—responsibility. The prison sentence is punishment but its execution is not vengeful. The prisoner's conviction was based upon his volition and now forms the basis for his treatment as a prisoner. The new prison pro-gramme can offer a reasonable array of services beyond the food-clothing-medical-shelter needs. We see the need for educational, recreation, conjugal visitation, work and vocational programmes.

Education (academic and vocational) in our new prison programme is akin to labour. There is no need for a full spectrum of remedial grade, high school and college programmes. Prisons rarely have them anyhow. Education should be offered on a contractual basis after a prisoner (or group of prisoners) has selected a programme he believes necessary for his own self-improvement. Counselling can also be accomplished in this manner. New programmes are simply added and old ones discarded in response to need, not for the purpose of keeping dozens of civil service academicians busy without reference to needs of the prospective student body.

All clinical programmes can be dismantled as well. The spectacle of organizing inmates into therapy groups or caseloads is embarrassingly tragic. It is best described as a psychic lock-step. When the indomitability of the human spirit could not be crushed by our 'break the spirit' forefathers we relinquished the task to the technology of psychiatry. It is our belief that a conception of the prisoner as volitional and his assumption of responsibility for his behaviour provide the best chemistry for mental hygiene. 'To punish a man is to treat him as an equal. To be punished *for an offence against rules* is a sane man's right' said W. F. R. Macartney, an English ex-prisoner.[71] If he feels he has an emotional problem requiring professional assistance the

15

PRISONS IN SOCIETY, OR SOCIETY AS A PRISON—
A Conceptual Analysis

Nils Christie

1. *Introduction*

I remember vaguely, far back in time, suffering from a bad bout of the common 'flu. It was bad, not because it was common, nor because of unbearable physical discomfort. It was bad because of the new-fallen snow. From the kitchen window, I could see one friend after another pass, bound for the forest and for ski-tracks so perfect that a cold became an unbearable pain. Warm words and chocolate from my mother did not make a bit of difference. My life was not worth living, and my home the most ugly prison I could imagine.

Later, I was brought to the understanding that my home could be seen as a prison for more than just me. In a feministic perspective, my mother would also have been incarcerated, the difference was only that she was a lifer while I left our common prison when the snow was still dry.

Most of the time she might have felt as a prisoner. But, and that ought to have added to the strain, she might also have felt like a prison administrator. According to Robert Frost, 'Home is the only place where when you go there, they have to take you in.'

2. *Words as weapons*

Words are free for use, and are used freely. We can *call* a prison a prison, or we can call it Gefängnis, or fengsel, or abracadabra. We can *define* what we call it according to a huge variety of attributes. And we can give various *reasons* for our choice of words and attributes.

There are no right definitions, nor any final source for the choice of attributes. Words are social phenomena. Words are acts with meaning to the participants. They are tools for social action. To understand society, it is as important to understand the choice and use of words as it is to understand the choice and use of weapons. Often words are weapons.

There are two major and easily-observable trends in the recent use of the noun 'prison':
  1. The all-inclusive (imperialism)
  2. The denial of existence (the minimizers)

3. *The all-inclusive strategy*

I have already given an example of the all-inclusive or imperialistic approach. But more can easily be added.

From Goffman, through the feminists, and over to many breeds of social critics, the *similarities* between prisons and other institutions have been underlined. The ship, the monastery, the hospital, the family, the factory, the school, the village—they all have embarrassing similarities to the prison, and it serves many an important purpose to underline these similarities. It gives power to many movements dear to many among us to define homes as prisons for females. It brings into focus important oppressive mechanisms *vis à vis* children and young persons to look at teachers in the grammar school as untrained prison guards. It highlights the ugliness of modern industry to compare the work at the oil rig with the working conditions obtaining in a state of slavery. Generally: it gives strength to movements for the abolition of bad phenomena to get these phenomena associated with prisons.

4. *The denial-of-existence strategy*

This all-inclusive strategy is not the only one. There is also another trend, directly opposed to the all-inclusive one. I have christened this counter-current 'the denial of existence strategy'. While the ideologists behind the all-inclusive strategy could be called imperialists in their use of the concept of prison, the protagonists of the denial-of-existence strategy could be called minimizers.

Most often they are prison officers, or close to the penal system of society. Of course they are. Social reformers are attempting to change unwanted conditions by pointing to similarities with prisons. Workers within prisons are attempting to improve their life situations by pointing to similarities between their core-area and other social phenomena.

Prisons are not called prisons, but institutions
                                                    improvement homes
                                                    special service centres
                                                    treatment units.
Prisoners are not called prisoners, but inmates
                                                    members
                                                    clients

or all terms are evaded and they are
called by their own names, which
add to the image of homeliness.

Again we know there are reasons behind these strategies.

First, it makes life somewhat easier for the personnel within these institutions. The hangman's job was never very popular. Those who got a chance,
slipped into the doctor's rôle as fast as possible. There are great amounts of
ambivalence in having direct responsibility for other people's suffering. There
is a need for a defence. Major strategies are to claim that what one is doing to
other people does not hurt, is intended to help, or actually is very efficient in
helping them even though it might hurt a bit in the beginning—just like so
many good cures.

Secondly, the minimizers, and I am here particularly thinking of the minimizers within the general area of criminal policy, the chief ideologists
within penal law, civil service and criminology; these minimizers are also
efficient in resolving dilemmas at the level of society. Study after study has
shown how penal measures and long-time incarceration have been made more
acceptable to society if they were disguised as treatment, training, or pure
help to suffering individuals in need of such measures. The more the element
of intended pain has been kept out of the picture, the easier it has been to
evade justice and legal protection. Special measures against young people,
against psychopaths, against supposedly dangerous people, against persistent
but very small troublemakers—such special measures are immensely more
easily accepted by society at large when they are seen as something different
from penal measures, and particularly when the institution where they are
carried out is not seen as a prison, when the guards are not guards and when
the prisoners are not prisoners.

5. *Three related examples*

Strategies as here described are far from unique. Let me give a short
description of three related examples. Through these examples, we might be
able to see some consequences of such verbal strategies, and thereby be
better equipped when it comes to an evaluation of them within the field of
prison terminology.

The all-inclusive strategy is particularly frequently used within the area of
violence and political conflict. Here, as with prisons, the point of departure
must be that nobody 'owns' the concept of violence. But violence is a highly
loaded word, and we can therefore find a lot of attempts to capture the word
for highly different purposes.

One rather successful case is represented by the concept of structural
violence. Norway is a peaceful country. We kill, through acts officially

P.P.F.—7

registered as murder, only one person where in the United States they kill fifty persons on the same population base. And we are proud of being peaceful, even though we realize this is combined with a considerable amount of dullness and a lack of vivacity. So, it makes us particularly upset when radicals tell us that we are not peaceful at all. On the contrary, we are violent to the extreme. We are violent when it comes to structural violence. We do not kill directly, but we kill at long distance through our high living standard at home, and through our trade policy. We create suffering in other parts of the world. Children die in Africa because of us. And we know it. We are violent. For those interested in changing our foreign policy, it might be useful to make us appear criminal to the utmost. This creates a need for improvement. It creates an incentive for reform. The disadvantages have to do with the 'war at home', with what happens within the ordinary crime control system. The uninformed public might, through broad definitions of violence, find added reasons to believe that traditional violence—old-fashioned murder— actually runs as high as some evening papers seem to indicate.

Another example of the imperialistic use of the concept of violence is to be found in the debate on police violence. To some political groups, the police represent the apparatus of violence for the State. That is fine for some goals, but becomes inconvenient when it comes to the question of how to differentiate between acceptable and unacceptable police behaviour. We are hampered in discussions of how to prevent the police from maltreating or killing apprehended persons. When all police activities are seen as violence, then we lose possibilities—and most often also interest—in discriminating between qualities in police work.

The drug debate represents a third classical case of terminological imperialism. Is marihuana a drug, is LSD a drug, is even alcohol perhaps a drug, and if not, why not? Those able to define a substance of some sort as a drug gain obvious advantages if they want to control that substance. Those able to define the substance so that it does not fit into the drug categories gain equally obvious advantages in keeping the substance out of the more rigid forms of control. If we look into the history of drug laws, and I have done that in a paper with my Finnish colleague Kettil Bruun, we can easily see how the definitions of drugs over time have been made more and more all-inclusive to make room for substances very different from the original ones. It started with definitions suitable to cover substances leading to strong physical dependence: opium is the classical case. It ended with a WHO definition of psychological dependence which could be applied to everything human beings wanted. But they were able to keep the old concept and transfer its horror. They were able to keep under the same bracket a huge amount of substances that a huge number of pressure groups wanted to fight. The old association with opium was, rightly so, seen as an important ally in the control of new substances. And again important distinctions were lost.

6. *Conceptual strategies*

The choice of words is not without consequences. Is it then, in a volume commemorating John Howard's great work, possible to think of conceptual strategies that might be good for prison reform?

I think the analysis so far allows us to come up with some suggestions. First and foremost, we have seen that both those calling many bad things prisons, and those not wanting to call anything prison, have in common *a lack of interest in specifying elements that might be peculiar to the type of prisons that most readers of this volume are particularly interested in.*

Are we able to specify such elements?

I have up to this point refrained from any specification. That was intentional. I have made an attempt to pay attention to other people's uses and definitions of words as well as to the consequences of variations in use. Too early an introduction of my own definition of the concept would mean that I was propagandizing for *one* particular understanding whereas it is of vital importance to underline that all uses are legitimate, but with different consequences for different segments of society. But sooner or later—preferably later—I will be forced to expose my own preferences.

Perhaps seven elements ought to be particularly mentioned:

A prison is
1. A physical structure
2. creating high internal visibility
3. with possibilities for some absolute restrictions in movements
4. where the stay is decided by other persons
5. independent of the wishes of those staying there
6. because those staying there are to blame
7. with the purpose of creating pain.

Elements 1, 2, 3, 4 and 5 are elements common to many social systems.

The old valleys in Norway were, in the true sense of Erving Goffman, total societies. They were areas where all activities took place within the same enclosed surroundings, where all activities were known to most participants, and where mutual obligations were strong indeed. Mutual obligation is a phenomenon related to mutual dependence which again is the precondition for everybody's control of everybody else. It creates restrictions independent of the wishes of any particular individual. So far, the valleys were prisons.

And so far the factories might be called prisons as well. A factory worker with five hungry kids at home and no other alternatives for work does not have much choice. He might hate every minute at the job, but would be glued to the place just as efficiently as if there had been a prison wall around him. A prisoner in an isolation unit might feel more free than the worker. And we can think of even more extreme cases. Subtle economic incentives might have been exchanged for brutal physical measures. Guards or guns or walls might force the worker to produce for the King, the Great Cause or for the Nation. His condition might border on, or transgress the border to, slavery.

Still, that would lack an important element of prison work. It would lack number 6 'because those staying there are to blame', and number 7 'with the purpose of creating pain'.

Within all penal philosophies, we find implicit or explicit elements of blameworthiness. These are most clear in retributive theories, but can also be seen within theories of general or individual prevention. General prevention is not applied to persons who have not done anything blameworthy, nor is treatment to prevent recidivism applied to persons without a record. A borderline case is represented by preventive measures carried out against so-called high-risk categories. Such measures, which are most often perceived by the receiver as retribution in advance, are controversial, rare, and most often carried out against persons with an earlier record. They are also often disguised as treatment for physical or mental defects. The great controversies regularly stirred up around the introduction of ideas of preventive detention are a good indicator of their problematic relationship to the phenomenon of guilt and to the whole set of mechanisms that regulate the distribution of formal blame in society.

Specifically, numbers 6 and 7 are also essential when it comes to our denying that prisons are prisons. Shame does not fit in with the medical model, nor does the pain make the analogy of the prisons with the care-taking institutions or with the schools any closer.

My general intention, then, is to underline elements 6 and 7 in my discussion of imprisonment. We must attempt to limit other pressure groups' attempts to call a lot of bad phenomena prisons, and we must not accept that prisons have no specific peculiarities. Prisons are peculiar institutions for the delivery of blame and pain. We ought to emphasize this point again and again in the public debates on imprisonment.

To some weak-spirited people, these are brutal suggestions. Is not the detention bad enough for the prisoners, should we also underline these particular features? Is it not better to protect prisoners by minimizing the emphasis on pain and shame? Is it not better to protect prisoners to the utmost against symbols of their defeat?

I do not agree. Prisoners do know the realities. They are reminded of them every day. It is the rest of society that needs a reminder. It needs it for reasons already suggested: to make sure that interest in prison reform is not undermined, and to make sure that legal safeguards are upheld. But in addition there is another important purpose: an accentuation of the pain aspect makes a rational debate possible as to *how painful the pain ought to be*!

This topic is generally evaded in discussions of penal policies. As with the servants, so with their masters. We the chief ideologists of the prison service —professors of law, penologists, criminologists, and some general reformers —all want to shy away from the central question and to ignore the fact that it is the infliction of pain that we are discussing.

So, how painful do we want the places to be?

Are there intentions behind the ugliness of most prisons? Is it intentional that a greater part of the prison population is placed in closed institutions compared to open ones? Is it to increase suffering? Is it intentional that prisoners so often are locked into their individual cells early in the afternoon, to remain there for endless hours of spare time? Are there intentions behind the restrictions on prisoners' sexual life, their aesthetic life, their intellectual life? Why do we limit leave of absence? Most often, most administrators will claim that there are no intentions of infliction of pain behind the restrictions placed on the life of the prisoner. Restrictions are created by administrative necessity, to limit the smuggling in of drugs, to protect weak inmates, to prevent escapes. And they are probably right. Sometimes, however, it appears as if the pain aspect also plays an important rôle. It seems therefore important to raise the question whether the purpose of inflicting pain actually creates limits for prison reform.

It seems difficult to find any.

Empirically, we experience enormous variations among prisons. They vary with regard to visibility, with regard to restrictions in movement, and with regard to inner self-government. But, overriding all possible variations, they are still prisons. They are prisons, precisely because it is shaming to stay there. And it is shaming to stay there because they are intended to create pain.

But if shame is of overriding importance, then we are also more *free* to manipulate the other elements. They are unimportant compared to shame, but not unimportant for the daily life inside prisons. As has been found during the last year in Denmark with their fancy new prison in Ringe, no revolution is created in ordinary society if prisoners get the maximum of decent, comfortable living, if the buildings are made beautiful, if it is left to the prisoners to organize their internal life, their money, their cooking, their shopping, their sex life and their general social life. It is still a prison. They are there because they are to blame. And they suffer sufficiently, because it is shameful to stay there. The scope for reform is much wider than we are accustomed to think.

But why stop here?

Several of the reforms direct us, step by step, to a situation where there is not very much left of the prison. Internal visibility is not of importance, nor is detailed direction, nor is type of work, nor is sexual deprivation. What remains seems to be compulsive restriction to certain areas which remind the one party that he is to blame. But the compulsive restriction does not need to be without vacations, nor to last through the twenty-four hours. We have day prisons, we have night prisons—why do we not soon get five-minute prisons? The minimum type of prison seems to approach a situation where the client appears at regular intervals just to receive a reminder that he is to blame.

Or, to put it bluntly: the logical final and extreme case of prison reform, the goal next to complete abolition, is the short encounter where the one person is compelled to attend to receive a reminder that he is to blame for some acts of transgression of norms. The necessary number of such meetings and the formal staging of them seem to become the next topic for discussion if we want to carry out an innovative discussion of prison reform.

Would society accept it?

Let my answer be an indirect one through some comments on the old problem of the relationship between type of society and volume of prisoners. The more I have worked with this problem, the more I have come to believe that we should not so much think in terms of a *push* from society to the prison. The type of prison, and the size of the prison population seems to be more easily explained by a *pull* from the prison system itself, than by a push from society. Maybe we operate with too coherent a picture of society when we expect society to 'produce' prisoners. Prisoners are produced by the prison service, or those interested in that service. Foucault has described how establishments for venereal diseases were converted into mental hospitals. A house is a structure that has to be filled. Annika Snare has written a history of the Swedish prison system. A preliminary title of the book is *The War at Home*. By and large, it is the story of how Sweden stopped being an imperialistic nation. That meant that an old institution had to be given a new content. In war, the underdogs served as soldiers and the overdogs as officers. In peace the underdogs were converted to prisoners, the overdogs to prison officers and the castles to prisons. Why should it not be like that? And why should it not be like that also for the inner life of prisons? Schools live their own life with regard to content, only vaguely related to the needs of children, the needs of commerce, or the needs of societies. Medical institutions do the same. It is much easier to understand the organization of the medical service when we take the interests of the medical personnel— particularly the professors of medicine—as our point of departure, than when we take the needs of the patients as our point of departure. My suspicion is that once prisons are there, at least one of the best explanations of the fluctuation of prison populations as well as of the organization of their inner life can be found in the need for bread and butter, in the need for employment of prison officers as well as prison administrators, in the need for commanders to have someone to command and in the need for the use of buildings that otherwise would stay there embarrassingly empty. In the last resort, buildings and personnel will prove more resistant to change than the public and the politicians.

Allow me one last remark on the often called 'need for incarceration', the need for keeping a specific segment of the population out of circulation—'at least they don't cause harm when they are behind walls.' My country is of course among the peaceful ones. All other populations are more evil. But let me at least suggest that on grounds of pure logic it is rather difficult to see that it would *matter* to society at large if the prison population went down to half, or doubled or tripled. In Scandinavia, we incarcerate by and large 50 per 100,000 of the population. Since there are nearly no females among the prisoners, this means about one per 1000 males. But would life change very much if we tripled the proportion to 3 per 1000 males so that the 1 per 1000 got two more to accompany him in his misery? It would not matter much with regard to crime. There would still be 997 males out to commit it. And it would not give the one much counteractive power if he were joined by two more. And most people would not know. The newspapers would continue their campaigns for law and order. There is no efficient feedback system in operation with regard to information. But it would not make much difference if we *reduced* the one in 1000 to one in 10,000 males either, except for those who were spared the suffering. There are no logical upper limits to the number. There are no logical lower limits either.

I have departed from a very simple analysis of some elements in a definition of a prison. Words are free for everybody. Families, factories or states might well be called prisons in the service of undermining them all. I have, however, tried to point out some dangers in that strategy. Instead of underlining the resemblance between prisons and other phenomena, I have, through my concluding remarks, opted for an analysis that purifies the specific aspects of prisons. By doing that, I hope to have been able to minimize the importance of those elements connected with traditional prisons that are not peculiar to prisons. To face honestly the fact that the central element of prison is the distribution of blame and pain, means that we are free to abolish prisons by abolishing all other elements of prisons except the encounter that conveys blame and shame to the offender. An analysis of what a prison 'is', becomes a necessary step in a policy of liberation from unnecessary suffering.

16

CONTROL WITHOUT REPRESSION?

Inkeri Anttila

The title of my contribution, 'Control without Repression', may seem to provide a suggestion about the future of the criminal justice system. However, at this stage I would prefer to add a question mark. Thus, I am asking—can we have 'control without repression'?

As broad an issue as this can be presented on different levels; and in the same way, the term 'the future' can apply to varying lengths of time, from a few years to hundreds of years from now. This allows us to consider quite a variety of ways and means, as is evident from the following:

1. If we regard 'control without repression' only from the point of view of prison administration, then it means developing new types of institutions.
2. If we examine the criminal justice system as a whole, we could consider the possibility of sanctions that are less repressive than the prison today.
3. We can of course go even further. It may be possible to imagine a society where crime can be controlled entirely, or almost entirely, in new ways. One could visualize, for example, a replacement of official control by unofficial control. Or we could adopt a system of positive sanctions so that law-abiding citizens would be rewarded, and there would be no need to threaten law-breakers with punishment.

Dealing with these different alternatives, I shall begin with the more limited aspects, and then go on to the broader ones.

1. Is it possible to have *prisons without repression*? Could we visualize a society where we send offenders to be treated, or a society where all offenders would voluntarily seek treatment?

The idea of replacing prisons with treatment institutions has intrigued experts for decades, and at times there have been attempts to put it into practice. I have no intention of inflicting a long exposition of the principles of 'treatment philosophy' on the reader. We are, after all, quite aware that the twentieth century has seen the 'rise and fall of the therapeutic prison philosophy'. There was a time when a small minority of penological experts believed that the average prisoner could be rehabilitated through scientifically-planned efforts and allowed to take his place in society as a law-abiding citizen. Despite strong opposition, the adherents of this philosophy gradually gained ground and attracted a growing number of supporters. For example in Scandinavia, support for this philosophy reached its peak during the 1940s and the 1950s. However, on the basis of controlled empirical studies, researchers reported time after time that no support could be found for the fundamental hypothesis, and so it today is regarded as erroneous. Now we know that the average prisoner will not benefit from treatment in prison regardless of its scope and nature. It has been clearly proved that prisons do not—and cannot—have any strong rehabilitative effect except in very unusual individual cases. It makes no difference, of course, what we call these institutions—an 'institution for psychopaths' or a 'reform school' has been just as unsuccessful as an ordinary prison.

What I have just said has to do, then, with prisons, or non-voluntary treatment in institutions. It would, of course, be possible to suppose that offenders would *voluntarily* seek care and treatment in institutions—for example psychotherapy, aversion therapy—and why not even electrotherapy? Would it be possible to use this approach to create a new system of control, control without repression?

In some exceptional cases it might be possible to do so. The necessary conditions for this would be that:
  a) the treatment would truly be voluntary;
  b) the results would be good enough to justify the use of the necessary resources.

These conditions are met in our present system in connection with an offender not responsible for his criminal conduct and willing to enter a mental institution for treatment. The general level of tolerance in society defines the limit to which we can exchange punishment for treatment. If the offence and the offender seem to be sufficiently exceptional, then we are prepared to accept this change-over from the rôle of the offender to the rôle of the patient. And even then the treatment should be truly voluntary.*

I have already noted that replacing punishment in exceptional cases with voluntary treatment in a hospital-like institution can be considered an alternative only when this treatment is obviously effective. There are of course cases where treatment must be given in an institution *for other reasons,*

---

* The reverse situation exists for example when an alcoholic is told to seek institutional treatment voluntarily 'because he could be forced to go there anyway', or when consent is obtained for example by promising compensation from national health insurance. Of course, this semi-voluntary system could be called 'control with *less* repression' than some other alternative; but it is not really 'control without repression'.

regardless of an offence: the offender may be insane or so severely mentally deficient that it is obvious that he needs treatment, and he is thus generally and unanimously regarded as a patient who happened to commit an offence. On the other hand, the punishment of offenders whose mental abnormality is only slight may be quite justified. The type of offence by no means automatically shows whether the offender is sane or insane, healthy or ill. Not every person guilty of homicide is a wanton murderer, nor are all rapists sexual psychopaths, all thieves kleptomaniacs nor all drunken drivers alcoholics. The great majority of those guilty of these offences do not belong in a hospital.

What attitude should we take to this large majority? We know that prisons are in use all over the world, including all those countries where the treatment ideology has met with failure. As a result, these countries have been forced to admit that the situation must be re-evaluated. Prisons are still supposed to fulfil significant societal functions in our society. What, then, will the future trend be?

We must start by redefining the problem. We must recognize the fact that in order to maintain our fundamental social norms, we need punishments, or at least public denunciation of morally unacceptable behaviour. By publicly denouncing certain behaviour as morally wrong we maintain standards of morality—regardless of whether these standards measure 'traditional' crimes such as embezzlement or 'new' crimes such as pollution. I repeat: *we need punishments, defined as public and authoritative denunciation by state organs of individual cases of wilful harmful behaviour.* Even a mild reproach may suffice to express this denunciation. Most punishments are and should be more lenient than incarceration in a prison.

By placing the offender in prison, society dramatizes the severity of the denunciation. Undoubtedly, the prison system primarily has a general preventive effect, with the exception of a few really dangerous criminals who must be constantly isolated. The future will certainly bring new alternatives to prisons: but if we are to limit ourselves to the next 10–20 years, we must admit that we do need prisons. *The main function of the prison is to deter.*

According to this line of thought, society needs prison sentences and prisoners because this strengthens and reinforces the contents of certain norms of conduct. The presence of the prisons guarantees that prison sentences will be executed according to the general expectations of those who maintain the system of social control.

In the short run, then, I presume that prisons will remain a part of our system. However, what I have said runs the risk of misinterpretation.

First of all, when I speak of general deterrence, I am not referring to *severe* punishments. The mechanisms of deterrence involve a large number of factors; the severity of punishment is only one element. Another important factor is subjective certainty of punishment. If the potential offender believes that there is a high risk of being caught, then even light punishments may be enough. We should attempt to achieve general deterrence through other sanctions than prison. When imprisonment is necessary we should primarily use short-term imprisonment; this system of punishment is already the rule in, for example, the Scandinavian countries, where the great majority of prison sentences are for only a few months.

Another risk of misinterpretation is related to the prison régime. The belief that prisons are primarily institutions that strengthen general deterrence is often erroneously connected with the idea that *strict discipline, inhumane treatment*, and *poor facilities* for medical and other treatment should be all that prisoners are offered. Thus, there is need to emphasize that even though the rôle of prisons in the criminal justice system can be defended on the grounds of general deterrence, prisons need not and cannot be institutions lacking in the proper care and treatment. As a matter of fact, the situation should be quite the reverse: it should be possible to provide prisoners with good care and treatment. We must remember that prisoners are the scapegoats of the prevailing system. In the first place, they suffer for all of those offenders who are never detected and prosecuted. In addition, they are sent to prison for all those members of society who do not become offenders due to their better education or social circumstances.

Because prisoners serve as a warning example, the burden now piled upon their shoulders should be lightened. The average length of prison sentences should be reduced. The prisoners should have good conditions in the institutions, they should have the opportunity to obtain psychological and psychiatric help when they want it, they should be provided with assistance and guidance when they are released; and some of them could even be pensioned after a very long sentence results in social inability. We should also direct our efforts towards minimizing the negative influences of the stay in prison, 'prisonization'. The longer the time in prison, the more important it is to normalize the prison conditions.

When the conditions in prisons are improved, this should take place only in order to ease the circumstances of prisoners. It should never be felt that we send someone to prison 'for his own good', for example in order to provide him with room and board for the winter. Care and treatment should be given only because the *prisoner would be in prison anyway*.

Nor should any supposed need for treatment give the authorities the right to lengthen the period of sentence, or the right to place the offender in a special institution where the term of punishment would be based on whether or not he is regarded as having been 'cured of his criminality'. Also, not even recidivism should on its own lead to the replacement of imprisonment with internment for an indefinite period, or to the labelling of the offender as a 'psychopath' who needs a special institution.

2. I have now come to the conclusion that prisons cannot be changed into treatment institutions. The next step would be to ask how the penal system as a whole should be changed. Should we try to find *punishments that are less repressive than the prison* of today?

This is a very serious question, and not at all at odds with what I have just said. There is reason to repeat that prisons are needed only as long as and to the extent that there are no other proper alternatives. Even though prisons cannot be dropped from the system, we should consider whether their use can be lessened.

It is the duty of society constantly to seek new alternatives to imprisonment, and the use of prisons should be minimized. Those who insist that all non-custodial sanctions are too lenient for effective general deterrence scarcely take into consideration the fact that the actual harshness of a sanction is constantly changing. Penological values meet with waves of 'inflation' and 'deflation', and a sanction that was regarded as lenient yesterday may be experienced as much harsher tomorrow.

What kind of punishments, then, should we consider? The Penal Law Committee in Finland, which delivered its report in March 1977, listed a few principles that would affect all punishments. I would briefly mention the following:

— the punishments should not be cruel
— they should reflect the principles of proportionality and equality
— the punishments should be directed at the offender alone
— the punishments should not cause needless suffering
— the sanctions should not cause unregulated cumulation of sanctions
— the system should be economical from society's point of view.

These principles, of course, can only serve as goals that cannot be reached in full very easily. If we examine imprisonment in their light, then we see that it does not meet the demands very effectively. Long terms of imprisonment can rightly be regarded as 'cruel', and many sentences of imprisonment have a tangible effect on other people besides the offender. There are many negative features connected with institutionalization. One must definitely try to develop the system so that imprisonment is used less often than today.

During the past few years, we have seen quite a number of meetings around the theme 'alternatives to imprisonment', and in them, many proposals have been made. The use of the 'old' type of non-custodial sanctions, for example suspended sentences and probation, should, according to many proposals, be increased. Doubtless, these are less repressive than imprisonment, and thus a step in the right direction.

A few years back, there was a great deal of discussion in Scandinavia on the characteristics of the systems of probation and parole. The conclusion that was drawn was that here also, coercion and service must be separated from each other. Coercion, in other words repressive control, is evident for example in parole, as the parolee is obliged to contact his supervisor; the sanction for neglecting to do this is a return to prison. The fact that the supervisor generally tries to help the parolee and give him psychological and material support does not remove the repressiveness. Therefore, obligatory supervision must be seen in the right light: it is an after-punishment, regardless of how much care and assistance is provided. One should even consider giving the elements of coercion and service to different officials, and perhaps demand that the request for help should always come from the ex-prisoner himself.

The attempts to separate the elements of coercion and service have led some planners to consider new types of non-custodial punishments. One possibility is a return to symbolic and admonitory punishments. A prosecutor's court's authoritative and formal *warning* would suffice in petty cases, primarily for first-time offenders. Another sanction that as an alternative to imprisonment may be applicable to a greater variety of offences would be so-called *punitive supervision,* that is intermittent reporting-in to the police for a period of a few months. Both of these sanctions are clearly repressive, as neither would be tied in with any treatment. They would, however, naturally be *less repressive* than imprisonment.

A sanction that is basically repressive, but also clearly less severe than imprisonment, is of course the *fine.* Fines are undergoing a definite renaissance in Scandinavia. In Sweden and Finland fines are set in accordance with the so-called day-fine system, in which they fulfil the demand for equality better than fines which are set in definite sums, and which thus favour the wealthy. Despite the obvious repressiveness of fines they have clearly been accepted by the general sense of justice. This is true especially if the payment can be put off for a while when necessary, and if the fines can be paid in instalments, both of which are possible at least in the Scandinavian countries.

Some proposals for alternatives to imprisonment have gone along different lines. One proposal is that we replace imprisonment with *administrative measures,* for example tax increases or deprivation (revocation) of driver's licence. Such a proposal could be supported as a way of rationalizing the criminal justice process; after all, this system is in use in many countries in the form of, for example, parking fines (tickets). However, in examining the system as a whole we must beware of hiding our head in a hole in the ground and imagining that merely using a new name would allow us to get rid of the repressive features in the system. It is important to note, for instance, that according to some studies drivers who have lost their licence for drunken driving regard this as a more severe sanction than short-term imprisonment. Giving the sanction a nice name will not make it any nicer. On the contrary, it may hide its true nature, and the situation may become more complex from the point of view of both the offender and the general public. Changing the system this way will not lead us very far in the direction we wish to go.

3. In the above, I have dealt with the possibility of replacing imprisonment with either new or newly adapted sanctions that are less repressive. But in planning the future, must we remain on such narrow ground? Would it not be possible to replace official control with other forms of control?

The idea that one should turn to *unofficial control* instead of, or in addition to, official control has naturally been presented quite often in the recent discussion, no matter whether the principal subject has been aboriginal tribes, the raising of children, internal discipline on the job, or the control directed at the members of a religious movement. In part, the situation has only been seen as a re-living of the olden days, and it has been observed that there can be no return to old village society.

Some writers have, however, gone so far as to make concrete proposals for the shifting of official control to the level of unofficial control. It has been suggested that the offender and the victim should be confronted with each other, and the authorities should not interfere in the matter. The idea is an attempt to lessen bureaucracy, and to return conflicts to the individual level where they originated. One could also change the present control system by increasing the number of offences for which charges can be made only when the victim wishes to do so, and by giving a more prominent rôle to compensation for any damage and to the willingness to give compensation; the courts' function would then be more to mediate than to punish. But this is possible only in selective offence categories. For example, a confrontation between the offender and the victim is possible only when the offence has a definable individual victim; after all, there is no one who could confront the offender when it is a question of, for example, careless driving, currency regulation offences or narcotics offences! In any case, most of the criminalizations that are included in modern penal codes would be left outside such a system.

Some reform plans have departed from the point of view that control should be *decentralized.* These reforms have definitely not regarded the offence as a matter solely between the offender and the victim, but as the internal affair of the immediate circle of both. In this way the Socialist countries of Europe have a great number of 'peer courts', for example within a factory. The petty offences that are committed within these circles are dealt with outside the general criminal justice system, although in an 'official' way. Those countries where this method is applied report that the results are positive. The matter is dealt with in the context of the everyday surroundings in which the offence took place, and the speed of the procedure as well as the severity of the sanction can be concretely seen by those within this circle. The efficiency is increased by giving the neighbours or the fellow workers the responsibility of supervising the offender in the future. However, 'peer courts' apparently require at the least an ideologically strong system as well as common values. A form of control that has been fairly successful in one country cannot as such be transferred to another; instead, in accepting a new system, other cultural changes would have to be accepted. This would be all the more true in going over to, for example, the criminal control system in the People's Republic of China, where—at least in the opinion of other countries—the system is based very strongly on unofficial control and the semi-official control of the immediate surroundings.

In speaking of control without repression, it would not do to forget the significance of the general level of tolerance. Repression is not needed if an act is no longer regarded as being worth punishing. The lively discussion that has been carried on the past few years on the possibility of *decriminalization* has been based specifically on the belief that penal codes contain a needless number of punishable acts. Unfortunately, even in decriminalizing we will soon run up against a wall. The principal topic of discussions on decriminalization has been the so-called morality offences, which according to the official statistics of many countries are already quite rare. At times decriminalization has also resulted in a situation where repressiveness has not been done away with; instead, it has been transferred from the criminal justice system to the hands of social welfare officials, and in this way the result has been less legal security.

It also seems that the future will bring with it a greater number of new criminalizations instead of decriminalizations as the official control in many countries increases, and as does the complexity of activities and related norms. Continuous decriminalization attempts are definitely needed to keep matters in balance. But they are not enough to solve the problems we are discussing now.

Perhaps the most exciting idea is that repressive sanctions can be replaced with *positive sanctions*. In other words, people would live in the hope of receiving the rewards given to law-abiding citizens, instead of—as they do now—in the fear of the punishment that awaits offenders. Is it possible to visualize a situation where punishment would no longer be necessary? Put in so radical a form, I believe that this will remain a Utopia. However, this does not mean that we should not think about changing the present balance between positive and negative sanctions. It must be admitted that we have grown used to thinking almost solely in terms of negative sanctions, and not in terms of positive sanctions. Rewards for law-abiding citizens are by no means common—a reward to an honest person who returns lost property, or a bonus to a careful driver are only exceptions to the rule. A reward system, supposedly, would definitely be 'control without repression'—as long as these benefits do not become so noticeable that those left without would regard themselves as being repressed!

I have tried to examine this topic from a wide point of view, but even so, I have been forced to limit myself to *the control system and its possible effects*. For this reason I would like to conclude by noting that this has represented only a part of the reality, and that the limits imposed have, in a way, been artificial. Our natural goal is the decrease or the regulation of criminality. In considering goals and methods we must therefore be aware of the limits of our possibilities. We should not expect our penal system to produce any miracles in the field of crime control. We should realize that no individual crime control system that has the individual offender as its focus has had a noticeable effect on the general crime situation in a given country. The amount and structure of criminality is determined by other social forces: the system of crime control plays only a modest rôle.

17

ETHICS AND EXPEDIENCY IN PENAL PRACTICE

Laurie Taylor

I suspect, on the basis of having attended a number of international conferences, that some of us at one time or another will have felt the need to
throw at least a modicum of doubt upon the value of the proceedings, upon
the likelihood of any actual change occurring as a result of the papers and
discussion. It is the same at all conferences but perhaps more so at those on
prisons, for we know that although we and our academic ancestors seem to
have been talking about the horrors of prison life for two hundred years, the
high walls and the institutions themselves still continue to mock our clever
words with their endurance. By regarding our inveterate conference-going
and paper-reading with a certain amount of detachment we can spread an
amiable, self-deprecating gloss over the actual inhumanities of prison life,
over the physical and psychological brutalities, the total deprivation of rights,
the multitude of frustrations, which constitute daily life in most penal
institutions.

This gentle cynicism just about enables us to maintain a slight moral glow;
nothing much may be happening, but somehow a bit of sceptical conversation
can give us the pleasant sense that most of the people we come into contact
with are reasonably humanitarian, relatively aware that some changes are
necessary, comparatively progressive and even, when judged towards the end
of the evening, somewhat radical. It must indeed be difficult for overseas
visitors to conferences in Britain really to believe the atrocity stories they
hear about British prisons; their overcrowded, deteriorated state; their
disturbing record of violent attacks by officers upon inmates; their most
systematic flouting of the most basic human rights laid down by the
European Commission on Human Rights.

But it is not just conversational cynicism which helps to maintain that
sense of possible change, that idea that something progressive might occur
even if nothing is actually happening. It is also, and this is more to the theme
of this brief paper, the particular coalescence of ethics and expediency which

has come to characterize all discussions of the penal system in the last hundred years or more.

Let me begin to explain what I mean by reference to a conference I attended recently in Montreal, although it could have been any one of a dozen such conferences. This had been called at the invitation of the Solicitor General of Canada by the International Centre for Comparative Criminology. It was being asked to pass on the 'benefits of its experience' on long-term imprisonment to the Canadian Government.

Now you might have thought that the idea of such a conference was really an excellent one. It is certainly quite novel. The idea of our own Home Office inviting a group of independent academics to meet and discuss in this informal way is hard to imagine. So how good that a government should be prepared to meet academics and researchers and discuss such matters with them; how flattering actually to be asked for 'the benefits of our experience' on the subject of long-term imprisonment. After all, this was surely what academic research was for, this was the relationship between theory and practice which we had heard so much about. Why, one actually felt good just sitting there, watching the man from the government making notes.

But, there was just one problem, a little fly in the ethical ointment, in fact a gigantic bluebottle, for the harsh truth was that we had all been called together to offer 'the benefits of our experience' on the subject of long-term imprisonment *after* the Canadian Government had already stipulated sentences of twenty-five years for first-degree murders and fifteen years for second-degree—some of the longest sentences ever to be agreed upon in the last hundred years of penal policy. And there we were, offering our advice. Only one piece of advice was out of order—you could not suggest that they abandon such a vicious sentencing policy—for the choice had already been made and of course no similar conference of liberal academics had preceded the decision. We had in fact been invited to paint our pretty ethical patterns and deck our humanitarian frills over an already completed structure.

In other words, the conference was being used to legitimate an action that had already been taken. The academics were there to make a collective sigh of sympathy for all those people who are locked up for twenty-five years, to put their ethics on display; the actual decision to give such sentences was however crudely expedient, a vulgar political trade-off which allowed capital punishment to be abolished, that hollow penal victory so beloved of liberals who, after abolition, suddenly lose all interest in the penal system and happily allow people to rot in cells for the rest of their natural lives. (As someone in Canada remarked, it might have been better if they had never formally abolished capital punishment, for then there would have been no need for the long sentence trade-off and the liberals could have effectively secured stays of execution for most condemned prisoners—as they had done in recent years.)

But, of course, the matter does not stop there. Conferences and academics and researchers are not just presented with political *faits accomplis* and then invited to make sighing noises, they are also invited to do something about the situation. What looks like a new ethical position comes sailing into view. Even though nobody likes the look of what is happening, even though the prisoners are screaming about their sentences, should not someone, some team of researchers, go in and really find out what it is like. After all, it might not be quite so bad as we think. Do we not need a few facts and fewer opinions—and by the way, although we agreed with the ethical line you took over long-term imprisonment, do not forget the higher ethical demands of scientific objectivity when you get inside, will you?

In Canada one government man said to me, referring to some early work I did with Stan Cohen on long-term imprisonment, 'Well, if you don't mind tightening up a bit on your methodology (in other words, get a bit objective) I can tell you that Canada is really ready now for a major research proposal from you.' Now that they have got them inside for twenty-five years, they are ready for a research proposal; what better time could there be?

Of course, the amazing thing is that there is no shortage of such objective researchers. They are falling over themselves to get inside and establish for certain that it is not too pleasant to be penned up in a cell for quarter of a century. They will tell you all about their ethical concerns, of course—that is an almost essential introduction to their papers. You know the sort of thing. 'God, imprisonment is terrible; three weeks in there would drive me mad; yes, I can understand why they commit suicide; but (pulling an objective face) I'm afraid my tests show no actual evidence of any measurable effects.' The absurdity of their enterprise screams to heaven. It is like attempting to prove that ten years of physical torture have had no effect on a man by producing objective evidence that his reflexes are still working perfectly (and that, believe it or not, was one of the actual tests used by one such group of long-term imprisonment researchers).

But it was not just research that was dragged in to put some ethical top-dressing on basic expedient practices. Also invited to the party were the programme innovators. In they came, also shaking their heads about the horrors of long-term imprisonment. Here is one such contributor, dripping with ethical concern.

> The negative effects of incarceration are all too well known to this group; the disruption of family life; the hardening process to assure survival; the compartmentalization of thought; the brutalizing adjustment to the lack of privacy and the lack of individual identity. But these depredations of the person's character

are of a mild order when compared to the effect of long periods of incarceration. Changes are more than a mere increase in the quantity of negative impact. With four or five years of incarceration to face the individual loses hope and in the process of serving long stretches of time begins to assume the role of the living dead, the zombie of the voodoo cults. Many of you have observed this fate amongst long-term prisoners, a manner of coping so abhorrent to some that suicide is considered a preferred alternative.

But my task is not to paint a picture of the horrors of long prison terms, my colleagues have or will amply depict the condition. But rather the powerful nature of the negative influences is highlighted, emphasizing the extreme need to work towards the improvement programmes and opportunities for those individuals who have been subjected to the highly ineffective punishment of long-term confinement.

Obviously he is totally against it; it is producing suicides and zombies: it breaks up family relationships: it brutalizes, takes away identity. But—at the same time—as it is here—let us just go along and see if we can produce some programmes which will ameliorate a few of those effects. And from there is only a short step—a couple of paragraphs, to the innovative programmes. This particular speaker was soon happily proposing a variety of ways in which prisoners might cope with a life in jail by getting stuck into a bit of technological innovation. Their talent could be applied to the growing interest in battery-powered transportation. It might be just the thing to produce new ideas for recycling sewage. And he cheerily quoted one example of an Illinois man who thought that small hydraulic cylinders might be placed under highways on downhill stretches which could both serve to slow vehicles without the use of brakes and also generate power from the pressure applied.

Inmates often have strong potential for attacking problems from unusual angles inasmuch as they have in some cases viewed the world differently from the rest of society for most of their lives.

So—good news. If you ever get in for twenty-five years they may put you on the hydraulic cylinder road project and the time will just fly by.

There was, I am afraid, little support for the brave idea advanced by Inkeri Anttila from Finland, who suggested quietly but bitingly that it might be more ethical to leave the prisons just as they were, so that no one could have any doubts about what they were doing or could be misled by the innovative programmes into thinking that they were somehow institutions which should be tolerated by any civilized society.

Actually ethics and expediency did manage to confront each other in a rather direct manner at the end of that particular conference. Someone who had heard each speaker express a horror of long-term imprisonment suggested that it seemed reasonable that we pass a motion condemning the practice, particularly as the man from the Solicitor General's office was present. And indeed we eventually did that, though not without producing a certain amount of disturbance from all those who felt that academic conferences should not pass resolutions. For while it seemed perfectly all right for some delegates that any hack writer on a daily national newspaper could produce accounts off the top of his head about what we should be doing with prisoners, the idea that a hundred or so people from all over the world who might know something about it, should make a collective statement about their abhorrence of the practice, struck some people as remarkably inappropriate. Were we not being asked to make—horror of horrors—a *value judgement?* A strange example of how we manage to separate our notion of ourselves as objective researchers from our humanitarian concerns.

Let us look at the mix in another way, this time with reference to a conference in Britain, the much publicized conference on Prison Overcrowding called by the Prison Governors' Association. This was the first time, as far as I know, that this organization has invited outsiders to any of its meetings.

Of course, such a conference has a close affinity with the Montreal one, overcrowding being directly related to long-term imprisonment, so that for example, Holland may imprison the same proportion of its population but still show a much smaller percentage of people actually in prison because of the length of the sentences dispensed. Well, we were quickly into ethics, speakers fell over each other to abhor the number of prisoners who were living two or three to a cell. (As I recall, the figure is approximately 15,000 out of the 42,000 total.) Words like 'warehousing' were actually being used by members of the prison administration. There was even agreement that rehabilitation was virtually a thing of the past, that it had now been dispelled by the realities of prison life. Somehow all the governors and deputy governors spoke so liberally that we almost forgot that their livelihoods depended upon the retention of the system.

Only gradually did it become clear that it was not actually imprisonment which exercised most of the people there, it was simply overcrowding. By the second day we had seen the kind of ethical-expediency slippage which I have already described at the Montreal conference, the blurring of the two approaches to life which does so much to create that peculiar sense that something pleasant, amiable and liberal is going on whilst simultaneously aware that very little is actually happening. So it emerged that there was not too much wrong with handing out long stretches of time to 25,000 or 30,000 men, making daily psychological attacks upon their humanity, identity, personal relationships, depriving them of all natural rights—just as long as they had room to walk around their cell while it was all going on. Anyway, the total expediency of the situation was finally captured in one of the key papers given to the delegates there. It was written by Dr. Ken Pease of Manchester University. This is in no way an attack on Dr. Pease—indeed he may well have had an ironic intent—and in any case his paper was the most intelligent and articulate given during the conference. I refer to it, however, as an example of the way in which a topic with obvious ethical elements can be treated in a totally expedient manner.

Specifically, asked Dr. Pease, could we not implement something like a sliding scale of remission? That is to say, the proportion of the prison sentence which can be remitted for good conduct should vary according to the rate of prison intake.

> The rate of intake which has applied recently has yielded a prison population of 42,000. Let us say that we wish the prison population to fall to a figure of 35,000. On the basis of the most recently available rate of receptions into prisons, and taking into account the distribution of lengths of sentences of those receptions, the amount of remission which would be required would be around forty-eight per cent. If we wish the target population to be set at 38,000 the remission required would be forty-two per cent.

This is, if you like, a hydraulic, cybernetic model of prison life, whereby, if a lot come in this end then a lot go out that end. Now it is pretty difficult to tie any ethical labels around that. It really is a pure piece of expediency, which has no *necessary* relationship to any concern about what prison is doing to people or to its incompatibility with contemporary humanitarian values. It was an idea which would ensure that prison staff and governors had a perfectly manageable population, an idea which performs the remarkable feat of squeezing every drop of ethical substance out of a problem that seemed so saturated as to forever deny such a possibility.

As the conference went on one other feature became more evident. I heard it one night in the bar and realized that another slippage was interestingly occurring between ethics and expediency. Once the population had gone down a bit, said one governor, we could get on with some 'proper rehabilitation'. In other words, we could start pretending once again that we were not just keepers, that we were making people better. Reduce prison population and we can all become specialists again: prison officers can become treatment officers and, who knows, we might eventually get rid of such nasty words as *cell, screw,* and even *prison.*

Still, at least the prison governors have one achievement to their credit. They did not, and who could expect them to, particularly dislike imprisonment, but their report does place them well to the left of the pathetic Home Office Advisory Council on the Penal System which, after due consideration, and taking all matters into account, and not wishing to upset anyone, or to run before it could walk, or leap before it had looked, *actually manages to say* (and this is the strongest remark in the recently published contribution to the great debate on penal policy):

> Are there not cases of two years' imprisonment where eighteen months or fifteen or even less might safely be passed, and sentences of twelve months when six months would do just as well?

My God, John Howard could never have predicted the arrival of such radical times.

What I have been trying to say is that we have become seduced into a way of regarding prison which forever compounds the ethical-expedient distinction. The only way to get out of the trap is to make a few changes in organization. Clever radical words at conferences will do nothing at all. Those who look forward to the abolition of imprisonment, and not just some tinkering with a few thousand prisoners here or there, should refuse to attend any future conferences on the subject unless they:

(a) called for a halt to all new prison building; so that we could allow the present structures to rot away;

(b) gave a detailed forecast of the cuts in prison staff which were envisaged for the coming years;

(c) only admitted research findings which were obtained not just from, but with the active co-operation of, prisoners, and which were not directly sponsored by the government body controlling the prisons;

(d) addressed themselves directly to the need for censoring the media treatment of crime. I am sorry that I do not have space to amplify on this, but I am referring to statements like those made a few days ago by the present Home Secretary about the necessity of considering public opinion before doing anything about long-term imprisonment, the vulgar notion that public opinion lies 'out there somewhere' when research shows us quite clearly that it is located in the editorial columns of the sensational press. (Steve Chibnall's recent book on crime reporting, for example, neatly demonstrates the relationship between sentencing policy and those law-and-order campaigns which were initiated by the press for a crude mixture of commercial and political profit.)

(e) announced the resignation of at least twenty criminologists and the closures of two research institutes;

(f) clearly revealed the sources of their funds;

(g) actually had present a number of prisoners who could quickly give the lie to any prophylactic, social-scientific verbalizing.

Without such safeguards we will stay on the merry-go-round for another hundred years, having our doubts about the system periodically assuaged by a minor concession here (no more drunks in prison) and a little liberal handout there (increased use of parole in order to make up for longer sentences handed out by judges in order to compensate for the increased use of parole). Without some action to change this state of affairs we will continue to regard prisons as rather like schools or hospitals, permanent institutional features of our society which occasionally need some internal reform, instead of staring behind the mumbo-jumbo and official secrecy and seeing the system of imprisonment for what it is—an institution more akin to slavery, a way of debasing and brutalizing our fellow human beings which persistently undermines our claim to be a civilized society.

18

MENTAL HEALTH SERVICES AND THE PENAL SYSTEM

T. C. N. Gibbens

This volume, I feel sure, will have shown that there is a crisis of confidence in the proper rôle and function of the penal system, and especially the prison system. On all sides there is a tendency to go back to fundamental considerations of liberty, human rights and ethics.

The current view was stated very clearly at the last United Nations Congress on Social Defence, by a representative of a Scandinavian country. He said in effect, 'The only duty of a prison administrator is to accept an offender on an order by a court. We have no obligation whatever to do more than detain him, and we have no right to require the prisoner to change in any way. We say to him "You can sit in your cell and do nothing if you want. If you want to do something there is trade or industrial training, or education, or group therapy available. They are there if you want, but you must ask. It's entirely up to you." ' These ideas were echoed at a recent meeting on the effects of long-term imprisonment, when a Canadian administrator went further saying, 'We now know that prison does not rehabilitate. We do not know how to rehabilitate and in any case it is very uncertain what it means.'

There was a second main theme at the UN Congress not directly related to the first. There are now 150 nations instead of 50 and very few are European. The majority tended to say, 'We have very few resources and they are urgently needed for schools and hospitals. Prisons are unproductive and now that people tell us that they do not achieve rehabilitation anyway, we are even less inclined to put money into them. In any case, the real threat to national safety comes from either external financial or ideological pressures, which tend to be divisive or corrupting. Compared with this, conventional crime is of very little importance.'

European nations may not feel so threatened from outside, but since ninety per cent of crime consists of property offences, and there is increasingly wide distribution of property and alteration in social values attached to it, it is also questionable whether the amount of crime is really threatening. The public certainly takes an interest in violent and sexual crime, but one study showed that half of all reports of crime in the newspapers were concerned with those offences, although they constitute only five per cent of prosecuted offences; so the public may have a very distorted picture.

The disappointing results of what is usually called the medical model of the treatment of crime—extending perhaps to all rehabilitative measures—and the advance of social sciences, have probably contributed to this scepticism. And since the medical model tended to support the extension of indeterminate sentences, it has come to be regarded as the source of quite unjustified interference with human rights. Doctors, who were once seen to help their more disordered patients to avoid the inappropriate rigours of the law, are widely accused of allowing themselves to be seduced from their medical ethical rôle and of becoming subtle and deceptive agents of law enforcement. Most of the sexual psychopath legislation in the United States has been repealed, as well as the 'defective delinquent' legislation in Maryland, and what remains appears increasingly inappropriate. In 1973 Denmark repealed its legislation for psychopaths which gave rise to the famous Herstedvester institution.

The working group on Forensic Psychiatry assembled by the World Health Organization in 1975 revealed that forensic psychiatrists show just as much disarray and confusion as the penologists. No one would say today what the German psychiatrist Strumpfl said in 1958, 'We have said that psychiatry and especially forensic psychiatry is the *central* core of criminology as science, and can add that in future research it will appear as its "royal road".'

Professor Walker in his extremely closely argued Sandoz Lecture on Treatment and Justice in Penology and Psychiatry has listed the many accusations which are made against the medical model of treatment of offenders, some of which can be made with justice in particular cases.

Firstly, there is the problem of *compulsion*. Under what circumstances is it ethical to compel a person to be treated? In psychiatry there has always been this issue and it is recognized that it is ethical to impose treatment on a mentally disordered person to the minimal extent necessary in three sets of circumstances: (1) where it is necessary to prevent violent and dangerous behaviour on the spot: (2) to save life and (3) to prevent the patient from deteriorating. But in what circumstances should this be applied to those who have the capacity to judge the situation? Secondly, there is the problem of *consent*—of 'informed consent', of consent under unethical inducements, real or imaginary. Added to these considerations is that of *indeterminacy of sentence*, extending possibly far beyond the length of any just sentence, for which the medical model has often been held largely responsible: of *spuriousness*—of imaginary or false promises of successful treatment, of *ineffectiveness of treat-*

ment and finally of *inhumanity or degradation* of the patient. A great many offenders, especially alcoholics, have such a sense of self-loathing that they will consent to almost any form of treatment—like the self-flagellating monks of the Middle Ages.

I think these criticisms need to be made and to be kept constantly in mind, though their solution is not easy and must constantly change. Certainly there is something wrong with any forensic psychiatrist who does not realize that there is a conflict which has to be constantly watched. But conflict is unavoidable. Psychiatrists are expected to be able to assess the risk of suicide, and are given the means to control it. They cannot really avoid the duty of assessing the risk of violence to others and the protection of the public, however difficult it is and however bad they are at it.

In one sense this re-examination of basic principles and ethical concerns is somewhat excessively purist. Real-life issues are never clear cut, and one might take the view that an essential aspect of civilization is that every individual in society has to maintain an awkward balance between a number of rôles. Medical confidence can be maintained in nearly all circumstances, but in the end must clash with public duty. The lawyer must defend his client to the utmost but not to the extent of proffering evidence which he knows to be false. It may be argued that there is no greater need for prison administrators or doctors in this field to beat their breasts and confess their sins than for other professions in society, since they are constantly confronted with human rights and ethical considerations.

If we turn to the modern rôle of forensic psychiatry in this new international setting of penology, we are faced with the constant difficulty that whereas the criminal law in Europe has evolved for a thousand years and has developed some intelligible similarities and basic concepts, the hundred years or so during which psychiatry has been on the scene have led to some very large differences in its legal applications, even though there is considerable agreement among psychiatrists about their basic doctrines. The legal means by which psychiatry can be made effective vary so much that it is difficult to make any generally valid statements. In Italy, I believe, psychiatric expertise tends to be concentrated at the stage of trial and refer to questions of criminal responsibility, since, if responsible, sentence on conviction is fairly closely prescribed by law. By contrast, in this country the judges have such discretion in their sentences that the focus of interest is mainly on influencing them in this respect, rather than on any questions of criminal responsibility. The judge can commit a mentally ill offender to hospital with or without any control over his ultimate discharge and in ninety-five per cent of all mental cases the question of responsibility does not arise in law, but only by implication.

Again, in Scandinavian countries, so much in the forefront of discussion of human rights, they preserve the surprising system by which the diagnosis of the mental state of an offender is decided only by a state psychiatrist. The offender has no right to obtain the opinion of a psychiatrist of his own choice. Examination is not always made by a trained psychiatrist, but sometimes by a public health doctor. If the report is criticized, the medico-legal board may appoint another doctor, but after that there is no further appeal. The approval of the report, as far as I can find out, is only made on paper— whether the report looks as if it made sense. In this country such a system could not be accepted: it would be regarded as an interference with human rights if an offender could not have access to psychiatric evidence of his own choice, though in practice the consultant psychiatrists (who are those who carry weight with the court) do not tend to differ seriously. No doubt in Scandinavia the system works out quite fairly: it is a question of the principle. Pre-sentence medical reports to the court are said to have become much fewer recently.

Psychiatric expertise within institutions will be profoundly affected also by the general sentencing policy of the courts. Professor Anttila said at a meeting recently that in the four Scandinavian countries, with 22 million inhabitants, there were only 200 offenders serving sentences of four years or more. In England and Wales we have many times that rate per head of population with 4,800 prisoners serving four years or more in 1975. Clearly if very few prisoners are serving more than three or four months in prison the need for medical services will be very different.

If these are some of the great variations in legal and penal policy, there are probably as many national differences in the mental health practice. The purpose of this volume is to celebrate the bicentenary of John Howard's work on the prisons. But it was the same humanitarian movement of which he was a part, which led a little later to the development of the great Quaker mental hospitals, which established the tradition of treatment of insanity without compulsion or restraint. It is only in very recent years that the physical detention of psychotics has been relaxed in many European countries or the United States, and still to an extent which is probably less widespread than in England, where only some five per cent of the mentally ill population is legally and in any real sense physically detained. One learns in time that Professor Penrose was right when he remarked that comparing one country with another, there is an inverse relationship between the numbers detained in mental hospitals and the numbers in the prisons. Those with a large prison population have a small mental hospital population and vice versa. South Africa shows both aspects of this phenomenon within one country for the socially disorganized blacks are mainly in prison and the disorganized whites mainly in hospital. This is not to say that the populations of each are equivalent; this is the mystery. It reflects something else. When one looks at the figures for the prison population one must never forget those who are officially in institutions for alcoholics, institutions for subnormals, or for mental disorders. The total institutionalized or socially incompetent populations should always be added together. In Sweden, I believe, it was at one period the normal practice to commit minor sex offenders to hospitals for treatment rather than to prison if it seemed necessary to institutionalize them somewhere. The relative ineffectiveness of this procedure for large numbers of them may have led to the present wave of scepticism about the scope of forensic psychiatry.

After these preliminaries I would suggest that there are three areas or issues which need rather separate consideration in the relation of the mental health services to penal services.

Firstly, there is the question of psychiatric treatment of offenders serving sentences in prison. They have an undeniable human right to receive the same quality of medical treatment that they would receive in the community outside. Countries vary as to whether there is, as in this country, a separate whole-time or part-time prison medical service, or not. In this country there is no doubt that prisoners receive better treatment for any physical disorders than they do outside in the Health Service—or at least they receive the same treatment, if necessary by specialists of every kind from outside, with less delay than there is in the general community where there are long waiting-lists for minor operations etc. In the case of mental illness there are some eighty part-time visiting consultant psychiatrists, but there is perhaps more uncertainty about what does or does not constitute a mental illness requiring treatment.

The one medical entitlement which the prisoner has removed from him by his sentence is the right to choose his own doctor, or to change his doctor if he wishes to have another one. That right raises extremely complex questions which we could perhaps leave to discussion.

In conformity with the new anti-rehabilitative principle it is emphasized, of course, that this treatment is *only* to make the prisoner more healthy and comfortable in prison and has nothing whatever to do with the prevention of further crime on release. It is certainly justifiable on those grounds, though it may seem extremely unrealistic to make such a limitation. Of course this view of the social neutrality of medical treatment is quite correct if we look at the reverse side of the balance. Removing tattoos, correcting physical deformities, etc., is carried out in the hope that it will assist rehabilitation, but it could be argued that it would also enable the man to become a more competent criminal if he so wished. A man once came to hospital asking for treatment for his alcoholism because it caused a tremor of his hands: it turned out that he was a professional forger and wanted to be cured because his tremor was beginning to make his forgeries much more easily detectable.

When treatment in prison is evidently motivated by an intention to help the offender not to commit further crime, rather than to support his mental health during a sentence, the situation undoubtedly becomes more complex. This applies especially to the treatment for alcoholism, drug addiction or sexual anomalies—the main areas in fact where there is some psychiatric expertise in the treatment of criminal tendencies; but they are all conditions from which the patient suffers a great deal less in prison than he does outside. We are then accused of allying ourselves unethically with the forces of repression and law enforcement, of imposing the 'tyranny of treatment'. And it must be admitted that there are ethical problems about consent. In spite of all warnings to the contrary, the offender may voluntarily undergo treatment in the belief that this will shorten his sentence; and become angry, and feel betrayed, if this does not occur. I will come back to this question later.

The second area—of great antiquity—is the question of those, mainly psychotic or severely disordered, who are clearly not criminally responsible. All countries have well-established provisions for this sort of offender and it is generally accepted by the public, and the legal and medical professions, that it is not moral or ethical that an irresponsible person should be punished, even if he has to be detained for the protection of the public. The problem here is, how are they to be released? And by whom? The justice system must take part, but it leans heavily on the doctors. The superintendent of our Broadmoor hospital has said he could release half the population tomorrow without risk, but he does not know which half. Mistakes invite enormous publicity. In this country the Butler Committee on Mentally Abnormal Offenders gave detailed consideration to the law relating to criminal responsibility and suggested changes in the tests to be applied, the methods of giving increasing flexibility to the court in passing sentence, and arrangements for controlling release. Most of these recommendations are of no concern to the penal or prison system since they deal with the diversion of mentally abnormal offenders away from the prisons. There are, however, two related aspects which do concern them.

A. First, the increased effectiveness of modern drug treatment for mental illness makes it increasingly possible for an offender who has a mental illness in the course of a prison sentence to be maintained and treated successfully in the prison hospital, or even as an 'outpatient' visiting the prison hospital from his ordinary prison location. There is less urgency to transfer the prisoner to an outside mental hospital or to regard him as a long-term problem quite unsuitable for a prison. Even when he is unsuitable for further detention in prison there is a great reluctance in outside hospitals to accept him, since they can offer no security, and have no means of detaining him to the end of his sentence. They also fear that his criminal tendencies, even if of a relatively minor kind, will lead to his committing crime in the neighbour-hood. When he evidently should be transferred—and one could take the view that prison or even a prison hospital is not a proper environment for a mentally ill person—application may be made for him to go to one of the secure Special Hospitals. These are already overcrowded with seriously dangerous cases sent by the courts, and they may consider that the offender is not dangerous enough for them to accept, and that he is quite properly treated where he is.

This situation is probably unique to this country since the general mental hospitals offer far less security than is common in most European countries, where the ordinary non-offending psychotic may be considerably restricted if he is unreliable in his behaviour. And the same applies to hospitals for the subnormal which in general offer no facilities for detention. In the light of this problem the government has decided to set up in each region a 'regional security unit' in a selected mental hospital for the detention of difficult but not dangerous abnormal offenders—a policy which has been received with mixed feelings and some resistance by the nursing and medical professions in the hospitals, since it runs counter to the prevailing open-door policy.

B. A second factor arises from a recommendation of the Butler Committee with regard to psychopaths. Our Mental Health Act of 1959 provided, like much legislation in the USA and elsewhere, for a category of psychopathic disorder defined here as 'a mental abnormality (whether combined with subnormality of intelligence or not) giving rise to abnormally aggressive or seriously irresponsible conduct which requires or is susceptible to medical treatment'. This category does not exist in the Mental Health Act in Scotland; such people are sent to prison if convicted. This category has rarely been used in ordinary mental hospitals mainly because such patients' behaviour makes them very unpopular and the doctor has to agree to accept them before the order can be made. But many cases were committed to the secure Special Hospitals under this label and it proved of some value under the Homicide Act where it could be cited as a form of diminished responsibility justifying reduction of the crime from murder to manslaughter. However, it never gave rise here to litigation as in the USA where patients sued the government for not providing treatment, because here treatment was sensibly defined as including not only nursing but also care and training under medical supervision.

Twenty years' experience has shown that although some types of person-ality disorder, usually the milder ones, can benefit from the available treat-

P.P.F.—8

ments of different kinds, there is no known treatment for some of the more severe examples. Since detention was for an indefinite period it became apparent that it was hypocrisy in terms of human rights to detain a person for a treatment that did not exist, and the doctors were equally reluctant to see themselves cast merely in the rôle of gaolers. The Butler Committee considered deleting this category of mental disorder from any future Mental Health Act, but emphasized that knowledge was always advancing and the more treatable examples should not be deprived of any right or possibility to receive whatever treatment was available. They tried to differentiate the treatable cases and the possible rôles of health and prison services by suggesting that committal to hospital should be subject to the proviso that 'no order would be made in the case of an offender suffering from psychopathic disorder with dangerous anti-social tendencies unless the court is satisfied that a previous mental or organic illness, or an identifiable psychological or physical defect, related to the disorder, is known or suspected and (2) that there is expectation of therapeutic benefit from hospital admission'. Otherwise they suggested that psychopaths should be committed to prisons, and clearly be seen as their responsibility. Grendon psychiatric prison, which selects moderate or treatable psychopaths who volunteer to go there, undoubtedly succeeds in greatly modifying their behaviour in prison and sometimes achieves a definite change in life style for some time after discharge, though it cannot be shown that the improvement is permanent. The Committee suggested that specialized training units should be set up in the prisons for other categories of personality disorder.

These considerations at least make it clear that whatever else is done there is going to be a need for considerable extension of psychiatric services within the prisons.

We can now turn to the final and most controversial aspects of the relation of mental health services to penal services—the so-called and much maligned 'medical model'—that psychiatry has a rôle both inside and outside prisons in not only making the patient comfortable in the situation he is in, but actually contributing to his adjustment to society. What is the future of this system? If it is not dead, how should it operate constructively?

First, one should perhaps remark that there is no medical model, but hundreds of different medical models. Is it a medical model to provide some form of behavioural or social treatment undertaken by psychologists or social workers without any medical contact? Is it a matter of imposing some sort of demand for a change, which is certainly not a medical intention, or merely offering a person a chance of using his time constructively? Or does it refer to any system which implies that some sort of change ought to be encouraged?

Dr. Peter Scott in his important paper on *Treatment and Punishment,* has pointed out that for very many years there have been some who were perceived to be treatable or helpable, the rest being only considered for detention as a form of punishment. Yet it is quite impossible for any civilized country to maintain a purely punitive system. One cannot find the staff to do it. Very soon they start to find a small group, which, they say, should be dealt with more constructively: these are first segregated for different treatment within the system, and later tend to be removed from the system altogether: and so the process begins again with an alleged hard core of untreatables until someone comes along to detect and split off a new treatable subgroup.

The present policy of keeping offenders out of institutions as far as possible naturally leads to a steady deterioration in the characteristics of those who reach borstal or prison. Good programmes find no suitable recruits; open prisons are much less used, partly because of the spread of drug smuggling. One would expect the reconviction rate to be rising dramatically but as far as I know it has not in fact risen as much as one would expect. Since the régime must be geared to the control of the most difficult section of the population it contains, it is likely to become increasingly restrictive, so that those judged likely to respond to some constructive policy need to be transferred to quite separate units, either to a prison such as Grendon psychiatric prison, or an industrial prison such as Coldingley, which tend to accept a relatively small proportion of all offenders. And since they are much more expensive, there tend to be criticisms about cost effectiveness. It is, however, very difficult to decide, for those who fall within the potential ambit of the medical profession, who is a 'medical case'. Dr. Gunn in his study of Grendon prison, and of samples of the general prison population, concluded that there were three criteria—previous mental breakdown, hospitalization or treatment; the presence of some current psychiatric symptoms; and thirdly *motivation* for treatment. The presence of the third factor—motivation—was in some respects the most important of all. Motivation, however, is unfortunately one of the most difficult things to assess accurately, especially perhaps in the criminal population. There are many cases where it turns out from experience of his response to a Grendon régime, that apparent motivation was spurious, a belief that it might be a soft option and so on. Many studies have shown however, for example in the treatment of alcoholics, that the most unlikely subjects may benefit and the distinguishing feature in such cases appears to be strong personal motivation. Since nearly all of the common recidivist property offenders give up crime soon after forty if not before (in this sense the ultimate outlook is always hopeful) either because drives and impulses weaken with age or perhaps more often, or in addition, because other relationships, especially marriage, build up increasing motivation not to lose what they have come to value. When Lee Robins asked offenders interviewed 30 years after their adolescent problems had been observed what they attributed their relative improvement to, they put getting older and wiser first and getting married a close second.

The major problem in the prisons, of course, is that they are places of isolation from the main stream of life, and from potentially motivational relationships, both for the prison and very often for the staff. It is difficult for prison staff to be concerned about what happens before a man comes to prison—in fact it is often said that it is deliberate policy to pay no attention to this to avoid prejudice, to wipe the slate clean, and to deal with him as you find him. Similarly there is in general no responsibility for a prisoner when he leaves, though Grendon and some other institutions have grasped this point by allowing the same staff to maintain contact with the released offender. There is increasing scepticism about the value of psychiatric treatment in prisons at all, except to make detention comfortable, mainly because there is no possibility of experimental or testing periods of release or decreasing supervision in partial liberty, apart from a few pre-release schemes for long-term offenders. In a sense this is natural enough. If a man is fit to be at liberty for longer than a few hours, why should he be the responsibility of the prison administration? It is only the probation service which can have any real conception of the process before a man goes to prison, while he is in prison, and when he comes out; and medical treatment tries to follow the same procedure or pattern of contact.

The present policy of keeping offenders out of prison as much as possible corresponds closely to the modern operation of the mental health services with regard to hospitalization. As also does the policy—less often discussed— of admitting them or sentencing them for as *short* a time as is necessary for their own or society's protection. All institutionalization has negative effects including hospitalization or even going to bed with flu, but this is not the same as saying that there are no other effects, which sometimes outweigh them. No society has ever found how to deal with quarrels between individuals other than to separate them, if necessary forcibly, until they 'cool off'. It has always seemed to me that the concept of 'cooling off' and the time necessary for conflict resolution to take place, deserved more consideration. Nowadays, a great deal is talked about the just sentence but no one knows what a just sentence is. Professor Anttila has said that we need more research into how the standard or habit arises and what factors change it, and how one country comes to have 'just sentences' twice as long as another.

At any rate the Butler Committee in its detailed consideration of the medical component in the management of crime, seems to me to have pointed in the direction in which development should occur. And it is no accident that this also attempts to deal with the most controversial problems of compulsion, of consent, and indeterminacy, beyond the just sentence. Many more of those offenders who were fairly evidently mentally ill should be diverted as soon as possible after arrest into the health services. This would be quite possible even for some who commit very serious offences, such as homicide. There would have to be better conditions of security and the regional security units could play a part in this, as well as being centres for the expensive equipment which is nowadays necessary for thorough investigation. In some cases a prison sentence might still be imposed when the offender returned to court.

However, the second series of recommendations was even more important —that it should be possible, without interfering with the duration of sentence, to transfer selected offenders to specialized treatment in the health service, if they consented. They could ask to return or be returned at any time. It would be analogous to the voluntary transfer within prison to the special prison of Grendon. For reasons mentioned earlier, it is unlikely that the prisons, which have to be organized to receive a very wide range of dangerous offenders and have no capacity to refuse, can ever be organized to provide the sort of environment suitable for certain classes of patient. In an outside hospital environment, with a rather different pattern of responsibilities, it would be possible to use a more liberal system of graduated release, with involvement in specialized or general employment arrangements which are used for non-offending members of the public. Of course, this sort of release from prison to hospital occurs extensively now, but always for psychotic or grossly handicapped individuals who cannot be maintained in prison and are expected to be ill for a long time.

The central problem, of course, is co-operation between agencies. In an increasingly complex society there must be defined agencies—police, courts, prison doctors, probation officers, who understand their limitations and rôles. But there is always a tendency for agencies to isolate themselves and set themselves rigid objectives. Professor Christie was partly referring to this when he told the assembled UN representatives, 'You are the main causes of crime.' In a large study recently of medical reports to the courts prepared either in prison or by psychiatrists outside with the offender on bail, we found that direct referral on bail to psychiatrists in the general health service resulted in four times as many being put on probation with a condition of treatment. When in custody the main emphasis, rather naturally, is on reporting the presence or absence of psychosis and other very serious abnormalities and there is less knowledge of local community resources for milder cases. Forensic psychiatrists see their main contribution to be in *community treatment*, sometimes taking a major part, more often a minor and ancillary one. They discuss the need to take off their white coats and leave the outpatient hospital departments and get an office in new community centres where agencies of several kinds can co-ordinate their work by personal contact. There is also a special rôle for them in helping with particular crises which precipitate crime, for they have additional persuasive facilities at their disposal. Finally, there is a growing rôle in *primary prevention* of delinquency in the diagnosis and treatment of special handicaps which require special treatment.

19

CONCLUSION

Marvin E. Wolfgang

I welcome the opportunity to complete this book by returning to the man whose bicentenary it celebrates. Sir Leon Radzinowicz opens the volume by writing about Howard, but most of the other papers deal with appropriate contemporary issues in corrections and penal policy. It is fitting, therefore, that I offer a closing on the topic that reflects or adds to Sir Leon's opening. In this way, he and I stand in the posture of being parentheses to the other statements.

These statements have presented us with some detail about John Howard's work and with some observations about the present and future conditions of prisons and the criminal justice system. I cannot avoid some redundancy with what has been said earlier, but I shall also try to recall some further things about the life and work of the man whose activity this bicentennial publication is to honour.

Unlike Antony who said he came to bury not to praise Caesar, I think we frankly admit that we have come together in this volume to praise Howard. In a summary perspective of John Howard, which I wish to offer, I am sure you realize that any work, including *The State of the Prisons*, is vulnerable to criticism. I wish neither to be negatively critical of the man and his work, nor to over-romanticize beyond the proper mettle of the man. And I hasten to add that I yield to my colleagues who are deeper authorities about Howard than I, should I draw the wrong inference or interpret this eighteenth-century man incorrectly in any of these remarks.

Howard has been contrasted with Bentham and Beccaria, and justly so. Beccaria, in 1764 with his famous *Dei deletti e delle pene*, dealt with monumental ideas of penal philosophy. And so did Bentham later. John Howard was more concerned with the details of physical life, less with the humanity of the penal system than with the humanity towards individual prisoners. Beccaria counted the seriousness of crime and the severity of sanctions; Howard counted the size of cells, the weight of bread, the amount of meat. Bentham had a felicific calculus regarding the risks of crime, the pain and pleasure principles of all human behaviour; Howard saw almost exclusively the pains of imprisonment and wished to reduce them.

But do not throw upon Howard any anachronistic labels, such as quantitative, positivistic, empiricist. He was a surveyor, an accountant of prison conditions, not an intellectual theorist. He contributed not to the intellectual history of the evolution of penology except by being an exacting reporter whose testimony cannot be ignored by any scholar in this field. He had no theory to accompany his data collection. But he did have a philosophy of what he noted as Christian compassion for fellow humans and a notion of what corruption means when he described the fee system under which gaolers benefited from their charges.

We cannot praise him for a Marxian thought system nor for the insights of Enrico Ferri. There are few among us who can bear such comparisons. What he did, however, must be classified in contemporary terminology as a breakthrough, as pioneering, as being driven by the zeal for reformation of the rattled, rutted routinization of persons viewed by the system as outcasts. He described more than he prescribed, and for this he deserves our abiding admiration and praise.

The character of this man and the written works he has left us are a beautiful blend in which each properly reflects the other. I shall not recount the well-known tale of his being a prisoner of French pirates in 1754 nor his becoming High Sheriff of Bedfordshire as having any influence on his later travels. I should like, however, to recall some of the incidents of his life that paint the portrait of a person who could do what no one before him had done —nor, perhaps, since him.

As Sir Leon Radzinowicz has mentioned, Howard was elected to the Royal Society rather early on and partly because of his physical science interests. Before he did most of his prison inspections he showed his concern for measuring in detail. In a letter to Lady Mary Whitbread in 1770 from Rome he wrote:

> I ascended Mount Vesuvius; and when I was up three parts of the hill, the earth was, by my thermometer, somewhat warmer than the atmosphere. I then took the temperature every five minutes till I got to the top. The heat was continually increasing. After I had stood the smoke a quarter of an hour I breathed freely; so with three men I descended as far as they would go with me, where the earth or brimstone was so heated that, in frequent experiments, it raised my thermometer to 240°, which is near 30° hotter than boiling water, and in some places it fired some paper I put in. As these experiments have never before been made. I thought the account of them might afford your ladyship some entertainment.[1]

Another indication of his concern for detail, even outside prisons, comes from the account of how excruciatingly involved he was in every step of the publication of *The State of the Prisons*. Edgar Gibson's description is revealing:

Lodgings were taken near to the printer's, and no journeyman printer could have worked harder than Howard himself did. He rose every morning at two, and worked at the correction of proofs till seven, when he breakfasted. Punctually at eight he repaired to the printing-office, and remained there until the workmen went to dinner at one, when he returned to his lodgings, and, putting some bread and raisins or other dried fruit in his pocket, generally took a walk in the outskirts of the town during their absence, eating, as he walked along, his hermit fare, which, with a glass of water on his return, was the only dinner he took . . . When he had returned to the printing-office, he generally remained there until the men left work, and then repaired to Mr. Aikin's house, to go through with him any sheets which might have been composed during the day; or, if there were nothing upon which he wished to consult him, would spend an hour with some other friend, or return to his lodgings, where he took his tea or coffee, in lieu of supper; and at his usual hour retired to bed.[2]

He was a stern, serene, somewhat severe man who was tolerant of the religion of others—he was a Congregationalist—but intolerant of deviance from the work ethic, intolerant of alcohol, whether sold by gaolers to their prisoners or abused by others. There is an amusing incident told by Brown about Howard's visit to a Capuchin convent in Prague where he

found the holy fathers at dinner round a table, which, though it was meagre day with them, was sumptuously furnished with all the delicacies the season could afford, of which he was very politely invited to partake. This, however, he not only declined to do, but accompanied his refusal by a pretty severe lecture to the elder monks, in which he told them that he thought they had retired from the world to live a life of abstemiousness and prayer, but he found their monastery a house of revelling and drunkenness. He added, moreover, that he was going to Rome, and he would take care that the Pope should be made acquainted with the impropriety of their conduct. Alarmed at this threat, four or five of these holy friars found their way the next morning to the hotel at which their visitor had taken up his abode, to beg pardon for the offence they had given him by their unseemly mode of living, and to entreat that he would not say anything of what had passed at the Papal See. To this request our countryman replied, that he should make no promise upon the subject, but would merely say that if he heard that the offence was not repeated, he might probably be silent on what was past. With this sort of half-assurance the monks were compelled to be satisfied; but, before they took leave of the heretical reprover of their vices, they gave him a solemn promise that no such violation of their rules should again be permitted, and that they would keep a constant watch over the younger members of their community, to guard them against similar excesses; and here the conference ended.[3]

We have some clues about his attitude towards women. His first wife, whom he married in 1752, was his landlady who nursed him through an illness and who was twice his age. He apparently was happy with her but she died three years later and left him a widower before he was thirty. His second wife, Henrietta Leeds, more his own age, he married in 1758. With her he took a very authoritarian attitude. He is reported to have said to her that 'to prevent all altercations about those little matters which he had observed to be the chief grounds of uneasiness in families, the decision on any question that might arise should rest with him'.[4] She accepted this dictum wholeheartedly and their life together was also a good one until she died four days after the birth of his only child, a son, John, in 1765. Howard attributed his son's insanity to the loss of the mother, but several biographies imply that the absence of an affectionate father, travelling over Europe and Asia, may have been a major contributing factor.

But I wish to comment more about Howard and women. During Howard's visit to Austria in 1786 the governor of Upper Austria made an

> inquiry as to the state of prisons in the province to the government of which he had been appointed. 'The worst in all Germany,' was [Howard's] answer, 'particularly in the condition of the female prisoners; and I recommend your countess to visit them personally, as the best means of rectifying the abuses in their management.' The lady who had accompanied her husband, exclaimed indignantly at this, '*I* go into prisons!' and abruptly quitted the room, retiring downstairs with such rapidity that Howard feared she would meet with an accident. He was not, however, deterred from shouting after her as she fled: 'Madam, remember that you are a woman yourself, and must soon, like the most miserable female prisoner in a dungeon, inhabit but a small space of that earth from which you equally originated.'[5]

In Florence, where he found the prisons large, clean and well managed, he left money with the governor to provide meat for the men and tea for the women.[6] He regularly advocated the separation of the sexes, but this the Florentines had done two centuries before Howard arrived.

What can we glean from his writings about penal prescriptions? What did he oppose? What did he favour? And how far removed from or how close to that of John Howard is the current mode of thought about penal philosophy?

Firstly, I should like to mention one or two issues on which he may have been a reflection of his own time but from our twentieth-century retrospection appears less advanced than we might have wanted him to be. He described torture rooms and instruments with obvious disdain. Yet, as D. L. Howard remarked, 'Howard's assumption that physical pain, greatly though it disturbed him, was of far less significance than spiritual salvation would not be readily accepted by all humanitarians today.'[7] His reactions to the slave ships at Naples illustrates this point. He made no adverse comments on the practice of slavery; he was more interested in the fact that there was a chaplain and Sunday worship. Slaves locked to each other and to their boats by chains were regarded as well treated so long as they were clothed, fed, given water and encouraged to praise God.

But a Philadelphian, such as I, dare not speak too loudly about this, for in 1777 the newly independent states did not abolish slavery, and even at the Constitutional Convention a decade later George Washington still had his slaves, however well fed and encouraged to praise God they may have been.

Moreover, the UN in Geneva last year had to frame a resolution against torture, for it still is used in many countries, some of which Howard visited, many of which he did not.

He opposed the long list of capital crimes, but he was not an abolitionist. 'I wish,' he said, 'that no persons might suffer capitally but for murder, for setting houses on fire, and for housebreaking, attended with acts of cruelty.'[8] For his time, this was a liberal comment. Even now, as I witness new legislation in about thirty states of the United States reinstating the death penalty, often for a longer list of offences than Howard's, his restricted list is as modest as the man himself.

The term 'separation' appears often in Howard's writings, and on this topic he was quite modern. He lamented the bunching together of men and women, of adults and children. He did not invent the idea of separation, of course, but he promoted it. Prisons he had visited in Ghent, Amsterdam, especially Florence, and others had maintained separation of the sexes for generations before Howard, at Le Stinche in Florence, for example, since the fifteenth century.[9]

More importantly, Howard spoke of separation in a way that reminds us of the Pennsylvania or separate system developed by the Quakers in Philadelphia at the beginning of the nineteenth century. This is separation as a philosophical basis for the treatment of offenders. Howard emphasized the use of separation for purposes of reflection and self-reformation. But he had some reservations which the fathers of the Eastern State Penitentiary in 1829 did not have and which Charles Dickens[10] in 1843 shared with Howard, but without reference to him. As F. H. Wines states:[11]

> He had seen separation practised in Europe. Of Holland he reports that 'in most of the prisons, there are so many rooms, that each prisoner is kept separate; they never go out.' In Switzerland, in every canton visited by him, felons each had a room to themselves, 'that they might not tutor one another.' In his chapter on permanent improvements, he expresses his own opinion: 'I wish to have so many small rooms or cabins, that each criminal may sleep alone. If it be difficult to prevent their being together in the day-time, they should by all means be separated at night. Solitude and silence are favourable to reflection, and may possibly lead them to repentance.' Elsewhere he had said that he wished 'all prisoners to have separate rooms, for hours of thoughtfulness and reflection are necessary,' and added that he meant day as well as night, but yet, 'not absolute solitude.' That he dreaded the effect of too protracted isolation is apparent from the following quotation: 'It should be considered by those who are ready to

commit for a long term petty offenders to absolute solitude, that such a state is more than human nature can bear without the hazard of distraction or despair.'

He was in favour of reformation, as several passages of his writings reveal. Again, he was not among the first to speak of reformation. The Hospice of San Michele in Rome attracted him because of the motto from Cicero about re-education. The prison in Renaissance Florence I have studied, Le Stinche, opened in 1300, had rules of governance that stipulated re-education of the prisoners. Howard knew these things and built whatever penal philosophy he had on these instances he found abroad. In contemporary terms—if they can be applied to his thinking and his period at all—it must be said that the current disillusionment with the rehabilitative model, or main rationale for captivity of offenders, is based upon *coercive* reformation. Howard believed in self or voluntary reformation, or what he called 'salvation', a concept now enjoying currency, albeit not with Christian biblical tracts alone. As he writes:[12]

> Our present laws are certainly too sanguinary, and are therefore ill executed; which last circumstance, by encouraging offenders to hope that they may escape punishment, even after conviction, greatly tends to increase the number of crimes. Yet many are brought to a premature end, who might have been made useful to the state.
>
> I the more earnestly embarked in the scheme of erecting penitentiary-houses from seeing cartloads of our fellow creatures carried to execution; [many of whom] I was fully persuaded might, by regular, steady discipline in a penitentiary-house have been rendered useful members of society; and above all, from the *pleasing hope* that such a plan might be the means of promoting salvation of some individuals—of which, every instance is, according to the unerring word of truth, a more important object than *the gaining of the whole world*.

Most contemporary thought about imprisonment suggests that only a small cadre of 'hard core', serious and violent offenders should suffer such limited life space as a prison cell. I have buttressed this contention with a study of *Delinquency in a Birth Cohort*[13] in which we found only six per cent of 10,000 boys born in 1945 to be responsible for the murders, most rapes and two-thirds of all violent crimes. Listen now to Howard's words 200 years ago:

> To the penitentiary-houses I should wish that *none* but old, hardened offenders, and those who have ... forfeited their lives by robbery, housebreaking, and similar crimes, should be committed; or, in short, those criminals who are to be confined for a long term, or for life.[14]

Surely Howard would agree with the current movements to divert many offenders from the indignity of imprisonment.

John Howard would, I believe, find affinity with the neo-classical revivalism now occurring in many Western countries, that is, a return to retribution, the just deserts model and sanctioning proportionate to the crime. But perhaps more importantly, our present emphasis upon humane treatment of prisoners, especially while recognizing the apparent inefficacy of coercive rehabilitation, is clearly and especially concurrent with Howard's great work. Clean, dry, ventilated housing, adequate food, water, sunlight, privacy, charity from the guards and warders—these were his physical claims for decency, and, like the Chicago School of Criminology in the 1920s and 1930s, he recognized the impact that the physical environment had on the emotions and mental health of the inhabitants. For him Holland was the country that expressed his humane impulses:

> I leave this country with regret, as it affords a large field for information on the important subject I have in view. I know not which to admire most—the *neatness* and *cleanliness* appearing in prisons, the *industry* and *regular conduct* of the prisoners, or the *humanity* and *attention* of the magistrates and regents.[15]

Howard's combined emphasis on proper food and desire to uplift the prisoners through the authority of the state reminds me of two recent conversations I had about this combination. Professor Edward Banfield, the urbanologist from Harvard and author of *The Unheavenly City,* recently asked and answered his own question about a punishment for prisoners that would at once be viewed by all society as humane yet would probably be considered by prisoners as a form of punishment. Prisoners like to have many potatoes, ice cream, lots of bread and other food high in calories and carbohydrates. A humane punishment, said Banfield, would be a perfectly nutritionally balanced diet with lots of spinach, green beans, fish, cheese and little starch. John Howard would probably agree.

The other conversation took place in a special model prison outside Mexico City.[16] The superintendent was a man with a missionary zeal not unlike John Howard's. He was gentle, serene, full of compassion for his charges who are serious felons, one-third of whom are homicide offenders. He has loud speakers stationed all over the prison grounds and buildings, and all day long, through the evening hours, only classical music is broadcast. Beethoven, Bach, Brahms, Mozart are the constant companions of each inmate who cannot escape their aural invasion of his privacy. At first the inmates find this music oppressive, for if any music was to be given them they wanted flamenco or rock. This was punishment, again, of a humane character. In time, the prisoners come to enjoy and even memorize the classics and become mini-authorities on the classical composers. As the superintendent remarked: 'If one has power he might as well use it to advantage.' Again, I think John Howard would approve.

The immediate effect of Howard's influence may be questioned, but there is some evidence of it. The long-term effect of his work is clearly evident in the existence of Howard Leagues and the Bicentennial Conference held in Canterbury. In his own time, there is no doubt that he was lauded throughout Europe and respected for his work.

In 1774, just a year after his becoming High Sheriff of Bedfordshire, he gave evidence before a committee of the House of Commons and received the thanks of the House. Almost immediately an Act was passed which provided for the liberation, free of all charges, of every prisoner against whom the grand jury failed to find a true bill, giving the gaoler a sum from the county in lieu of abolished fees. This was followed by another Act requiring justices of the peace to see that walls and ceilings of prisons were scraped and whitewashed at least once a year, that rooms were regularly cleaned and ventilated, that infirmaries were provided for the sick, that underground dungeons were to be used as little as possible, and that measures were taken to restore and preserve the health of the prisoners. At his own cost, Howard had the provisions of the new legislation printed and sent to every gaoler and warden in the kingdom. Moreover, the information he obtained from his travels and presented to Parliament resulted in a Bill for building two penitentiary-houses.

He apparently had an influence on foreign penal systems wherever he went. Emperor Joseph II was affected, as were many other dignitaries. Had he been at Attica he might have had the influence he had when he quelled a riot in the Savoy. Edgar Gibson reports the following:

> Two hundred of the prisoners had broken loose and killed two of their keepers, nor dare anyone approach, till Howard, in spite of the remonstrances of his friends, calmly entered in among them, and such was the effect of his mild and benign manner, that they soon listened to his remonstrances, *represented their grievances* [emphasis added], and at last allowed themselves to be quietly reconducted to their cells.[17]

On all his travels he was never stopped by highwaymen, never robbed, never insulted by prisoners or keepers, never even lost anything.

He was eulogized by the conservative Burke in a speech in 1781 in which he said that Howard

> visited all Europe—not to survey the sumptuousness of palaces or the stateliness of temples; nor to make accurate measurements of the remains of ancient grandeur; nor to form a scale of the curiosity of modern art; nor to collect medals, or collate manuscripts—but to dive into the depths of dungeons, to plunge into the infection of hospitals, to survey the mansions of sorrow and pain, to take the gauge and dimensions of misery, depression, and contempt; to remember the forgotten, to attend to the neglected, to visit the forsaken, and

compare and collate the distresses of all men in all countries. His plan is original: it is as full of genius as it is of humanity. It was a voyage of discovery, a circumnavigation of charity. Already the benefit of his labour is felt more or less in every country; I hope he will anticipate his final reward by seeing all its effects fully realized in his own.[18]

William Cowper spoke of Howard in his poem on 'Charity' when he said:

> To quit the bliss thy rural scenes bestow,
> To seek a nobler amidst scenes of woe,
> To traverse seas, range kingdoms, and bring home
> Not the proud monuments of Greece or Rome,
> But knowledge such as only dungeons teach,
> And only sympathy like thine could reach, . . .[19]

John Wesley, the Methodist leader, said, 'I had the pleasure of a conversation with Mr Howard, I think one of the greatest men in Europe.'[20]

Howard had an influence on the construction of the 'D' building, or penitentiary-house of the famous Walnut Street Jail in Philadelphia in 1790, through correspondence with the Quakers there, and indirectly on the construction of the outside cell block of the Eastern State Penitentiary in 1829. Howard died of the gaol fever in Kherson, a small town in the Crimea, on 20 January 1790. The man at his bedside when he died, Admiral Mordvinoff, a Russian, later persuaded John Haviland, a native of England and a distant cousin of Howard, to emigrate to America, where he became the architect and designer of Cherry Hill, the Eastern State Penitentiary in Philadelphia, in which some of Howard's ideas were put into practice.

The extent to which Howard was acclaimed may be seen in the fact that two thousand people attended his funeral in Russia and the first statue admitted to St. Paul's in London was not that of a sovereign or statesman or saint; it was that of John Howard. His neighbour and probably closest friend wrote the inscription that appears at the base of the statue now; Samuel Whitbread, founder of the brewery of that name, was his benefactor, which is especially interesting since Howard was a teetotaller. The inscription says:[21]

> This extraordinary man had the Fortune to be
> honoured whilst living,
> In the manner which his Virtues deserved;
> He received the thanks
> Of both Houses of the British and Irish Parliaments,
> For his eminent services rendered to his Country
> and to Mankind.
> Our National Prisons and Hospitals,
> Improved upon the Suggestions of his Wisdom,
> Bear testimony to the solidity of his Judgement,

And to the Estimation in which he was held
In every Part of the Civilised World,
Which he traversed to reduce the sum of
Human Misery

If John Howard did not directly and immediately influence legislation for prison reform, he certainly has had an enduring influence on us all, even 200 years hence. He was a first, a pioneer; none before him was his model. As Melville has said, 'It is better to fail in originality than to succeed in imitation.' If Howard failed to promote prison reform at once, he could never be accused of imitation.

I end by offering my own tribute, in blank verse, to this modest man who asked to be forgotten.[22]

JOHN HOWARD (1726–1790)

He measured the bread and the cell
As none before him.
From his own imprisonment
He learned the miseries of others.

Blessed by inheritance
He built not castles and halls
To adorn his name,
But a catalogue of how
The social contract functioned
When violators were captured and constrained.

No one before or since
Has done so well
In giving us description and design
Of democracy's deprivation of liberty.

Saturated with this mission,
He gave his life and fortune
To the cause of prison reform.

His chronicle remains,
His activism sustains
All of us who wish well
For the art of healing

The miseries of those caught
By the net of criminal justice.

Among us today,
John Howard would count
The calories and cry out
For help from Attica to Pentonville,
From Herstedvester in Denmark
To the Serbsky Institute in Moscow.

His work lives on
In the minutiae of the present.
For no architect can draw a cell
Without being in his debt.
No diet for the restrained
Can contain his absence.

John Howard is the Sermon
On the Mount of each imprisonment
From Philadelphia to the Gulag Archipelago.
In two hundred winters
Since him
We still need his instruction
And his compassion.

He was scrupulous, gentle and gentile,
A religious libertarian and free spirit,
Yet a stern, steady man
Always rational and thoughtfully logical;
With two wives he loved
But who left him to enter
Early graves.

Their departure
And his unsuccessful political venture
Left him free to explore
His passion
To become our first student
Of descriptive detail
Of how prisoners fare.

References

1. Gibson, Edgar C. S. (1901), *John Howard*, London, Methuen and Co.: pp. 24–5.

2. ibid.: pp. 53–4.

3. Brown, James Baldwin (1831), *Memoirs of Howard*, Boston, Mass., Lincoln & Edmonds: p. 142.

4. Gibson, *John Howard*: p. 12.

5. ibid.: p. 160.

6. Howard, D. L. (1958), *John Howard: Prison Reformer*, London, Christopher Johnson: p. 70.

7. ibid.: p. 74.

8. (1929), *State of Prisons*, E. P. Dutton & Co., Inc., Everyman Edition: p. 261, cited by Barnes, Harry Elmer & Teeters, Negley, *New Horizons in Criminology*, New York, Prentice-Hall: p. 482.

9. Wolfgang, Marvin E. (1960), 'A Florentine Prison: Le Carcere delle Stinche', *Studies in the Renaissance*, Volume VII: pp. 148–66.

10. Dickens, Charles (1842), *American Notes for General Circulation*, London, Chapman and Hall: pp. 119–20, cited by Eriksson, Torsten (1976), *The Reformers: An Historical Survey of Pioneer Experiments in the Treatment of Criminals*, New York, Elsevier: p. 70.

11. Wines, F. H. (1895), *Punishment and Reformation*, New York, Thomas Y. Crowell Co.,: p. 144.

12. *State of Prisons*: p. 261.

13. Wolfgang, Marvin E., Figlio, Robert & Sellin, Thorsten (1972) *Delinquency in a Birth Cohort*, Chicago, University of Chicago Press.

14. *State of Prisons*: p. 261.

15. Gibson, *John Howard*: p. 91.

16. This prison was also visited by Geis, Gilbert, 'Epilogue', in Wolfgang, Marvin E. (1977) (ed.), *Prison Reform*, Lexington Books, in press.

17. Gibson, *John Howard*: pp. 203–4.

18. A speech delivered at Bristol, cited by Stoughton, John (1884), *Howard, The Philanthropist and his Friends*, London, Hodder and Stoughton: p. 206.

19. Quoted by Gisbon, *John Howard*: p. 42.

20. ibid.: p. 162.

21. See Brown, James Baldwin, *Memoirs of Howard*: p. 336; also Gibson, Edgar C.S., *John Howard*: p. 184

22. As quoted by Gibson in *John Howard*: p. 181, Howard said: '. . . let me beg of you, as you value your old friend, not to suffer any pomp to be used at my funeral; nor any monument or monumental inscription whatsoever to mark where I am laid; but lay me quietly in the earth, place a sun-dial over my grave, and *let me be forgotten*' [emphasis added].

INDEX

The letter-by-letter system of alphabetization has been adopted throughout.

The term 'prison' is used in the index irrespective of any acceptable alternatives which may be used in the text, such as gaol. The entry itself is divided into sections as follows:

prisoners—matters affecting convicts;

prisons—general references to prison establishments;

prison officers—matters affecting staff;

prison system—matters relating to the running of prisons;

Prison Acts—Parliamentary Acts by year of enactment;

prison bodies—pertaining to Commissioners, Service College, etc.;

Prisons—titles of books including the word 'Prison'.

Quasi-prisons (Borstal, approved schools, etc.) are individually indexed as are extra-mural functions such as Parole and Probation.

The entry 'sentence' is split into four sections as follows:

(i) effects of receiving;

(ii) handed down by the courts (including non-custodial types such as Community Service Orders);

(iii) prison disciplinary;

(iv) views, other than the courts, expressed about.

Compilers: R. and R. Haig-Brown, Sherborne, Dorset.